The ICSA
**Company Reporting
Handbook**

The ICSA
Company Reporting Handbook

TONY HOSKINS

Published by ICSA Publishing Ltd
16 Park Crescent
London W1B 1AH

© ICSA Publishing Ltd, 2007

All rights reserved. No part of this publication may be reproduced, stored in a retrieval system, or transmitted, in any form, or by any means, electronic, mechanical, photocopying, recording or otherwise, without prior permission, in writing from the publisher.

Typeset in 9.75 on 13pt Goudy and Vectora by RefineCatch Limited, Bungay, Suffolk
Printed in Great Britain by Hobbs the Printers

British Library Cataloguing in Publication Data
A catalogue record for this book is available from the British Library

ISBN 978-1-86072-368-1

Contents

Foreword *xi*
Preface *xiii*
Acknowledgements *xv*

1 Background to corporate reporting *1*
What is corporate reporting? *1*
Purpose of corporate reporting *2*
A brief history of corporate reporting *4*
Regulatory authorities' role in corporate reporting *6*
Different accounting standards *7*

SECTION 1
Regulatory requirements for financial and narrative reporting *11*

2 Corporate reporting under Companies Act 1985 *13*
Introduction *13*
Reporting requirements *14*
Companies Act 1985 – its impact on corporate reporting pre-2005 *14*
Operating and Financial Review (OFR) – 1993 and 2005 *16*
Reporting Statement *18*
Reporting Statement and key performance indicators *22*
Business Review 2005 *24*

3 Impact of Companies Act 2006 on corporate reporting *30*
Background to the Act *30*
Objectives of the Act *31*
Changes to duties owed by directors *33*
Accounts and reports *35*
Various forms of accounts *37*
Duties of companies regarding reports and accounts *39*
Separate requirements dependent on nature of company *44*
Compliance *47*
Enforcement *51*

4 Audit requirements of Companies Act 2006 — 54
General approach — 54
Exemptions and variations — 55
Appointment of auditors — 57
Auditor's report — 58
Auditor's duties — 59
Auditor's rights — 62

5 Codes of Governance — 65
Combined Code of Corporate Governance (July 2003) — 66
Key principles relating to corporate reporting — 67
Disclosure of corporate governance arrangements — 69
Audit committee – reporting requirements — 70
Remuneration committee – reporting requirements — 75
Nomination committee – reporting requirements — 80

6 Stock Exchange rules — 83
Listing Rules — 83
Alternative Investment Market – corporate reporting requirements — 96
Introduction of the Transparency Directive — 102

SECTION 2
Managing the process — 107

7 Developing the annual report – traditional processes — 109
Opportunities provided by publishing a company's report and accounts — 109
Processes — 110
Delivering audited accounts on time — 110
Producing other relevant board committee reports — 113
Producing designs for annual reports and delivering them on time — 115

8 Developing the annual report – Business Review — 119
Producing the directors' report and incorporating the Business Review — 119
Required elements of Business Review – and what each means — 120
Additional requirements of Companies Act 2006 and Business Review — 125
A practical approach to develop Business Review — 127
Alternative approaches to producing Business Review — 133
Producing statements from chairman and chief executive — 138
Key steps to assess progress in planning — 140

SECTION 3
Best practice and future developments — 143

9 The value of better quality reporting — 145
Introduction — 145
Company law reform arguments — 146
Academic research — 148
A practitioner's view – PricewaterhouseCoopers ValueReporting team — 149
Some conclusions on the value of better quality reporting — 152

10 Understanding how companies meet their Business Review corporate reporting requirements — 154
Background — 155
Research findings — 155
ASB's analysis — 167
Conclusions and ways forward from both reports — 172

11 Corporate reporting – current developments — 175
Developments in the United States — 175
Output from Big Six summit in November 2006 — 177
Convergence in accounting standards and the management commentary — 179
New version of ABI Guidelines — 181
Development of ISAE3000 — 183
Report Leadership initiative — 184
Conclusion — 187

12 Current state of corporate reporting – views from the users — 189
Background — 189
Introduction to interviewees — 190
Current state of corporate reporting — 192
Value and purpose of annual reports — 196
Best practice in corporate reporting — 197

13 Challenges of the Business Review – views from the users — 201
Introduction — 201
2005 Business Review – process and experience — 202
Forward-looking statements — 205
Reporting – KPIs and risks — 208
Style of Business Review — 210
Impact of Companies Act 2006 on Business Review — 211
Best practice for Business Review reporting — 214

14 Future of corporate reporting – views from the users   *218*
Introduction   *218*
What is the future for corporate reporting?   *219*
Opportunities offered by electronic communications   *223*
Real time reporting and other new forms of reporting   *227*
Other issues   *229*

15 Some thoughts on the way forward   *234*
Introduction   *234*
Compliance or a tool for investors?   *234*
Effective communications?   *236*
Future for the annual report   *236*
Does this all matter?   *238*

Appendices   *240*
Appendix 1: Form and content of company as established under Companies Act 1985   *240*
Appendix 2: Comparing the requirements of the OFR and Business Review (Companies Act 1985 and Companies Act 2006)   *244*
Appendix 3: Financial Reporting Council Combined Code on Corporate Governance   *248*
Appendix 4: Company Secretary Checklist – annual report and accounts   *261*

About The Virtuous Circle   *273*

Index   *275*

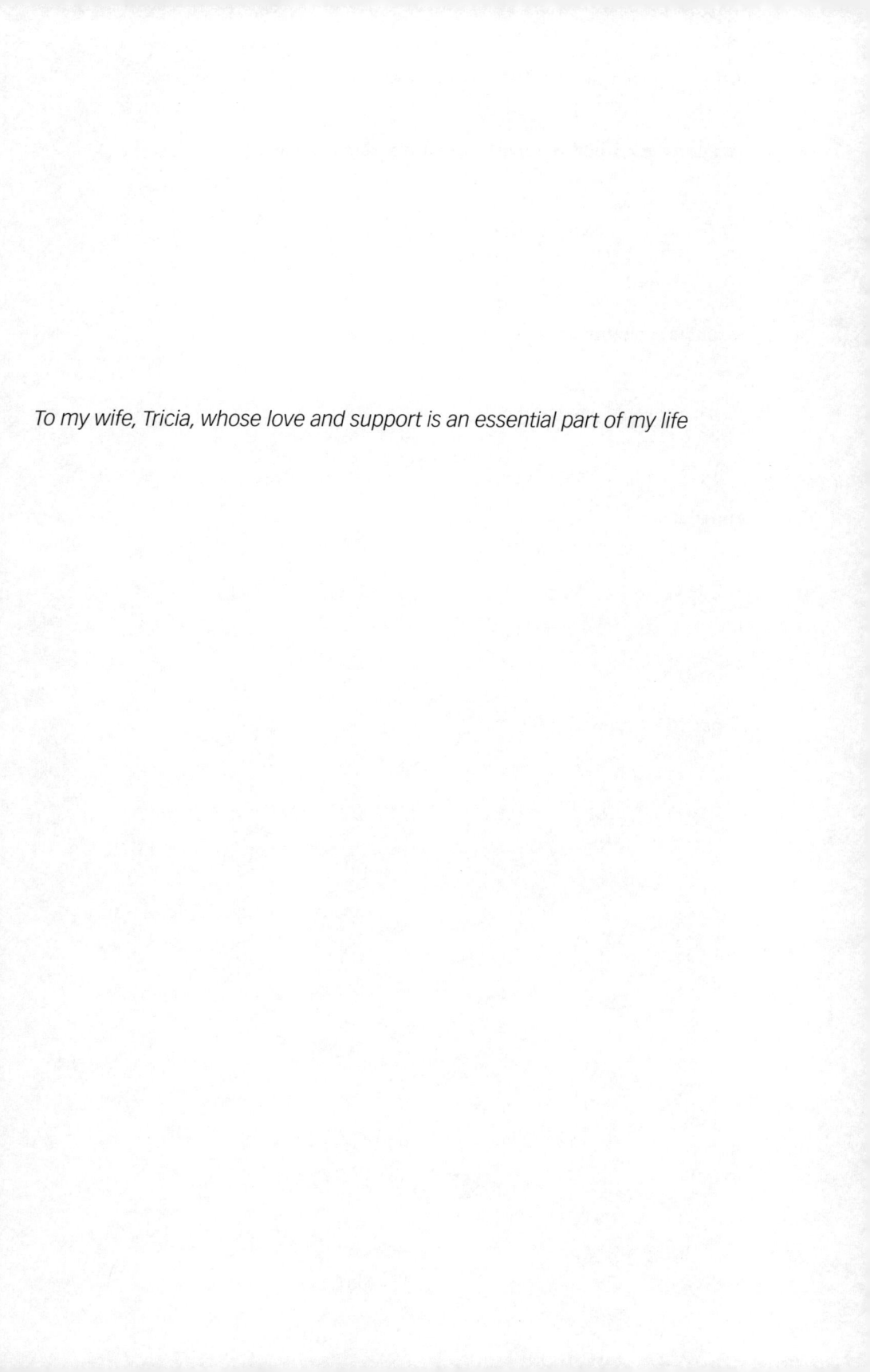

To my wife, Tricia, whose love and support is an essential part of my life

Foreword

There can be little doubt that the quality of corporate reporting is in itself a driver of shareholder value that is increasingly reflected in share prices today. With a developing requirement for directors to provide greater insights into their company's strategy, values, risks and prospects, stakeholders of all persuasions are rightly paying more attention to what is said and how it is said. For better-run companies, this development is to be welcomed as yet another means by which they can differentiate themselves from those that are unable to articulate their performance as clearly.

The challenge for boards is, of course, to convey their key messages in a balanced and succinct fashion to discerning readers who have different interests, whilst at the same time complying with a multitude of legal and accounting requirements, some of which at first sight seem to be in conflict. Navigating this maze is made more difficult by the constant tide of new regulation and the fast-changing views of what 'good' looks like.

For such an important aspect of a company's relationship with the outside world, it is perhaps a little surprising that a practical guide to the topic has not been written already; in this respect, this Handbook is long overdue. In charting the journey that companies are on, both retrospectively and prospectively, and more generally the different forces that are shaping the reporting landscape in the United Kingdom, this book will do much to de-mystify the topic for both authors and readers alike.

Drawing out the learning from others and examining best practice, it sets out the current requirements for both financial and non-financial performance reporting in the United Kingdom, and signals clearly the direction in which such reporting is headed. It defines the boundaries within which companies must operate, whilst offering insights into the options available for those keen to tailor their reporting to their audience.

Despite many articles and publications on this topic, until now there has been nothing quite as accessible or readable. It is inevitable that further editions will be required and desired by the business community.

Phil Hodkinson
Group Finance Director
HBOS plc

Preface

I volunteered to write this book after I had given a presentation at the ICSA Annual Conference in October 2006 on the implications of the latest form of corporate reporting – narrative reporting as required under the Companies Act 1985 (Operating and Financial Review and Directors' Report etc) Regulations 2005 ('the Business Review Regulations'), which were introduced to ratify the European Accounts Modernisation Directive.

When I came to look at the entire subject matter, the complexities became much more evident – and the challenges more daunting. One challenge I found when researching the book was that guidance on the relevant pieces of legislation relating to corporate reporting was seldom to be found in one reference work. In attempting to overcome this challenge, I hope that the book will serve as a readily accessible reference work for all those interested in the various aspects of corporate reporting.

In writing this book, I have positioned it as a guide. I anticipate that the likely readers will be those directors and company secretaries who are or may become involved in producing corporate reports. The book is not intended to be either an accountancy or legal textbook – of which there are enough already. One of the challenges of corporate reporting is the flow of different standards (accounting and legal) that seem to continue to be introduced unabated. Those that are responsible for the accounting or legal aspects of corporate reports should rely on the latest pronouncements from the relevant bodies to ensure that their own company reports meet the latest mandatory requirements.

The book provides the background to the various forms of reporting and offers guidance for those individuals producing them. It also looks at the changes resulting from the Companies Act 2006. These are particularly relevant for UK listed companies, but given the changes in directors' duties, this aspect is relevant to all directors – regardless of the size or nature of their company. In addition, it discusses the process necessary to deliver the final annual report and accounts and considers best practice in corporate reporting.

In the last section of the book, I have looked at what changes may be introduced for corporate reporting. These are more extensive than I had first thought. However, the intention of the changes is to provide greater clarity and to avoid the charges of over-complexity, such as those made by Robert Herz, Chairman of the Financial Accounting Standards Board (FASB) – the leading US accounting regulator:[1]

> So we have both a complexity and a transparency issue. On the one hand, for preparers and auditors, I think the complexity starts with trying to determine which standards, rules or regulations apply in a particular circumstance. . . . On the other hand, investors and other users face a lack of transparency relating to the analytical complexity.

The comments of the CEOs of the international audit networks are also indicative of some of the changes that will be forthcoming in the future, suggesting that there is a need for 'A new business reporting model . . . to deliver relevant and reliable information in a timely way', and that 'The world is changing quickly. It is time for business and the methods for assuring investors of the quality and reliability of business information to change as well'.[2]

With the magnitude of the changes suggested by these commentators, the subject of corporate reporting will remain one that will require all those involved to maintain their knowledge of the mandatory requirements and of best practice to ensure that their reports do justice to the companies – and for the shareholders for whom they are prepared. The nature of corporate reporting has changed, and will undoubtedly continue to change. It is no longer used merely as an historic record, but now includes information that assists the users of these reports to assess how well a company is performing and how well it will perform in the future.

In this respect, it is highly relevant to assess the views of both the users and the producers of corporate reports, in order to understand how they have changed and may change in the future, and this is covered in the final section of the book. I have been fortunate to have access to some of the leading practitioners and influencers in the field of corporate reporting, who gave up their time to discuss their opinions with me. I found their rich mix of opinions and experiences to be highly valuable. Based on interviews with each of them, I have written their views in a common style. If this has led to any misinterpretation, then my apologies to the individuals involved.

NOTES

1 Robert H Herz, speech made to the AICPA National Conference on Current SEC and PCAOB Reporting Developments on 6 December 2005.

2 *Global capital markets and the global economy – A vision from the CEOs of the international audit networks* (November 2006); also available on the Pricewaterhouse-Cooper's website.

Acknowledgements

A book is usually a team effort, even if the author is the one who does the writing. This book is no exception.

Thanks are due to the support given to me during the development and completion of this book. Thanks to my publisher, Isabel Gillies, and to the individuals who reviewed parts of the book. It is always important for an author to have independent insights into both the content and the style, and their input has been invaluable.

In addition, I thank the interviewees featured in Chapters 12–14 for their willingness to contribute their personal views, and for the time they gave during and after the interviews.

Finally, writing a book can be an absorbing activity, particularly when you have an active business life and a fulfilling home life. My thanks go to all the team at The Virtuous Circle for their support and patience whilst I have been writing this book. But most importantly, my thanks go to my wife for putting up with me, both in the time spent and in the ever-changing temperaments that writing a book can cause!

Tony Hoskins, 1 June 2007

CHAPTER 1

Background to corporate reporting

KEY ISSUES

- What is corporate reporting?
- Purpose of corporate reporting
- A brief history of corporate reporting
- Regulatory authorities' role in corporate reporting
- Different accounting standards
  - GAAP
  - IFRS

What is corporate reporting?

For the purposes of this book, the term 'corporate reporting' is defined as being any form of communication between a company and its shareholders. In this respect, this would include:

- annual report and accounts;
- interim statements;
- listing prospectus (for new issues, rights issues or merger or acquisition documents).

Given the changes to corporate reporting included in the Companies Act 2006, the term will also include those documents from the list above that are presented on a company's website – either as a regulatory requirement or as a voluntary inclusion.

Having defined 'reporting', it is also important to define what is meant by 'corporate'. This book focuses on those corporate entities that are regulated under the UK's Companies Act. As such it does not directly cover any of the reporting issues that arise for those companies that have dual listing, such as on the New York Stock Exchange (although the requirements under the Companies Act 2006 Business Review do affect UK companies listed on EU, New

York Stock Exchange and National Association of Securities Dealers Automated Quotations (NASDAQ) stock exchanges).

This includes limited companies (quoted and unquoted) and limited liability partnerships (which are increasingly being used by professional partnerships, such as large firms of solicitors and accountants). It excludes other forms of corporate body, which fall under other forms of reporting regulations, including:

- sole traders and partnerships (which do not have a legal status or personality separate from the owners);
- co-operative bodies (which fall under the Industrial and Provident Societies legislation);
- charities (whose reporting requirements fall under the Charities Act);
- government bodies (which, whilst having some common themes for reporting to limited companies, have to provide their reports in the form of management commentaries).

In total, approximately 1.6 million companies are registered at Companies House. However, the greater majority are small companies (over four million employing less than 50 employees), and only about 6,000 companies are considered to be large (employing over 250 employees).[1] Even then, many of the large companies are subsidiaries of larger groups. There are only about 2,600 companies that have their stocks publicly traded on the London Stock Exchange. However, even this figure can be misleading. About 300 are overseas listed (companies like Boeing and IBM). Of those that are UK companies, many are investment trusts or investment entities, whilst some are the preference share or debentures of listed companies. These total about 700, which leaves about 1,600 companies that could be regarded as operationally active UK listed companies.

The reporting requirements for companies have changed significantly as a result of the passing of the Companies Act 2006. However, much of this commenced with the Business Review Regulations that came into effect for financial years beginning on or after 1 April 2005. In particular there are differences in the nature of reporting based on the size of companies, and for this purpose the book will look at the different reporting requirements for small, medium and large companies, both under the 1985 Act and under the recent legislation.

Purpose of corporate reporting

It is worthwhile reviewing the purpose of reporting and financial statements so that there are some reference points on which other parts of the book can develop. There are four areas to focus upon:

- **Making a report to the shareholders** – to enable shareholders to review the performance of the company in which they have invested. In this respect, a key issue for those companies whose shares are traded is that the report should be audited by an independent and qualified auditor in order to assure shareholders that the directors of the company have been fair and honest in their management of the company and its assets and liabilities. The new Companies Act varies this requirement for small companies.
- **Providing information to other financial stakeholders** – insurers and lenders use corporate reports as part of their evaluation of a company for its credit worthiness and insurability. Again, the availability of audited accounts is an essential element in terms of assuring these financial stakeholders that the company is being run and managed with appropriate levels of probity.
- **Providing the basis on which tax charges are assessed** – as will be seen below on the history of corporate reporting, this purpose is a relatively recent introduction for corporate reporting. However, with the availability of accredited audit professionals, governments and their tax collecting authorities have used the completion of the financial statements as the basis for determining tax charges.
- **Enabling regulators and governments to review the nature of a business or (in aggregate) its business sector** – since the end of the Second World War, governments across the world have recognised the need to regulate certain markets and to assess competitive positions within business sectors. For this purpose, companies' corporate reports are the platform from which governments can assess the size and performance of individual industrial sectors. From these evaluations, they can request further investigations if they believe that there is a regulatory case to be developed, based on their findings.

As will be seen, having audited accounts is important in each of the four areas. This highlights that whilst there may be trust in company directors, there is seen to be a need for checks and balances to ensure that there is no fraud or duplicity on their part. Fraud is an extremely complex issue, and the checks and balances designed to ensure that it does not arise are equally complex. They include the corporate governance system (which is the Combined Code for listed companies), as well as audited accounts. Auditors play an important role in this process.

To be an effective means of communicating across these four areas, corporate reporting needs to be seen to have:

- **reliability** – by which is inferred that the information contained within the reports has been verified to some extent or other, ideally using independent auditors. However, this becomes more challenging when dealing with narrative reporting, and when forward-looking statements are involved;

- **relevance** – if shareholders, investors and creditors are likely to wish to make financial decisions based on the reports they have to hand, then the information contained within the report must be seen to be relevant as a basis on which to make this decision;
- **consistent comparability** – most financial decisions are made on the basis of the evaluation of past performance as a means of interpolating future results. As a consequence, the information contained within these reports needs to have been produced on the same consistent basis. It must be capable of enabling comparison to be made over several financial periods to ensure that track records can be established.

Whilst audited accounts will go some way to assuring shareholders relating to these four areas, a further form of checks and balances is provided by the methods of corporate governance applied. These are particularly relevant in the case of quoted companies.

A brief history of corporate reporting

The names of Enron and Tyco will be fresh in the minds of many readers. However, inappropriate behaviour by directors and officers is not a recent phenomenon. Much of the history of the development of corporate reporting can be seen to have arisen as a result of previous financial scandals. These have necessitated improvements in reporting disclosure to avoid the pitfalls that arose in the past.

The first of these scandals was probably the South Sea Company, whose excesses led to the passage of the Bubble Act of 1720. However, the effect of the growth of the industrial revolution in the United Kingdom led to the advent of companies operating in the fields of canals and docks, railways, banks and mining and quarrying. This growth led to the first real requirement to provide disclosure about the public state of the business to its shareholders. Until that time some of these new companies were incorporated, whilst many, especially banks, were unincorporated. Their constitutions made different provisions for the auditing of accounts with differing rights of access of shareholders to the companies' books.

To address this inconsistency, the Joint Stock Companies Act was passed in 1844. The term 'joint stock' reflects the fact that companies were set up by a number of 'members' or shareholders who jointly held the shares in the component. The Act required all new businesses with more than 25 participants to be incorporated, and have a legal status and personality of their own.

A significant development was that the Act permitted that all companies could be set up by the simple process of registration – rather than by use of an Act of Parliament or by Royal Charter. This provided a significant degree of flexibility to enable the economy to become more competitive. The Act provided for the post of Registrar of Companies (which survives to modern times with the establishment of Companies House). The Act also required companies to provide for 'publicity' (or disclosure) with the requirement for companies' constitutions and annual accounts to be filed with the Registrar of Companies.

In 1855 the Limited Liability Act introduced the concept of general limited liability for shareholders. This further improved disclosure, with the requirement that companies make their creditors aware of this status by including 'limited' or 'ltd' in their names.

These two Acts led to sharp increases in the numbers of incorporated businesses, with 65,000 registered by 1914. This figure rose to about 200,000 by 1945. Since the end of the Second World War, there have been significant rises, and today there are approximately 1.6 million incorporated companies.

However, the two Acts were the last pieces of legislation of a reforming nature for some time. What followed next could be described as a patchwork approach to address perceived deficiencies and shortcomings. Roughly every 20 years, the Board of Trade (the predecessor of the Department for Trade and Industry) appointed committees to review company law. 'Amending Acts' were then passed based on the reports of these committees. Consolidations took place in 1908, 1929 and 1948. In 1948 the company secretary was defined for the first time as an officer of the company, and was made legally liable for complying with the Act.

The last large review took place in 1962 with the report of the Jenkins Committee. Again the outcome of the findings of this committee resulted in a range of piecemeal legislation with amending Acts being passed in 1967, 1980 and 1981.

A major change in the approach to corporate reporting took place with the UK's accession to the EU. Under its company law harmonisation programme the UK Government had to ensure that UK company legislation harmonised with EC directives. The combination of piecemeal legislation and compliance with European legislation meant that the overall effect was close to that of individual pieces of sticky tape trying to hold together a large paper parcel – or what some of the interviewees later in the book described as 'an elastoplast approach to incremental legislation'.

The Companies Act 1985 was a consolidation of all the legislation up to 1985 and was followed by the Insolvency Acts 1985 and 1986 and the Financial Services Act 1986. A further Companies Act was passed in 1989 to implement the Seventh EC Company Law Directive on consolidated accounts and the Eighth Directive on Audits.

Whilst the United Kingdom was adopting this piecemeal approach, other countries, especially those ex colonies that had traditionally seen UK legislation as their model, were taking more radical approaches. Canada, Hong Kong, New Zealand, South Africa and Australia all undertook major reviews of their company law legislation in order to make their own legislation more up to date and tailored to their own local circumstances.

In 1998 the UK Government instigated a consultation on company law reform, with the objective of modernising company law in the United Kingdom. This consultation led ultimately to the Companies Act 2006. The reform process, which started with the first consultation paper in 1998, took a considerable length of time to come to its final conclusion because of the high level of complexity involved. As a result, the 2006 Act is probably the longest Act ever produced.

In Section 1, which follows this chapter, the reporting requirements of the 1985 Act are described, together with the changes that have been introduced under the new Companies Act 2006.

Regulatory authorities' role in corporate reporting

It is necessary to emphasise that although UK company law is an important factor influencing the development of corporate reporting, it is not the only influence, and international legal and accounting standards have had their impacts.

As was mentioned above, much of UK company law is required to follow EU directives. A good example is the European Accounts Modernisation Directive (EAMD). This was passed in June 2003, and EU states had to pass ratifying legislation by 1 January 2005. The UK Government ratified this legislation with the passing of the Companies Act 1985 (Operating and Financial Review and Directors' Report etc) Regulations 2005 ('the Business Review Regulations').

The reason behind the harmonisation programme was to create comparability in the form of a common European capital market across the financial and business community in the EU. To achieve this objective, the EU was able to leapfrog existing legislation, such as that of the United Kingdom, and use the most up-to-date standards available. As an example, the EAMD was developed to respond to the requirements of the International Accounting Standards to have a single set of accounting standards.

Such standards come from a range of bodies. In the United Kingdom, the Accounting Standards Board (ASB) is part of the Financial Reporting Council (FRC). This is the UK's independent regulator for corporate reporting and governance. Its objectives are to promote high quality in terms of:

- corporate reporting;
- auditing;
- actuarial practice;
- standards of corporate governance;
- integrity, competence and transparency of the accountancy and actuarial professions.

Within the FRC, there are also the Auditing Practices Board, the Financial Reporting Review Panel (FRRP), the Professional Oversight Board, the Accountancy Investigation and Discipline Board and the Board for Actuarial Standards.

However, it is the ASB that determines the nature of corporate reporting requirements. It was responsible for the development of the Operating and Financial Review (OFR) and the guidelines for its implementation in the form of its Reporting Statement (originally Reporting Standard 1). The ASB provides guidance to the FRRP on how it should evaluate the quality of individual company reporting. It is essential to understand the extent of this guidance because the FRRP has the legal responsibility to impose criminal or civil penalties on companies if the quality of company reporting is low.

The ASB is an active member of the International Accounting Standards Board (IASB). The IASB is paramount over the ASB, and the latter would be required to introduce as its own standard anything the IASB declared formally to be an international standard. The example quoted in Chapter 14 of this book – the management commentary – is such an instance. If the IASB decides that something is to be a mandatory requirement as a common part of all company reports, the ASB would be required to implement this within the United Kingdom.

Different accounting standards

Whilst the work of the ASB and IASB is providing greater consistency in accounting approach, there are different accounting standards that probably serve to confuse the uninitiated.

GAAP

Until January 2005, generally accepted accounting principles (GAAP) were the basis for all UK accounting practices. This changed with the introduction of International Financial Reporting Standards (IFRS) for all UK listed companies. The phrase 'generally accepted accounting principles' should be familiar to avid readers of annual reports, except that the words 'generally accepted' need to be considered from a geographic perspective. GAAP, as the phrase is commonly known, means different things on opposite sides of the Atlantic. Even with the word 'International' in its title, the IASB is somewhat of a misnomer. Whilst the US accounting regulators are a constituent part of the IASB, they have different sets of standards to the rest of the world.

There are many useful documents available describing in detail the differences between the US GAAP and the UK GAAP, including Deloitte's IAS Plus[2] from which the following main differences have been derived. In this instance, the focus is upon how corporate reports are presented. It should be noted that given its complexity (and the frequency of new exposure drafts being presented) it cannot be claimed to be an exhaustive list.

In terms of **the general approach**, US GAAP tends to be more rules-based, with some forms of application guidance, whilst the IFRS tend to be principles-based, with limited forms of guidance.

Within the report, there is a difference in terms of **the requirement for comparisons**. Whilst the IFRS require a prior year comparison, this is not the case under the US GAAP. However, under the US Securities and Exchange Commission (SEC), listed companies are required to present three years' comparative financial information in their annual reports (although for balance sheet data, this requirement is only for two years' data).

Statements of **changes in equity** are required under, for example, the IFRS, and a grand total of 'comprehensive income' is permitted but not required. This is a calculation that combines net income with losses or gains that are recognised directly in equity. However, in the US GAAP, 'comprehensive income' is a required statement.

Similarly there will be differences in how the **reporting of segment information** is declared. Within the IFRS, the requirement is for lines of business and geographic areas. Under US GAAP, the only requirement is for those components that are the basis for internal management reporting. The accounting basis for such reporting is based on IFRS GAAP measures for those companies reporting to the IFRS, but is based on the internal measures for US GAAP.

Minority interests are also reported on different bases. The IFRS require minority interests to be reported within the equity statement, whereas US GAAP requires them to be reported outside of equity, between liabilities and equity.

Investments in unlisted equity instruments are treated very differently. For the US GAAP, they are valued at cost, whilst the IFRS measure them at fair value.

To give a view of the extent of the differences, the Deloitte document referenced nearly 50 areas of difference. Some were technical, relating to dates of actions, whilst others, such as the valuation of unlisted equity, could have a serious impact upon how the corporate reports are evaluated.

IFRS

In 2001, the EU passed a Regulation that required all listed companies (that is, those companies listed on an EU regulated stock exchange) to prepare their consolidated financial statements based upon the International Financial Reporting Standards (IFRS)[3] for all consolidated financial statements for accounting periods commencing on or after 1 January 2005. Apart from the EU, there are over 70 countries that permit or require the use of IFRS by some or all of their listed companies. In the United Kingdom, the AIM market requires its traded entities to use IFRS (although AIM is not a regulated market and hence the companies traded on it are quoted, but not listed).

One significant change introduced by the IFRS was the 'fair value' measurement. This requires the accounting of assets and liabilities to be on the basis of what is the 'fair value' – this can be based on market value, replacement value or by comparison and reference to market prices of other similar items (as well as by other means such as discounted cash flow). The traditional historical basis for costing is no longer in place. The challenges for 'fair value' lie with those assets or liabilities for which there is no easy means of establishing a market-based comparison, such as intangible assets. From an investor's perspective, there is the possibility of confusion, unless the basis for measurement is clearly stated.

UK unquoted companies are not required to present their statements to IFRS, although the Department of Trade and Industry has indicated that they are permitted to do so should they wish. The most likely candidates to take this option are companies considering becoming quoted companies at some stage in the future. The DTI has also stated that it will review this position in 2008. Other UK unquoted companies must continue using UK GAAP for the presentation of their accounts.

The main differences between UK GAAP and the IFRS lie in the accounting treatment of the following areas:

- pension costs for defined benefit schemes;
- deferred tax;
- financial instruments – especially on derivatives and accounting for fair value;
- goodwill amortisation;
- proposed dividends;

- finance leases;
- preference shares and convertible bonds;
- merger accounting.

However, the ASB has indicated that it does not believe that there is a case for the use of two different standards within the United Kingdom and will make a concerted effort to bring UK GAAP into line with the IFRS, so that, ultimately, UK GAAP will be virtually identical to the IFRS. However, in response to a consultation paper issued by the ASB in March 2005, the Institute of Chartered Accountants in England and Wales (ICAEW) called for reconsideration of this convergence[4] because the IASB is planning to introduce a simplified form of the IFRS for unquoted companies – or, as the IASB describes them, 'entities without external accountabilities'.

For the remainder of this book, we will refer only to the current UK accounting practices – the IFRS for listed companies or UK GAAP for non-listed companies. However, at the end of the book, we will discuss the attempts of the US and IASB accounting bodies to arrive at some consolidation of approach, and review the possible implications.

NOTES

1 Office of National Statistics Press Release URN06/92 (31 August 2006).
2 IAS Plus: Deloitte (August 2005); available at www.iasplus.com/usa/ifrsus.htm.
3 The IFRS were developed by the IASB and implemented in the United Kingdom by the ASB. The reader should understand some of the name and title changes. The IASB replaced the International Accounting Standards Council (IASC), which had produced International Accounting Standards (IAS). Following the introduction of the IASB, the IAS were renamed the IFRS.
4 ICAEW press release, 'No more changes to UK GAAP please'.

SECTION 1
REGULATORY REQUIREMENTS FOR FINANCIAL AND NARRATIVE REPORTING

CHAPTER 2

Corporate reporting under the Companies Act 1985

KEY ISSUES

- Reporting requirements
- Companies Act 1985 – its impact on corporate reporting pre-2005
- Operating and Financial Review (OFR) – 1993 and 2005
  - OFR: 1993 version
  - OFR: 2005 version
- Reporting Statement
- Reporting Statement and key performance indicators
- Business Review 2005

Introduction

In Chapter 1, the changes planned under the Companies Act 2006 were briefly discussed. However, the Government has announced that much of this Act will be implemented via secondary legislation. This is legislation that does not have to undergo full Parliamentary scrutiny (as is the case with Acts of Parliament). The date for the implementation of the last phase of the Companies Act 2006 is 1 October 2007.

As a consequence, it is likely that the 1985 Act will be in force at the time readers will be using this book. Therefore they will need to take the regulations under the 1985 Act into account in terms of producing their corporate reporting. Indeed, the intention of the Companies Act 2006 was not to make wholesale changes but to consolidate and modernise previous legislation. As a consequence, much of the 1985 Act will still have relevance, even when the 2006 Act is fully in force – and some parts may even have been embodied in their entirety within the 2006 Act.

Reporting requirements

The reporting requirements are defined by the Companies Act for all companies. In addition, the Listing Rules will impose additional requirements for listed companies. International Accounting Standards will impact upon reporting, especially those that apply as a result of regulations laid down by the EU (such as the IFRS for listed companies) or directives, which have been ratified by UK legislation, such as the European Accounts Modernisation Directive.

EU regulations do not require UK legislation to be approved by Parliament and are self-standing – although the IFRS requirements are embodied within the 2006 Act, as will be seen later. However, directives require approval of legislation by Parliament, such as the Companies Act 1985 (Operating and Financial Review and Directors' Report etc) Regulations 2005 ('the Business Review Regulations') relating to the Accounts Modernisation Directive, which falls under the auspices of the Companies Act 1985.

Companies Act 1985 – its impact on corporate reporting pre-2005

The corporate reporting requirements were largely prescribed in the original Companies Act 1985. Some elements of the Act were amended subsequently to ensure that it harmonised with EU legislation as it took effect.

An example of this is the Companies Act 1989, which updated the 1985 Act to comply with the EU Seventh Company Law Directive. This Directive defined the circumstances in which consolidated accounts were to be drawn up and regulated the contents of the consolidated annual report. It also established the system of auditing and laid down rules on disclosure.

The 1985 Act required that for each financial year of the company 'the directors of every company shall prepare accounts for the company for each of its financial years' and that 'the balance sheet must give a true and fair view of the state of affairs of the company as at the end of the financial year; and the profit and loss account must give a true and fair view of the profit or loss of the company for the financial year'.

Schedule 4 to the Act described the required form and content of the balance sheet and the profit and loss account, together with the additional information to be provided in the notes to the accounts – the detailed structure of these accounts is set out in Appendix 1. The notes to the accounts were intended to provide clarification to ensure that the accounts represented a true and fair view. If directors were unable to comply with the requirements sufficient to provide a true and fair view, they were required to provide an explanation, similar to the principle of 'comply or explain', which is used in the 2006 Act in relevant areas.

The 1989 Act included the requirement for group directors to produce consolidated accounts, dealing with both the parent company and its subsidiary undertakings. Schedule 4A described the form and content of the consolidated balance sheet and profit and loss account. This included exemption from producing group accounts if the company was a subsidiary of a parent established elsewhere in the EU.

The Act required that a company's annual report (which includes both financial and non-financial information) should include the following elements:

- profit and loss account;
- balance sheet;
- cash flow statements;
- statement of accounting policies, included within the notes to the accounts;
- general topics;
- auditors' reports;
- historical summary;
- directors' reports.

The directors' report is a requirement of the 1985 Act and is intended to give shareholders a more comprehensive picture of the company's current position as well as the nature of the board's governance.

The statutory requirement is that all companies should provide a report that includes:

- a description of the principal activities of the company during the year, together with a comment on any changes in these activities;
- the names of the directors in office during the year, together with their interests in the company's shares (including share options);
- details of any purchase of its own shares made by the company;
- details of any charitable or political donations (in excess of £200);
- any payments to the auditors for non-audit work.

In addition, the Act requires directors of large and medium-sized companies to include additional information, including:

- a fair review of the business, its position at the year end, together with any likely future developments;
- the recommended dividend;

- a statement on any significant post-balance sheet events;
- details of the company's research and development;
- policies on trade creditors;
- policies on the employment of people with disabilities;
- a statement of employee involvement in the company;
- comments on the degree of exposure to financial risks – price, credit, liquidity and cash flow, together with financial risk management policies.

The content of the directors' report has been extended with the introduction of the Business Review, which has undergone two iterations since 2005.

Operating and Financial Review (OFR) – 1993 and 2005

Whilst some observers may have gained the view that the Operating and Financial Review (OFR) was a reporting methodology that emerged out of the company law reform process, it stems from an earlier existence.

OFR: 1993 version

The OFR was first introduced for listed companies in 1993 by the ASB and offered a framework for reporting by listed companies.[1] It was a non-mandatory approach and asserted that there are certain essential features of an OFR which should:

- be clearly written;
- be balanced and objective;
- refer to comments in previous statements that have not be borne out by events;
- provide an analytical discussion;
- follow a 'top down' structure;
- explain the reasons for and effect of any changes in accounting policies;
- make it clear how ratios or numerical information relate to the data included within the financial statements;
- discuss trends and events that have affected or are expected to affect the business.

The directors were permitted to exclude confidential or commercially sensitive information, provided that, as a result, the OFR did not become unbalanced or incomplete.

The OFR was clearly targeted at investors and shareholders, and, as such, the information to be included was only that which was relevant to the needs of the shareholders. Of particular relevance to investors was the section entitled 'Dynamics of the Business' covering the principal risks and uncertainties, for which the ASB provided guidelines as to the nature of possible content, which could include:

- scarcity of raw materials;
- health and safety;
- environmental protection costs;
- product liability;
- skills shortages;
- dependence on a few large suppliers or customs.

As a result, directors were expected to provide qualitative comments on the nature of these potential risks and how they could impact upon the company's results.

Whilst this was a first for such non-financial reporting, the extent of adoption of the OFR occurred mainly in the FTSE 100 companies. Beyond this category, there was evidence that there was a failure to comply with the ASB's guidance. The DTI's view[2] of the quality of OFR reporting was that it was 'falling well short of meeting the ASB's recommended practice'.

Nevertheless, the existence of the OFR was a significant platform for further developments as part of the company law reform, which commenced in 1998.

OFR: 2005 version

As a result of the development of company law reform, a new OFR was developed by the ASB, which gave far greater consideration to other stakeholders, such as employees and customers, as well as requiring more non-financial information that was relevant to shareholders.

The intention of the company law reform was that the OFR should become a mandatory requirement for UK listed companies (and optional for other companies). However, because of the requirement that the Government comply with the European Accounts Modernisation Directive (EAMD) (to be ratified by Member States by January 2005), the introduction of a mandatory OFR was brought forward in advance of the Companies Act. Perhaps significantly (because it led to later confusion), the Government introduced combined legislation for a mandatory OFR for listed companies together with the enabling legislation to introduce the Business Review (which was the key element of the EAMD). This became effective for financial years starting on or after 1 April 2005.

To help guide listed companies in their production of the mandatory OFR, the ASB produced its Reporting Standard 1 (RS1). This was defined as the standard on which the mandatory OFRs should be produced.

However, before the first mandatory OFR was produced, the Chancellor of the Exchequer, Gordon Brown, announced the removal of the statutory requirement to produce an OFR for listed companies. This action was surprising in several respects. First, the Chancellor did not have the legislative brief for the OFR, which lay with the DTI. The second surprise surrounded the circumstances of the announcement, which came at the CBI Conference. This led to accusations of political interference – a charge even more relevant given the fact that the Chancellor did not appear to realise that the OFR was not a 'gold plating' of EU regulations (as he had asserted it to be) but had been borne out of considerable consensual dialogue across many different parties over six years.

The reaction of companies that had spent considerable amounts of time preparing for the OFR was dismay (and concern) that a piece of legislation that had been formulated on a genuine consensus approach could be dismantled so easily. On the other hand for those companies that had not been so diligent in their preparations for their own OFR, there was a huge sense of relief. This relief was based on the assumption that non-financial reporting had disappeared from the corporate reporting agenda. However, these companies were largely unaware of the requirements of the EAMD. As a result, their view that the OFR had been rescinded as a mandatory requirement did not take into account the fact that the statutory instrument under which it had been introduced had only been amended – but not withdrawn. The amendments took out all references to the OFR as a mandatory requirement, but left in the requirements to produce a Business Review.

The OFR was left as a voluntary form of non-financial reporting and the ASB modified its RS1 to become a Reporting Statement,[3] i.e. guidelines for listed companies considering producing an OFR[4] on a voluntary basis. Much of the modification came from changing the word 'would' to 'should' to demonstrate the voluntary nature of the OFR; its content remained otherwise identical.

Reporting Statement

The Reporting Statement remains in place. Its objective is to lay down guidance on best practice for completion of an OFR. This has to be a balanced and comprehensive analysis, as appropriate to the size and complexity of the business. The OFR should include a review of the following components:

- the development and performance of the business during the financial year;
- its position at the end of the financial year;
- the main trends and factors underlying its development, performance and position;
- the main trends and factors likely to affect its future development, performance and position.

The purpose of the review is to assist members (i.e. shareholders) to assess the strategies adopted by the business and the potential for those strategies to succeed.

It is this review of the strategies that marks out the OFR as a new approach to company reporting, which had previously focused on the historic performance of a business. As such, it was perceived as giving little away to the shareholders that would help them to understand how the business functioned and how it might perform over the short and medium term. Even though the OFR was seen to be innovative, there was some concern (particularly from fund managers such as Hermes) about the extent to which the Reporting Statement was considered to be too prescriptive.

Perhaps the bigger issue was that many external stakeholder groups (including unions and NGOs) saw the OFR as providing significant information about a company's approach to its impact on society and the environment. However, what they had failed to appreciate was that the OFR sets out an analysis of the business through the eyes of the directors. The only information that needs to be provided in the OFR is what is relevant to understand the business and its strategies.

An example of organisations attempting to use the OFR to further their own agenda is DEFRA (the UK Government's Department for the Environment and Rural Affairs). When the OFR was first formulated as a mandatory form of corporate reporting, DEFRA produced a report[5] with recommendations on the nature of environmental information that it believed companies should be reporting upon. This report included a total of 25 areas that it considered potentially relevant, but added the proviso that it believed that 80% of companies should be reporting on only five or less of these areas.

The reality, as can be seen later in this book, is that directors were much more challenging as to which areas should be reported upon from the perspective of gaining a greater understanding of their business. They focused on the OFR's intention to provide information relevant to the interests of the shareholders.

The Reporting Statement suggested that the OFR should disclose information relating to its subsidiary undertakings, including issues specific to business segments. This should include forward-looking views, but the Reporting Statement acknowledged that such statements may require a statement asking the shareholders to treat such elements with caution. This relates to the issue of offering a 'safe harbour provision' for directors to enable them to make forward-looking statements based on judgment, without suffering possible litigation from investors and others. Such litigation could arise if they have made decisions based on these statements, which are subsequently found to be inaccurate. Initially, the Government appeared to be unwilling to introduce such a provision, although it was persuaded to do so finally in the Companies Act 2006. Until such time, companies had to provide wording that ensured that any forward-looking statements were treated with caution by shareholders and investors.

As an example of the nature of the wording relating to forward-looking statements, the following were some of those used by companies that produced their first Business Reviews (based on 31 March 2006 year ends) in the form of OFRs based on the Reporting Statement:

- **Vodafone:** In its 2006 annual report, forward-looking statements are referred to at the beginning of the report, with a reference to a section later in the report. In total, one page of the report is devoted to 'A Cautionary Statement Regarding Forward Looking Statements'. Within this page, the areas in which forward-looking statements have been included are discussed, and the risks inherent for each of these areas are described. At the end of the page, the following words are used: 'No assurances can be given that the forward looking statements in this document can be realised. Neither Vodafone nor its affiliates intends to update these forward looking statements'.

- **National Grid:** In its 2006 annual report, a note at the beginning of the report emphasises that 'this report contains statements that are neither reported financial results nor other historical information'. A cautionary statement is also included at the end of the report which states that 'Because these forward looking statements are subject to assumptions, risks and uncertainties, actual future results may differ materially from those expressed in or implied by such statements'.

- **Tate & Lyle:** In its 2006 annual report a 'Cautionary Statement' is included on the first page which states 'There are a number of factors that could cause actual results to differ materially from those expressed or implied by these forward looking statements or profit forecasts. Nothing in this Annual Report and Accounts should be construed as a profit forecast'.

Both National Grid and Vodafone refer to legislation relating to forward-looking statements. Vodafone has a dual listing and refers to having to take account of US legislation, stating that its forward-looking statement falls under the 'US Private Securities Litigation Reform Act (1995)'. National Grid describes its forward-looking statement as falling under the 'Securities Act (1933), as amended', and the 'Securities Exchange Act (1934), as amended'. Tate & Lyle makes no reference to any relevant legislation.

Based on these examples, and the wordings used, it is clear that companies did not find excessive difficulty (although their legal fees for this purpose may have suggested otherwise) in providing forward-looking statements in the OFR, provided appropriate cautionary statements were included.

In addition, the Reporting Statement suggests that the OFR should be used to provide additional explanations of the information included within the financial statement.

However, the overwhelming intention of the Reporting Statement is that the OFR should be comprehensive and understandable, and that the emphasis is on the quality of the explanation of the business rather than the quantity of information provided. This last point was missed by some of the early reports, as will be seen in the coverage of the research relating to these reports, described later in this book. In addition, the Reporting Statement emphasises that the OFR should be balanced and neutral, with an even-handed treatment of both the good and bad aspects of the business's development. In this respect, the intention is that the OFR should be comparable over time, although the length of time envisaged as the basis for reporting is not prescribed in the Reporting Statement.

The ASB has included a disclosure framework within the Reporting Statement. The following are the main elements considered necessary to be included in this framework:

- a description of the business – including a description of the market, its competitive and regulatory environment, and its strategies and objectives;
- the development and performance of the business, both in the current financial year and for the future;
- the resources, principal risks and uncertainties and relationships that may affect the business's long-term value;
- the financial position of the business, including its capital structure, treasury policies and objectives, and liquidity – both for the current financial year and the future.

As part of the above, the OFR is expected to include information about the business's involvement in:

- environmental matters;
- employee matters;
- social and community issues;
- persons with whom the business has contractual (or other) arrangements that are essential to the business;
- receipts from and returns to the shareholders;
- any other matters deemed relevant by the directors.

All of the above are required subject to the phrase 'to the extent necessary', which again focuses on the directors' interpretation of what is necessary to help the shareholders understand the business's strategy and its development.

However, if the directors comment on environmental, employee or social or community issues, the OFR requires that the directors comment on the policy for each area – and the extent to which these policies have been successfully implemented. This last point is a significant issue that will be referred to later in the discussion on the approaches to handling the various reporting requirements.

Reporting Statement and key performance indicators

The OFR requires that key performance indicators (KPIs) should be included to enable shareholders to assess the business's progress against its stated objectives. KPIs should cover both the financial and the non-financial aspects of the business. Again, the OFR uses the phrase 'to the extent necessary' to ensure that it is the directors' interpretation and analysis of the business that is applied, rather than that of a third party.

The business is expected to define each KPI (with an explanation of the method of calculation), describe its purpose and provide a quantification or commentary on future targets. If there are any differences between information included within the financial statements and a version of the same included in the OFR, these differences need to be explained and reconciled. Prior year data for the KPI should be provided wherever possible (although, as will be seen later, this may not be sufficient to provide adequate explanation for a shareholder to understand the nature of the business).

The Reporting Statement gives a selection of 23 KPIs that may be considered for inclusion in an OFR, but makes the point that these are neither exhaustive nor required, since it will be important to fit the choice of the KPIs to the nature of the industry in which the business operates.

The KPIs have been chosen to relate to each area of the OFR, as can be seen below:

- **Nature, objectives and strategies of the business:**
    - return on capital employed;
    - incremental returns on investments;
    - economic profit;
    - organic rates of growth and returns.
- **Market positioning:**
    - market share.
- **Development, performance and position:**
    - average revenue per user;
    - number of subscribers;
    - sales per square foot;
    - percentage of revenue from new products;
    - numbers of products sold per customer;
    - products in the development pipeline;
    - cost per unit produced.
- **Resources, principal risks and uncertainties and relationships:**
    - customer churn;
    - environmental spoilages;
    - CO_2 emissions;
    - waste;
    - employee morale;
    - employee health and safety;
    - monitoring of social risks in the supply chain;
    - noise infringements;
    - reserves;
    - market risk;
    - business continuity management;
    - economic capital;
    - cash conversion rate.

When looking at this list, it may be easy for directors to say that 'they are not relevant to my business', but the challenge for directors is to determine the KPIs that reflect the main business drivers for their business, and in this respect the word 'key' is the critical descriptor, which emphasises the quality of measurement.

In a similar manner, when the Reporting Statement refers to the 'Principal risks and uncertainties', the emphasis is on the word 'principal'. It is not intended that the OFR should include the business's entire risk register. In contrast, it is intended to cover financial, commercial, operational and strategic risks. This range of risks covers areas that companies often had not fully disclosed in the past, focusing instead on financial risks, such as treasury, currency and interest rates, and excluded areas such as reputation risks.

Finally, the Reporting Statement suggests that directors should include in the annual report a statement that the OFR has been prepared in accordance with the Reporting Statement. This is treated as a matter of best practice, whereas when the OFR was a mandatory form of reporting, this was a requirement as a formal confirmation.

Business Review 2005

The Business Review (also known as an enhanced directors' report) was established under the Companies Act 1985 and introduced via Regulations in March 2005.[6] However, as described earlier, these Regulations included the requirement for a mandatory OFR. The Regulations were repealed in January 2006,[7] with new Regulations deleting all reference to the OFR, leaving the (now more skeletal) 2005 Regulations referring only to the Business Review.

The Business Review was introduced by the UK Government in order to ratify the EAMD.[8] The Directive was formulated in June 2000, when the Commission published its communication entitled 'EU Financial Reporting Strategy: The Way Forward', which proposed that all listed companies prepare consolidated accounts in accordance with one single set of accounting standards – the International Accounting Standards. The deadline for achieving this was set for 2005. The impetus behind this communication was the EU Lisbon Summit, which, amongst other matters, urged that 'steps be taken to enhance the comparability of financial statements prepared by Community companies whose securities are admitted to trading on a regulated market'.

The EAMD consolidated previous directives, as well as taking into account the concerns of the Lisbon Summit. As a result, it was held to apply to all forms of companies. The deadline for its ratification by Member States was 1 January 2005. All of the 25 Member States have ratified the EAMD with their own enacting legislation, with the exception, as at December 2006, of Italy and Greece, whose governments are being taken to the European Court of Justice for their non-compliance with the Directive.

The ratifying Member States have introduced legislation similar to the UK's Business Review, and any UK group company with European subsidiaries will be required to produce a similar form of Business Review reporting. The exact format of the equivalent of the Business Review will be defined by local country legislation since the EAMD does not specify where the information will be held – merely that it be included 'in the annual report'. The UK Government determined that within the United Kingdom the Business Review should be considered to be part of an enhanced directors' report.

The Business Review Regulations require a company to produce a directors' report (or a consolidated or enhanced directors' report) that includes the following information:

- names of persons that held the position of director at any time during the financial year;
- principal activities of the company;
- amounts recommended as dividends;
- a Business Review;
- with regard to Sch. 7 to the Companies Act 1985, disclosure of:
  - matters of a general nature, such as changes in asset values, directors' shareholdings and other interests, and contributions for political and charitable purposes;
  - acquisition of its own shares (or a charge on them);
  - employment, training and advancement of disabled persons;
  - involvement of employees in the affairs, policy and performance of the company;
  - policy and practice of the payment of amounts due to creditors.

Essentially, the Business Review is the new element in the requirement for the production of the directors' report. The required content and approach of the Business Review is as follows:

- It must contain a fair review of the business and a description of the principal risks and uncertainties facing the company.
- It must be a balanced and comprehensive analysis of the development and performance of the business during the financial year and the position of the company at the end of the financial year.
- It must (to the extent necessary to ensure understanding of the business) include an analysis using financial KPIs and, where appropriate, analysis using other KPIs, including information relating to environmental and employee matters.

- It must (where appropriate) include references to, and additional explanations of, amounts included in the annual accounts.

These requirements apply to all UK companies – listed and unlisted, group companies and subsidiaries, UK-owned and foreign-owned – but there are different applications dependent upon the size of the company concerned. The definition of the size of the company is one that is used consistently across the EU. A company will determine its size if, at each level, it meets two out of three qualifying criteria (turnover, balance sheet total or employee numbers):

- A small company is one whose turnover does not exceed £5.6 million, whose balance sheet total is no more than £2.8 million, and which has no more than 50 employees.
- A medium company is one whose turnover does not exceed £22.8 million, whose balance sheet total is no more than £11.4 million, and which has no more than 250 employees.
- A large company is one whose turnover exceeds £22.8 million, whose balance sheet total exceeds £11.4 million, and which has more than 250 employees.

It should be noted that the definitions emanate from the EU,[9] and the financial criteria are actually stated in Euros and are inflation linked. Hence these precise financial definitions will vary over time.

The difference in application of the requirements relate to the need for submission of a directors' report and the need to provide KPIs. Small companies must produce a directors' report but do not have to file it with Companies House if they choose to submit abbreviated accounts. Medium companies must submit a directors' report but do not need to comply with the requirement to provide non-financial KPIs.

These different applications do not apply if the company in question is a public company.

In addition, the small companies' exemption did not originally apply to a company operating under Part 4 of the Financial Services and Markets Act 2000, carrying on a regulated activity or carrying out an insurance market activity. However, in November 2006, new Regulations[10] were passed which allowed certain categories of small-sized financial services and insurance companies to take advantage of this exemption. This was an unsurprising turnaround, given that one of our client's contacts – a bank – told us that it had to produce 400 Business Reviews because of this anomaly. Bearing in mind the Government's objective of reducing bureaucracy, this was a situation that could be best described as having contravened the delivery of the objective.

Companies that are part of a group must produce a group directors' report covering the parent and those subsidiaries included in the consolidated accounts. However, there is no 'group exemption' and all UK subsidiaries have to produce their own Business Review (and for their EU subsidiaries, its equivalent in each Member State).

Under these Regulations, companies that distribute full accounts to shareholders are required to distribute the directors' report (including the Business Review) to those shareholders. However, companies that send summary financial statements are not required to include a summary of the directors' report – although they may choose to do so, either in the form of selected information or the full directors' report. However, shareholders are entitled to request and obtain a copy of the directors' report from the company.

An enforcement regime was put in place under the Business Review Regulations. Companies deemed to be in breach of any aspect of the Business Review Regulations are liable to criminal penalties (for financial years beginning on or after 1 April 2005) and to civil penalties (for financial years beginning on or after 1 April 2006).

The Financial Reporting Review Panel (FRRP) (a sister body of the ASB, and part of the Financial Reporting Council) was given legal authority under the Regulations to review directors' reports for financial years beginning on or after 1 April 2006, and, if necessary, to go to court to comply a company to review its report.

Based on discussions with these bodies, it seems unlikely that the Panel would ever find it necessary to pursue its rights until it took a company to court. The more likely scenario would be a series of discussions where a company 'voluntarily' revises its report. Any company so involved would find its financial and corporate reputation seriously affected, and the mere request for information from the FRRP would lead a company to modify its report. However, there needs to be an enforcement regime even if, at this stage, there is no case law to demonstrate how the Panel would operate and at what point it would take a company to court.

The guidance given in April 2005 about how the Panel would be expected to act with regard to a questionable OFR was that if the Panel came across something in (or an omission from) the OFR, it would take several courses of action. In the first instance it may contact the company for further information or explanation. Then, if still dissatisfied, it may request evidence of the basis on which the company compiled its OFR, and how it reached its conclusion on the issues causing concern. If the results of these two sets of actions fail to satisfy the Panel, it may ask the company voluntarily to revise its OFR or make a corrective statement. Only where the company fails to act voluntarily would the Panel apply for a court order to compel the company to revise its OFR.

In order to obtain a satisfactory explanation to its investigation regarding a particular issue in a company's report, the Panel has the power to request the production of documents from the company itself, any officer, employee or auditor of the company, as well as anyone who had been an officer, employee or auditor at the time to which the request for information or documentation refers.

This wording relating to the Panel's approach and the powers it has to request information suggests that it would be wise for all companies to document their process and decisions reached in developing their Business Reviews. As a consequence, in the event of the Panel making an investigation into any aspect of its Business Review, a company would be able to answer any questions and provide evidence of the nature of the decisions reached and the process under which they were made.

Perhaps a more interesting point is that the Business Review Regulations are not prescriptive in terms of what information should appear in a Business Review. The challenge for the Panel is to establish how it would evaluate company reports and to decide what is best practice and what is unacceptable practice.

As it stands, the only point of reference available to the Panel is the OFR Reporting Statement produced by the ASB. It seems, based on experience of the early Business Reviews, that using the Reporting Statement could be a useful framework on which to develop the Business Review. It acts as a helpful checklist for companies to ensure that they are confident that their reporting comes close to complying with the Business Review requirements.

NOTES

1 ACCA, *The operating and financial review – a catalyst for improved social and environmental disclosure*, Research Report No. 89 (2005).

2 DTI, *Draft Regulations on the Operating and Financial Review and Directors' Report – A consultative document* (2004).

3 Accounting Standards Board, *Reporting Statement: Operating and Financial Review* (January 2006).

4 It should be noted that whilst the OFR is intended for voluntary use by listed companies (and any others for which it may be an appropriate framework for reporting) it is a mandatory framework for some government bodies. In these cases, the OFR is described as a Management Commentary. Such bodies are those bodies that receive funding from government and include organisations such as NHS Trusts and the Post Office.

5 *Environmental Key Performance Indicators – Reporting Guidelines for UK Business* (DEFRA, 2005).
6 Companies Act 1985 (Operating and Financial Review and Directors' Report etc) Regulations 2005 (SI 2005/1011).
7 Companies Act 1985 (Operating and Financial Review) (Repeal) Regulations 2005 (SI 2005/3442).
8 Directive 2003/51/EC of 18 June 2003.
9 The latest financial criteria can be found on the EU website at ec.europa.eu/enterprise/enterprise_policy/sme_definition/index_en.htm.
10 For details of which categories of financial services and insurance companies can claim this exemption, readers are referred to the Companies Act (Small Companies' Accounts and Audit) Regulations 2006 (SI2006/2782), which apply to companies whose financial years end on or after 31 December 2006.

CHAPTER 3

Impact of Companies Act 2006 on corporate reporting

KEY ISSUES

- Background to the Act
- Objectives of the Act
- Changes to duties owed by directors
- Accounts and reports
  - Size matters
  - Group size criteria for small companies
  - Quoted or not
- Various forms of accounts
  - Statutory and non-statutory accounts
  - Summary financial statements
  - Abbreviated accounts
- Duties of companies regarding reports and accounts
- Separate requirements dependent on nature of company
  - Company size
  - Private and public companies
  - Quoted and unquoted companies
- Compliance
  - Penalty – imprisonment or fine
- Enforcement
  - Court orders and civil penalties
  - Secretary of State's notices

Background to the Act

The Companies Act 2006 took almost eight years from initial development and consultation. Looking back, it was a long drawn-out affair. The process started in 1998 with the Company Law Review, followed by Green Papers and, in 2001, a Final Report. In 2002 an initial White Paper was produced, followed in 2005 by a further White Paper and further clauses. In November 2005, the Bill was published, but it took a further year until it arrived on the statute books in November 2006.

However, even at this stage, the process is incomplete, because the Government has indicated that much of the intent within the Act will be translated into law via secondary legislation. The details of the intentions established under the Act will be worked upon by government departmental officials, who will then draft the legislation, usually in the form of a statutory instrument (SI). This will be put before a Standing Committee of the House of Commons (i.e. a group of MPs who have been brought together for the express purpose of reviewing the clauses within the SI). The Committee will amend the SI as appropriate and lay it before the House for it to be passed into law. This is a much faster way of enacting legislation, but can generally only be used if there are Acts in place that describe the underlying intention of the Houses of Parliament.

The Government has stated that all of this secondary legislation will have been completed by October 2008, and that the entire Act will be in force by that date. Some legislation elements came into force as early as January 2007. One relates to the EU's Transparency Directive and came into force on the Act being given Royal Assent. Another relates to electronic communications, which came into force on 20 January 2007. The provisions to implement the Takeovers Directive came into force on 6 April 2007.

The timing of the effective dates of the remainder of the Act is being phased over the period up until 1 October 2008[1] – partly because of the sheer size of the Act (over 70 sets of regulations will be required) and partly because of the need to establish how it will affect the legal position of existing companies – for example, as regards their articles and memoranda – for which the Government is conducting consultation with business.

In terms of those parts of the Act that relate to corporate reporting, the new directors' duties regime takes effect from 1 October 2007, as does the section relating to the Business Review. This covers both the enhanced reporting requirements for quoted companies and the new statutory purpose requirements that cover all forms of business entities that have to produce Business Reviews – quoted and unquoted companies. Table 3.1 overleaf is a tabular form of the implementation timetable for those parts of the Act that relate to corporate reporting.

In its finished form the Act is one of the longest ever to become law, comprising 44 Parts, 1,300 clauses, 16 Schedules and 701 pages (excluding the index of contents, which runs to 59 pages).

Objectives of the Act

The Government stated its aims for the company law reform at the outset of the course of development of the Act. Its purpose was to improve existing framework to ensure that the United Kingdom remains 'an excellent place to operate a

Table 3.1

Parts of the Act and description	Introduction date
Sections relating to the Transparency Directive (electronic and website communication)	20 January 2007
Part 10 (company's directors – including general duties of directors, but excluding directors' conflict of interest duties, directors' residential addresses and underage and natural directors)	1 October 2007
Part 15 (Accounts and Reports – s. 417 only – Business Review)	1 October 2007
Part 42 (statutory auditors – naming of auditors)	6 April 2008
Part 10 (company's directors – remaining sections)	1 October 2008

business'. Its intent was to consolidate, update and deregulate company law, making it as clear and modern as possible. Its approach was to restructure and redraft in far clearer language most of the Companies Act 1985 and 1989.

At its heart is the concept of directors taking account of 'enlightened shareholder value'. This was first stated in the report of the Steering Group, and represents 'an obligation on directors to achieve the success of the company for the benefit of the shareholders by taking proper account of all the relevant considerations for that purpose'.

Included within these considerations are 'a proper balanced view of the short and long term, the need to sustain effective ongoing relationships with employees, customers, suppliers and others; and the need to maintain the company's reputation and to consider the impact of its operations on the community and the environment'.[2]

Four key objectives were set by the Government. It was expected the Companies Act would result in a business law environment that:

- enhances shareholder engagement and a long-term investment culture;
- ensures better regulation and a 'Think Small First' approach;
- makes it easier to set up and run a company;
- provides flexibility for the future.

As regards enhancing shareholder engagement (a key outcome for company reporting) a main aim was to assist in improving shareholder dialogue. This was considered important especially as regards enfranchising indirect investors (such as those who held their shares through nominee accounts). The latter would normally lose their voting rights by placing their shares in nominee holdings. In this respect, the Government wanted to improve shareholder engagement by facilitating e-communications. A further aim of the Government's objective for enhancing shareholder engagement was to improve the quality of narrative reporting for listed companies.

Other aims included regulating directors' conflicts of interest, dealing with derivative claims and auditors' liability.

Changes to duties owed by directors

From the perspective of company reporting, perhaps the most significant development was the link provided in the Companies Act 2006 between narrative reporting and the new codified directors' duties. However, the impact of this new description has been questioned by some, as will be seen in Chapter 13 on interviews with key practitioners.

In total, there are seven codified general duties of directors. In framing the duties, the Government's aims were to improve clarity and accessibility, correct defects in the law in relation to the duties of conflicted directors, and ensure that directors would take account of 'enlightened shareholder value'.

These duties include the duties to act within powers, to exercise independent judgment, to avoid conflicts of interest, not to accept benefits from third parties, and to declare interest in proposed transactions or arrangements.

However, it is the final duty that has the most impact within the context of company reporting. This is the duty 'to promote the success of the company'. The exact wording of the first subsection of the relevant provision[3] is as follows:

> A director of a company must act in the way he considers, in good faith, would be most likely to promote the success of the company for the benefit of its members as a whole, and in doing so have regard (amongst other matters) to –
>
> a) the likely consequences of any decision in the long term,
> b) the interests of the company's employees,
> c) the need to foster the company's relationships with suppliers, customers and others,

d) the impact of the company's options on the community and the environment, the desirability of the company maintaining a reputation for high standards of business conduct, and

e) the need to act fairly as between members of the company.

The duty to promote the success of the company has its origins lying firmly within the concept of enlightened shareholder value. Effectively, it replaces the previous fiduciary duty of directors 'to act in the best interests of the company, having regard to the interests of shareholders'.

This new duty provides an express statutory purpose for the Business Review – namely to help members assess how effectively the directors have performed their duty to promote the success of the company. This express purpose is relevant in relation to the approach under the enforcement regime of the Financial Reporting Review Panel.

From a board perspective, the new duty will require directors to consider to what extent they are aware that the managers of the company are running it in a manner that supports them in this duty.

The challenges become far greater when we consider the position of non-executive directors, especially in quoted companies. In these instances, the non-executives may outnumber the executives, particularly in larger companies. However, they are unlikely to be as familiar as the executive directors with the quality of the company's management as regards the non-financial areas.

In the past non-executive directors would expect to receive financial reports of the company's progress, but they must now familiarise themselves to a possibly greater extent with the operational activities of the company of which they are director. There is a need for non-executives to be more probing of management's actions and to understand the context in which they operate. This is particularly significant bearing in mind that the Act requires all directors to certify to the auditors that they have been provided with all the information they need to know about the company. A greater degree of interactivity between executives and non-executives could be regarded as more beneficial to the company as a whole, but may be seen as somewhat frustrating by the management and executive directors.

This challenge is amplified when a multinational business is considered. In such circumstances, the directors of overseas subsidiaries should be aware of the duties of the directors of their UK parent (even if it has no comparable statute in their own country's company law) in order for them understand the obligations placed on the UK parent board and the non-financial reporting requirements.

Accounts and reports

The accounts and reports section[4] of the Companies Act 2006 has been schemed to reinforce the Government's 'Think Small First' approach. The intention is that smaller companies should not be overburdened by legislation that is more pertinent to larger companies. In essence the Act has been constructed in the manner of building blocks, but there is also an order for the Act's contents. The provisions applying to small companies appear before those applying to other companies. In a similar manner, the provisions applying to private companies appear before those relating to pubic companies. The same applies to quoted companies, with their provisions appearing after those relating to all other companies.

Nevertheless, for those reading the Act, its presentation may remain a little confusing. To simplify matters, in this chapter, those aspects relating to differing sizes of companies have been grouped.

Size matters

The Act sets out clearly how to determine the size qualifications for small companies (discussed earlier in relation to the Business Review 2005).

First, the Act states that a company is qualified as small in its first financial year of operation if it meets the size criteria. In subsequent years, a company is qualified as small if the 'small company' qualifying criteria were met in that year and in the preceding financial year.

The definition of the various criteria is also clarified.

For **turnover**, where the financial year is not a full calendar year (as may be the case for the first financial year) the criteria for the maximum figures for turnover must be proportionately adjusted.

The **balance sheet total** refers to the aggregate amounts of assets shown in the balance sheet.

The **number of employees** is in fact an average – and not the year-end figure. This average is calculated by taking the numbers of persons employed under contracts of service in each month (and this could be based on numbers employed throughout), adding these numbers for each month in the financial year, and then dividing by the total number of months in that financial year.

Group size criteria for small companies

If the company is a parent of a number of other companies, that company qualifies as small only if the group of companies (that it heads) qualifies as small.

The qualifying criteria are modified slightly to take account of any set-offs or adjustments to eliminate group transactions, but the figures are quoted both net and gross:

- turnover – not more than £5.6 million net (or £6.72 million gross);
- balance sheet total – not more than £2.8 million net (or £3.36 million gross);
- employees – not more than 50.

These net figures are calculated, in the case of Companies Act accounts, in accordance with s. 404 of the Act, and, for IAS accounts, in accordance with international accounting standards (IFRS).

As with the Business Review 2005, there are exclusions to this small company regime for any company that has been (at any time with regard to the financial year in question):

- a public company;
- a company that is an authorised insurance company, a banking company, an e-money issuer, an investment firm that has its registered office (or, if it has no registered office, its head office) in an EEA state, an undertaking for collective investment in a transferable securities (UCITS) management company, or a company that carries out insurance market activity;
- a member of an ineligible group – which would be the case if any member of the group is a public company, or whose shares are traded on a regulated market within a European Economic Area state,[5] or is a person (other than a small company) who carries out a regulated activity under Pt 4 of the Financial Services and Markets Act 2000, or is a small company that is an authorised insurance company, a banking company, an e-money issuer, an ISD investment firm or a UCITS management company, or is a person who carries out insurance market activity.

It should be noted that the reporting position for small companies operating under Pt4 of the Financial Services and Markets Act 2000 was changed as a result of the Companies Act (Small Companies' Accounts and Audit) Regulations 2006 (SI 2006/2782) which enabled some small financial services companies operating under this Act to claim the small companies exemption.

Quoted or not

In defining whether a company is deemed to be 'quoted', the timeline is whether it is a quoted company immediately before the end of the financial year. A quoted company is one whose equity share capital:

- has been included in the official list in accordance with Pt 6 of the Financial Services and Markets Act 2000; or
- is officially listed in a European Economic Area state; or
- is admitted to dealing on the New York Stock Exchange or NASDAQ.

Any company not meeting any of these criteria is de facto 'unquoted'. This means that for this purpose, companies registered on other markets, such as Alternative Investment Market (AIM), are not quoted.

Various forms of accounts

Accounts can be produced in several different forms, dependent on their purpose and the nature of the business. The following gives some explanation about the different forms.

Statutory and non-statutory accounts

Statutory accounts are those accounts required to be submitted to the Registrar of Companies. Such accounts must be accompanied by an auditors' report (unless they are exempt from an audit, and the directors have taken advantage of this exemption). If a company is the parent of a group, it must publish its group accounts with its individual accounts.

Non-statutory accounts may be produced for non-filing purposes, such as obtaining loans or preparing a prospectus. They may be either a balance sheet or a profit and loss account, or both. If they are published, a statement should accompany them that indicates that they are not statutory. The statement must also state whether any statutory accounts (relating to the same period) have been delivered to the Registrar of Companies. In addition, it should state whether any auditors' report has been made on the statutory accounts, and whether it was qualified or unqualified. The auditors' report for the statutory accounts must not be published with the non-statutory accounts.

Unlike the 1985 Act, where specific format of the profit and loss accounts and the balance sheet are provided,[6] the 2006 Act is not prescriptive about the format of these financial statements. This is partly because of the introduction of International Accounting Standards (IAS), which provide the more prescriptive requirements.

The Act requires individual accounts to be produced in compliance with regulations regarding their form and content (with the need for additional information in the notes to the accounts), or, where the directors prepare IAS individual accounts, this must be stated in the notes to the accounts.

For group accounts, the Act states that certain companies have to prepare their accounts in accordance with art. 4 of the IAS Regulations, whilst other group accounts should either comply with regulations laid down by the Secretary of State or be prepared in accordance with the IAS.

Summary financial statements

Summary financial statements may be sent out instead of the full set of accounts and report. If a company uses this option, all persons entitled to receive the accounts and reports must be sent a summary financial statement if they wish to receive it.

The summary financial statement for an unquoted company must state that it is only a summary of information derived from the company's annual accounts. It must also state whether it contains additional information derived from the directors' report (and, if this is the case, that it does not include the full text of the directors' report). It should also include an auditors' statement that the summary is consistent with the full annual accounts (including the excerpts of the directors' report, if appropriate). Furthermore, it must state whether the auditors' report for the full accounts was qualified or unqualified (for both the accounts and the directors' report).

The statement should also state how a person who is entitled to the full report and accounts and directors' report (the 'statutory accounts') can obtain a copy, should he or she wish to do so.

For quoted companies producing a summary financial statement, this follows the same requirements as for unquoted companies, but with the addition of references to the directors' remuneration report as well as those relating to the directors' report.

Abbreviated accounts

Small and medium-sized companies are entitled to submit abbreviated accounts to the Registrar of Companies. However, whilst such accounts can cut costs and save time, their use should be based on careful consideration since potential customers, suppliers, investors and lenders may check a company's accounts before doing business with it.

For a small company (including a small limited liability partnership – LLP) abbreviated accounts must include an abbreviated balance sheet with notes explaining the make-up of the figures in the balance sheet in more detail, together with a special auditors' report. The latter must state that the company is entitled to submit abbreviated accounts.

For medium-sized companies (and LLPs) the abbreviated accounts must include an abbreviated profit and loss account, a full balance sheet, a directors' report (although this is not required for LLPs), notes to the accounts and a special auditors' report (as for small companies).

If a company chooses to produce abbreviated accounts, these must be approved by the board and signed on behalf of the board by a director, whose signature must appear on the balance sheet. Prominently above this signature must be a statement that the balance sheet has been prepared in accordance with the provisions of the Act relating to abbreviated accounts.

For full information on abbreviated accounts, the Business Link website[7] offers useful information for small and medium companies.

Duties of companies regarding reports and accounts

The Act consolidates existing legislation and regulations. Within these are requirements regarding duties relating to reports and accounts, together with details of the penalties for directors and companies for non-compliance.

The table below sets out the list of duties regarding a company's report and accounts, together with a detailed description of related activities. A description of the separate requirements that depend on the nature of the company follows. Penalties for directors for non-compliance with these duties are then detailed, and details of the enforcement regime for companies that do not comply are set out.

Table 3.2

Duties relating to report and accounts	Detailed description
Duty to keep accounting records	Every company must keep **adequate accounting records**, covering monies received and expended and a record of the assets and liabilities of the company, plus, if goods are traded, a statements of stocks held in these goods.
	Every company must **keep its accounting records** at the registered office (or other place, as seen fit) and these records must be open to inspection by the company's officers.
Duty to prepare individual and/or group accounts	Directors should be satisfied that sets of accounts that they approve are a **true and fair view** of the assets, liabilities, financial position and profit or loss of the company (or the group if this is the case).
	A company's **individual accounts must be prepared** either in accordance with s. 396 of the Companies Act 2006 or in accordance with International Accounting Standards.

Table 3.2 continued

Duties relating to report and accounts	Detailed description
	Once preparation of the accounts in accordance with IAS is begun, this should continue (with a note to the accounts stating that this is the method of preparation), unless there are relevant changes of circumstances.
	Companies Act accounts must comprise a balance sheet (as at the end of the financial year) and a profit and loss account for that year.
Information to be included in notes to accounts	**Information about related undertakings** is required to be given in the notes to the accounts.
	However, **information about related undertakings need not be disclosed** if the undertaking is established outside the United Kingdom, or does business outside the United Kingdom and the directors are of the opinion that such information would be seriously prejudicial to the business of that undertaking, the company and it subsidiaries or any other business included in the consolidation. However, such exemption requires the agreement of the Secretary of State. If such an exemption is taken advantage of, then there must be a note to that effect in the annual accounts.
	If the directors believe that the number of undertakings on which information should be disclosed would result in **an excessive amount of information being included in the notes to the accounts** an 'alternative compliance' approach is available, for which the notes to the accounts would include only those undertakings that principally affected the figures in the company's annual accounts or are excluded from consolidation into group accounts.
	If this 'alternative compliance' approach is adopted, the notes to the accounts should state that this is the case (and include the basis for inclusion of principal undertakings). In addition, the full information relating to related undertakings (i.e. both those companies included in the notes to the accounts and those excluded) must be annexed to the full report and accounts delivered to the Registrar of Companies.
Information about company's employees	Information about the company's employees must be provided and **comprise the average numbers employed during the financial year and the average number based on a selection determined by the directors** as being relevant to the way in which the company is organised. If not stated elsewhere in the accounts, the aggregate sums for wages and salaries, social security costs and pensions should be stated.

Information about directors' remuneration	Information about the directors' remuneration must be provided and cover details of the various **remuneration components**, including gains made on exercise of share options, benefits received or receivable under long-term incentive plans, payments for loss of office, benefits receivable in respect of past services as a director or in any other capacity, and consideration paid to or receivable by third parties for making the services of the person available as a director.
Information about directors' benefits	Information about directors' benefits must be provided and **relate to a person either as director of a company not preparing group accounts, or as a director of a parent company** – detailing advances and credits granted by the company to its directors and guarantees of any kind entered into by the company on behalf of its directors.
Approval and signing of accounts	**A company's annual accounts must be approved** by the board of directors and signed on behalf of the board by a director, with the signature appearing on the balance sheet.
Duty to prepare directors' report	**The directors must produce a directors' report** for each financial year, and if the company is a parent, and group accounts are prepared, the directors' report must be a consolidated report, known as a 'group directors' report'. In such cases, the report may give greater emphasis to those matters significant to the undertakings included in the consolidation, rather than focusing solely on matters relating to the parent.
	The contents of a directors' report comprise the names of the persons who were directors during the financial year and the **general activities of the company. In addition, the report must state the amount recommended as payment as a dividend.**
	The directors' report must also include **a Business Review**, which must contain a fair review of the company's business and a description of the principal risks and uncertainties facing the company. The Review should be a balanced and comprehensive analysis of the development and performance of the company's business during the year and the position of the business at the year end. The content of the Review should be consistent with the size and complexity of the business of the company. The Review should, to the extent necessary, include analysis using financial key performance indicators and, where appropriate, other key performance indicators, including information relating to environmental and employee matters. The selection of these key performance indicators is determined by the directors, and should be based on the ability to enable an understanding of the development, performance

Table 3.2 continued

Duties relating to report and accounts	Detailed description
	and position of the company's business. It should also include references to and additional explanations of amounts included in the annual accounts – where appropriate. The directors are not required to disclose information about impending developments or agreements in the course of negotiation if they deem them to be seriously prejudicial to the interests of the company.
	The directors' report should also include a **statement of disclosure to auditors**. This statement should indicate that, for those directors in office at the time the report was approved, there is no relevant audit information of which the auditors are unaware and that all relevant steps have been taken to identify any relevant audit information and to establish that the company's auditors are aware of such information. Whilst this is a statement in the directors' report, the responsibility falls individually upon each of those individuals who were directors at the time of the approval of the accounts.
	A director will have been deemed to have discharged his or her duty if enquiries have been made of fellow directors for that purpose and any other steps have been taken, as appropriate. In so doing, each director will have fulfilled his or her duty to exercise reasonable care, skill and diligence.
	The **directors' report must be approved** by the board and signed on behalf of the board by a director or the company secretary.
Duty to circulate copies of the annual report and accounts	Every company must ensure that it sends a **copy of its annual report and accounts** to every member, every holder of debentures and every person entitled to receive notice of general meetings, provided the company has a current address for that individual or entity. The time allowed for sending out the report and accounts will vary dependent upon the nature of the company.
	A company may provide **a summary financial statement** instead of copies of the accounts and report (see earlier in this chapter for a description of the form and content of such summary statements).
Requirements as to website publication	The requirement to **publish the report and accounts on their website** applies only to quoted companies. The detailed requirements will be dealt with later under the section on quoted companies' requirements.

Rights of member or debenture holder to demand copies of annual report and accounts	For an unquoted company, **a member or a debenture holder is entitled to be provided on demand, and without charge, a copy of the last annual accounts and directors' report together with the auditors' report relating to those accounts**. It should be noted that this relates to a single copy only, and is in addition to the requirement to send a copy of the documents to these persons. In the case of a quoted company, the directors' remuneration report must be provided in addition to the directors' report.
Requirements in connection with publication of accounts and report	**Every copy of a document published** by or on behalf of a company must state the name of the person signing on behalf of the board. The nature of the documents involved will vary with the nature of the company.
	There are also requirements in respect of the publication of **statutory and non-statutory accounts**. These are dealt with in the previous section entitled 'Various forms of accounts'.
	Publication occurs if a document is published, issued, circulated or made available for public inspection, with the express intention of inviting members of the public to read it.
Duty to file accounts and reports	The directors of a company have **a duty to file the accounts and reports** with the Registrar of Companies. The period allowed for filing these accounts will also depend on the nature of the company.
Annual accounts in Euros	If the directors regard it as appropriate, the **amounts included within the annual accounts may also be translated into Euros**, and directors may deliver to the Registrar of Companies an additional copy of their company's annual accounts with the amounts translated into Euros.
Revision of defective accounts and reports	If directors believe that the annual accounts, directors' report (and the remuneration report in the case of a quoted company) or the summary financial statement **do not comply with the requirements of the Act** (or of Art. 4 of the IAS Regulations, if this is appropriate), they may prepare revised documents. **If copies have been sent** to members, delivered to the Registrar of Companies, or (for a quoted company) laid before a general meeting, these revisions are confined to corrections of those aspects of each document that failed to comply, together with the making of any necessary consequential alterations.

Separate requirements dependent on nature of company

The Government claims that it is concerned to avoid unnecessary burden, especially as regards small companies. As a consequence, under its 'Think Small First' strategy, there are different requirements for some aspects of the Act that relate to reporting requirements. These are described below, with differences first described by size of company (small, medium and large) and then by whether a company is quoted or unquoted, and by whether it is private or public.

Company size

The criteria used to delineate between small, medium and large companies were outlined in the previous chapter.

Small companies need not include within their annual report and accounts:

- information relating to employee numbers and costs;
- the amount recommended by directors to be paid in the form of dividends in the directors' report;
- a Business Review in the directors' report.

However, if a directors' report is prepared in accordance with the 'small companies' regime' there must be a statement to this effect (placed prominently in the directors' report) before the signature of the person signing the report as being approved.

As regards filing accounts with the Registrar of Companies, a small company must deliver a copy of the balance sheet, and **may** also deliver a copy of the profit and loss accounts as well as a copy of the directors' report. It must also deliver a copy of the auditors' report relating to both the accounts and the directors' report

Medium companies need not include key performance indicators relating to non-financial information within their Business Review; but financial key performance indicators remain mandatory (to the extent necessary).

For **large companies**, there are no exemptions from requirements laid down in the sections in the main body of the Act relating to annual reports and accounts.

Private and public companies

To be a public limited company, the company's articles and memorandum of association must state that it is a public limited company and the company must include these words or the abbreviated form 'PLC' at the end of its name.

A public limited company may, but need not, have its shares listed on the Stock Exchange or quoted on the unlisted securities market. Once it has traded for three years or more, a company can apply for its shares to be listed. However, should it prefer to be quoted on the unlisted securities market, its length of trading is reduced to a minimum of two years.

Other aspects that differentiate a private company are as follows:

- A private company is prohibited from offering its shares for purchase to the public at large.
- A private company's funds can be used to assist in the purchase of shares of the company when a member wishes to leave the company (but this redemption can only be made out of the distributable profits or from the proceeds of a fresh issue of shares).
- Private companies up to a certain size can be permitted to file abbreviated accounts with the Registrar of Companies.

In certain respects, the Companies Act imposes different requirements on private and public companies:

- A public company cannot claim exemption under the small company regime.
- A private company must keep its accounting records for three years from the date on which they are made. However, for a public company this requirement is increased to six years.
- A private company must send out copies of the accounts and reports to shareholders and other relevant parties before the end of the period for filing accounts and report (or, if this is achieved earlier, by the date on which it files them). However, a public company must do so at least 21 days before the date of the relevant accounts meeting with its shareholders, at which the accounts are laid.
- The directors of a public company must lay the report and accounts before a general meeting, which is to be held not later than the end of the period for filing the accounts and reports.
- The period within which the directors must deliver their accounts and reports to the Registrar of Companies is nine months after the end of an accounting period for a private company and six months for that of a public company.

Quoted and unquoted companies

A quoted company is one whose equity share capital is:

- included in the official list in accordance with Pt 6 of the Financial Services and Markets Act 2000; or
- officially listed in an EEA State; or
- admitted to dealing on either the New York Stock Exchange or NASDAQ.

As a result, an unquoted company is any company that does not meet any of the above criteria. As an example, in relation to the London Stock Exchange's secondary markets, a company that is only traded on the AIM is not included in the official list.

As such, for the purposes of the Companies Act, an AIM company is not treated as quoted (although under the AIM Regulations, it is required to produce and present an IFRS report and accounts, as is the case for listed companies). Details of the rules relating to AIM companies can be found the London Stock Exchange's AIM website.[8]

To give an idea of the differences in scale, over 2,500 companies have chosen to join the AIM (although, because of companies leaving the exchange or merging, the current membership is around 1,600). This compares to approximately 1,200 companies that are listed on the London Stock Exchange's main market.

A company is defined as being a quoted company if it is quoted immediately prior to its year end.

Again, in certain areas, there are different requirements for quoted and unquoted companies:

- For a **Business Review**, a quoted company must (in addition to that required for unquoted companies) include information (to the extent necessary for an understanding of a business's development, performance and position) on the following areas:
  - the main trends and factors likely to affect the future development, performance and position of the business;
  - information about environmental matters, the company's employees and social and community issues, including information about the policies relating to these matters, and the effectiveness of these policies;
  - information about persons with whom the business has contractual or other arrangements that are essential to the business (subject to the exemption[9] from disclosure if the directors regard such disclosure as being seriously prejudicial to that person and contrary to the public interest).
- For quoted companies, the directors must prepare a **directors' remuneration report**. This has a wider remit than the requirement for unquoted companies to provide information about directors' remuneration and benefits.

- For companies producing **summary financial statements**, there are additional requirements for a quoted company to include statements about whether the directors' remuneration report is qualified or unqualified by the auditors in their report, and, if qualified, to include the report in full. In addition, there is a requirement to comment on whether the auditors' report contained within it a comment that stated that the directors' remuneration statement did not agree with the records and returns.
- Quoted companies must ensure that their **annual reports and accounts are available on a website** maintained by or on behalf of that company, and continue to be available until the next year's report and accounts are posted on the website. Access to the website must be freely available.
- A member (shareholder) or debenture holder of a quoted company should be able to **request and receive without charge a copy of the last directors' remuneration report**, with the auditors' report in the remuneration report, in addition to those reports normally made available to members and debenture holders.
- For quoted companies, in addition to stating the name of the person signing published copies of accounts and reports, **the list of documents must also include the directors' remuneration report**.
- For quoted companies, members must be given notice of the intention to move a **resolution to approve the directors' remuneration report** at a general meeting, and the existing directors must ensure that the resolution is put to the vote of the meeting.
- In addition to the normal documents delivered to the Registrar of Companies, a quoted company must also **deliver a copy of the directors' remuneration report**, together with the auditors' report on this report.

Compliance

The Companies Act specifies a variety of penalties for non-compliance. These penalties apply to the directors responsible. The required duties, and the aspects of related required compliance, are set out below, and have been categorised by the nature of the penalty, with the heaviest penalties featured first.

Penalty – imprisonment or fine

In the event that a person is found guilty of any of the following offences, then, on conviction or indictment, the penalty is imprisonment for a term not exceeding two years, or a fine, or both. On summary conviction, the penalty is imprisonment for a term not exceeding 12 months, or a fine, or both, in England and Wales; and in Scotland and Northern Ireland, the term is a maximum of six months.

Table 3.3

Requirement	Detailed compliance – and defence/mitigation if appropriate
Duty to keep accounting records	In the event of non-compliance, every officer who is in default has committed an offence. It is a defence that the officer had acted honestly, and that the circumstances in which the business carried on the default was excusable.
Where and for how long records are to be kept	In the event of non-compliance, every officer who is in default has committed an offence. It is a defence that the officer had acted honestly, and that the circumstances in which the business carried on the default was excusable.
Contents of directors' reports – disclosure to auditors	If a directors' report includes a statement of disclosure to auditors but the statement is false, every director who knew that the statement was false and failed to secure compliance is guilty of an offence.

Penalty for conviction and continued contravention – fine not exceeding level five

In the event that a person is found guilty of any of the following offences, the penalty is liable on summary conviction to a fine not exceeding level five on the standard scale (£5,000 as at 2005) and for continued contravention to a daily default fine not exceeding one-tenth of level five on the standard scale:[10]

Table 3.4

Offence of failure to lay accounts and reports (public companies)	If the requirement to lay the accounts and reports before a general meeting is not complied with before the end of the period allowed, every person who was a director immediately before the end of that period has committed an offence. It is a defence if a person took all reasonable steps to secure compliance, but it is not a defence to claim that the documents were not prepared as required.
Default in filing accounts and reports	If the requirements for small, medium, unquoted and quoted companies to file accounts and reports are not complied with within the necessary time period, every person who was a director before the end of that time period has committed an offence. It is a defence if a person took all reasonable steps to secure compliance, but it is not a defence to claim that the documents were not prepared as required.

Penalty for conviction and continued contravention – fine not exceeding level three

In the event that a person is found guilty of any of the following offences, the penalty is liable on summary conviction to a fine not exceeding level three on the standard scale (£1,000 as at 2005) and for continued contravention to a daily default fine not exceeding one-tenth of level three on the standard scale:

Table 3.5

Requirement	Detailed compliance – and defence/mitigation if appropriate
Information about related undertakings	In the event that the full information relevant to related undertakings is not annexed to the company's next annual return (delivered to the Registrar of Companies after the accounts have been approved), both the company and every officer who is in default has committed an offence.
Right of member or debenture holders to receive copies of accounts	If a demand is not complied with within seven days of receipt by the company, both the company and every officer who is in default have committed an offence.

Penalty for conviction – fine not exceeding level three

In the event that a person is found guilty of any of the following offences, the penalty on summary conviction is a fine not exceeding level three on the standard scale (£1,000 as at 2005):

Table 3.6

Requirement	Detailed compliance – and defence/mitigation if appropriate
Information about directors' benefits: remuneration	In the event that any director of a company (or a person who is or has been a director within the preceding five years) has not given notice to the company of such matters relating to him, this is an offence.
Contents of directors' remuneration reports (quoted companies)	In the event that any director of a quoted company (or a person who is or has been a director within the preceding five years) has not given notice to the company of such matters relating to him, this is an offence.
Summary financial statements	In the event that there is a default in compliance with the required form and content of summary financial statements, or their sending out to members if requested, both the company and every officer who is in default have committed an offence.

Reports and accounts on a website (quoted companies)	In the event that the annual report and accounts are not made available on a website, an offence is committed by every officer in default. Failure to comply is disregarded if the documents are available for part of a period or if circumstances arose that could not have been prevented or avoided.
Name of signatory to be stated in published copies	If a copy of accounts and reports is published without the required statement of the signatory's name, both the company and every officer who is in default have committed an offence.
Requirements in respect of publication of statutory accounts and of non-stateroom accounts	If a company contravenes any provision of this section, an offence is committed by the company and every officer who is in default.
Members approval of the directors' remuneration report (quoted companies)	In event of default in notice being given of the resolution for approval, every director of the company has committed an offence. Similarly, if the resolution is not put to the vote of the general meeting, each existing director has committed an offence. It is a defence in respect of the latter if a person can prove that he took all reasonable steps to ensure compliance.

Penalty for conviction – fine

In the event that a person is found guilty of any of the following offences, the penalty on either conviction to indictment or summary conviction is a fine:

Table 3.7

Requirement	Detailed compliance – and defence/mitigation if appropriate
Approval and signing of accounts	If annual accounts are approved that do not comply with the Act (or with the IAS, if the accounts are prepared to these standards), every director who knew that they did not comply or who failed to take reasonable steps to secure compliance will have committed an offence.
Duty to prepare directors' report	If there is a failure to comply with the duty to prepare directors' reports, every person who was a director in office immediately before the filing of the report and accounts and failed to secure compliance is guilty of an offence.
Duty to prepare directors' remuneration report	If there is a failure to comply with the duty to prepare a directors' remuneration report, every person who was a director in office immediately before the filing of the report and accounts and failed to secure compliance is guilty of an offence.

Approval and signing of directors' report	If a directors' report is approved but does not comply, every director who knew but did not comply and failed to secure compliance is guilty of an offence.
Approval and signing of directors' remuneration report (quoted companies)	If a directors' remuneration report is approved but does not comply, every director who knew but did not comply and failed to secure compliance is guilty of an offence.
Default in sending out copies of accounts and reports	In the event that there is a default in compliance, both the company and every officer who is in default have committed an offence.
Approval and signing of abbreviated accounts	If abbreviated accounts are approved but do not comply, every director who knew that they did not comply and failed to secure compliance is guilty of an offence.

Enforcement

For this purpose, enforcement requires government bodies taking statutory powers to enforce companies to change matters relating to their annual reports and accounts. Usually these powers will have been granted by the relevant Secretary of State (currently for Trade and Industry), but in a few instances they may relate to court orders being granted. There are several areas where such enforcement occurs, and these relate to companies as distinct from individuals, for whom the previous section on penalties applies.

Court orders and civil penalties

In the event of a company being in default of filing its accounts and reports (for which there is also a penalty for the persons involved in such an offence), and if the directors fail to make good this non-compliance within 14 days of a notice being served on them, any member or creditor of that company may apply to a court for an order under which the directors are required to make good this default. The court order must be complied with within a specified timescale, and may provide that all costs related to this application are borne by the directors.

In addition to the penalties for which the directors may be liable, the company is liable to a civil penalty for failure to file its accounts and report within the specified period. It is not a defence to claim that the documents had not been prepared as required under the Act. The amount will be determined in relation to the length of the period between the date when the report and accounts are required to be submitted and the date when they are finally filed, and whether the company is private or public. The penalty may be recovered by the Registrar of Companies and is paid into the Consolidated Fund.

Secretary of State's notices

Once copies of a company's report and accounts have been circulated to members or delivered to the Registrar of Companies, or, for quoted companies, laid before a general meeting for approval, if it appears to the Secretary of State that there is a possible question as to whether they comply with the requirements of the Act, then notice may be given to the directors. Such accounts and reports include those that had been revised by the directors on a voluntary basis.

This notice will indicate the areas where such a question arises. The timescale for response to this notice is one month or more, during which the directors are required to provide an explanation regarding the specified area, or to prepare revised accounts or report.

Failure to provide a satisfactory explanation, or to revise the accounts or report to comply, will result in a court order being applied for, which will include direction as to the preparation of revised accounts or a revised report, as appropriate.

Costs may be ordered, including any reasonable expenses incurred by the company in respect of the preparation of the revised report and accounts. These costs will be borne by the directors who were party to the approval of the defective report and accounts. However, the court is able either to exclude some directors, or to order different levels of payment between the directors, based on the extent to which any director can demonstrate that he or she took all reasonable steps to prevent the approval of non-compliant reports and accounts.

The Secretary of State is empowered (via an 'authorisation order') to authorise another body to make the above applications to a court. Whilst not specified in the Act, the Financial Reporting Council could be such a body. This authorisation enables the specified body to approach HM Revenue and Customs to request disclosure of information, which would assist in discovering whether there were grounds for an application to the court. Similarly, this authorised body has the power to request any document, information or explanations from the company, its officers, employees and auditors (including those who fell into these categories at the time of approval of the relevant documents). If anyone fails to comply with this request, the authorised person can apply for a court order.

NOTES

1 Full details of the implementation timetable, together with updates on consultation on the secondary legislation, can be found in the Better Business Framework section of the DTI's website at www.dti.gov.uk.
2 UK Company Law Review Steering Group, 2000
3 Companies Act 2006, s. 172.
4 Ibid., Pt 15, 'Accounts and Reports'.
5 The EEA comprises all of the EU states (currently 25) plus Norway, Iceland and Liechtenstein.
6 Schedule 4 to the 1985 Act contains two formats for the balance sheet and four formats for the profit and loss account, and is included as Appendix 2.
7 See www.businesslink.gov.uk/bdotg/action/detail?type=RESOURCES&itemId=1073791915.
8 See www.londonstockexchange.com/en-gb/products/companyservices/ourmarkets/aim_new/About+AIM/rulesandregulations.htm.
9 This exemption was included originally because of concern over challenges by activists, such as those supporting animal rights welfare, that might target companies supporting medical and pharmaceutical industry with research and testing facilities.
10 The Government has introduced schemes for fixed and variable monetary administrative penalties, for regulators and enforcers of regulations, that are compliant with the Hampton and Macrory Principles and characteristics. Fixed monetary administrative penalties (FMAP) schemes are set against a series of levels (1–5). Further information can be found on the Cabinet Office website at www.cabinetoffice.gov.uk/REGULATION/reviewing_regulation/penalties/index.asp.

CHAPTER 4

Audit requirements of Companies Act 2006

KEY ISSUES

- General approach
- Exemptions and variations
  - Small company exemption
  - Time limits
  - Exclusions
  - Dormant companies
  - Auditor's report for small companies' abbreviated accounts
  - Other forms of variation
- Appointment of auditor
  - Private company
  - Time periods
  - Process for appointment of auditor
  - Public company
- Auditor's report
  - True and fair view
  - In accordance with reporting framework
  - Unqualified or qualified reports
  - Directors' remuneration
- Auditor's duties
  - Undertaking investigations to form opinion
  - Duties relating to directors' remuneration
  - Duties relating to small companies
  - Signing the auditor's report
  - Who can be an auditor?
  - Auditor's signature
- Auditor's rights
  - Access to records
  - Offences relating to statements to auditors

General approach

The 2006 Act states as one of its paramount duties of the directors of a company that the company's accounts must give a true and fair view of its 'assets, liabilities, financial position and profit or loss'. This can relate either to the individual accounts of a company, or, in the case of a group company, to those undertakings incorporated within the group accounts.

The company auditor is required to have regard to this directors' duty during the undertaking of the audit function. However, it is important to recognise that, as regards the auditor's duty, there are exemptions to the requirement that a company must have its accounts audited.

Exemptions and variations

Small company exemption

Small companies[1] are exempt from being **required** to have their accounts audited. But to ensure that they follow the letter of the law, small companies' filed accounts must include a statement from the directors in the company balance sheets. This must state that advantage has been taken of the exemption. A group company may be entitled to exemption if it meets the criteria for a small group company (as detailed in Chapter 3).

The exemption does not preclude the members of a company (which is entitled to exemption) from making a request of the directors to obtain an audit of the company accounts for any financial year. Members must have shares representing not less than 10% of the issues share capital (independent of the class of the shares). If there is no defined share capital, the right of request applies to any individual or group of members that represent less than 10% of the members in the company.

Time limits

The notice for an order to obtain an audit must not be given before a financial year to which the order relates – and must be given not later than one month before the year end. In other words, it must be made within the financial year, and give sufficient time for an audit to take place as part of the year-end process. If a notice is made, the company's accounts must include a statement to that effect. As a result of the notice being granted, the company is not entitled to exemption for that financial year.

Exclusions

Small companies are not entitled to claim the small companies' exemption if, at any time during the financial year, they have been either a public company or have been involved in financial services or insurance market activity, or are a special register body, such as a trade union or employers' association.[2]

Dormant companies

Dormant companies may be entitled for exemption from audit if they have been dormant since the company's formation or the end of the previous financial year. By implication, a company that falls dormant during its current financial year cannot claim exemption for reasons of its being dormant at the year end, since accounts will need to be presented for part of that year.

To be eligible for exemption, the company should either have been entitled to prepare its accounts in accordance with the small companies' regime, or would have been eligible but for having been a public company or a member of an ineligible group. However, this entitlement for exemption is not available if for any time during the financial year in question the company was involved in financial services or insurance market activity.

Other bodies that are able to claim exemption from audit include non-profit-making companies and public sector companies subject to public audit – either from the respective Comptroller and Auditor General for England or Northern Ireland or the Auditor General for Wales or Scotland.

Auditor's report for small companies' abbreviated accounts

Where a company is subject to the small companies' regime and chooses not to take advantage of the audit exemption (or is unable to do so, for example if it is a public company), the auditor's report must be delivered to the Registrar of Companies, together with the set of accounts.

If this company chooses to submit abbreviated accounts,[3] the auditor's report is described as the 'special auditor's report'. This is a report in which the auditor states that the company is entitled to deliver abbreviated accounts, and that they have been properly prepared in accordance with the Companies Act requirements.

However, any qualification in the auditor's report must be set out in full, together with any necessary explanation. This requirement also applies to any comment in the auditor's report that there was an inadequacy or inconsistency in the accounts or records, or that there had been a failure to obtain the necessary information.

Other forms of variation

Non-statutory accounts may not include an auditor's report. However, as was mentioned above, if non-statutory accounts are published for any purpose, such as an attachment for a listing prospectus, the publication must not include an auditor's report relating to previous statutory accounts.

Appointment of auditors

Private company

The auditor of a private company must be appointed for each financial year, unless the directors are able reasonably to agree that audited accounts are unlikely to be required, for example for small or dormant companies. Auditors are not permitted to overlap with previous auditors who are still in office. Furthermore, they cease automatically to hold office at the end of the period for which they have been appointed, unless they are reappointed.

Time periods

The 'period for appointing auditors' is defined as being within 28 days of the time allowed for sending out the prior financial year's annual accounts and reports, or within 28 days of the day on which the annual accounts and reports were sent out, if earlier.

Process for appointment of auditor

The appointment of an auditor can be made by directors or by members.

A directors' appointment may occur before the first period for appointment, to fill a casual vacancy or following a period during which the company was exempt from audit. However, a members' appointment requires an ordinary resolution to be passed, either during the 'period for appointing auditors' or at other times if the directors or company failed to make an appointment.

The Secretary of State can appoint an auditor if a private company fails to do so. Where a company fails to appoint an auditor within the 'period for appointing auditors', the company must, within a week of that period, give notice to the Secretary of State of this power becoming exercisable. If such notice is not given, an offence is deemed to have been committed by the company and by every officer who is in default in this respect. The penalty is a fine not exceeding level three; if contravention continues, the penalty is a daily defaults fine not exceeding one-tenth of the level three fine.

Where no auditor is appointed by the end of the next period, any incumbent auditor will be deemed to have been reappointed. There are exceptions to this automatic reappointment where the auditor was appointed by the directors (as may be the case if there is a casual vacancy).

Where the company's articles require reappointment, this requirement must be followed. In addition, the company's members may prevent a deemed reappointment by notice from members representing at least 5% of total voting rights. Alternatively, they may resolve not to reappointment in a general meeting. Finally, the directors may resolve that it is not necessary to appoint auditors for the next financial year, for example where the company is entitled to a small company exemption or the company is dormant.

Public company

The regulations applying to a public company are broadly similar to those of a private company except that the 'period for appointing auditors' is before the end of the accounts meeting of the company.

The ability of directors or members to appoint an auditor is the same as with private companies, as is the default power of the Secretary of State to appoint, except that the period when this power becomes exercisable is defined by reference to the fact that auditors had not been appointed by the end of the company's accounts meeting.

Auditor's report

The company auditor is required to make a report to the company's members. This must relate to all of the company's accounts, copies of which are sent to members (in the case of a private company) or laid before a general meeting, also known as an accounts meeting (in the case of a public company).

True and fair view

Since the requirement of the auditor relates directly to the directors' duty to provide a 'true and fair view', the report must state clearly, based on the auditor's opinion, whether the annual accounts provide a true and fair view of the state of affairs of the company. This is based on the balance sheet and the profitability of the company via the profit and loss account. Where the company prepares group accounts, these must apply to all the undertakings included within the consolidation.

In accordance with reporting framework

The report must also state, again based on the auditor's opinion, whether the accounts have been prepared in accordance with the relevant financial reporting framework and in accordance with the Act.

The report must identify all the annual accounts covered in the audit, together with the means by which the accounts have been prepared, i.e. the UK GAAP or the International Accounting Standards. In addition, the report should describe the scope of the audit and the auditing standards on which the report has been based.

Unqualified or qualified reports

The auditor's report is defined as either unqualified or qualified. However, even if the auditor decides not to qualify the report, it must include a reference to any matters about which the auditor wishes to bring attention. This would be done by way of emphasis, rather than formally qualifying the report.

Directors' remuneration

For unquoted companies that are not required to produce a remuneration report, the auditor's report must state whether the information included in the directors' report is consistent with the information provided in the annual accompanying accounts. This applies also to the Business Review, which is part of the directors' report.[4]

All quoted companies must produce a directors' remuneration report. In this respect, the requirement on the auditor is slightly different. The auditor's report must report to the members on the auditable part of the remuneration report, i.e. on aspects such as financial remuneration and benefit (as defined by Sch. 7 to the 1985 Act). However, the auditor is also required to state whether, in his opinion, the remuneration report was completed in accordance with the 2006 Act.

Auditor's duties

Undertaking investigations to form opinion

The auditor acts on behalf of the members as a monitor to review that appropriate financial management is in place. This duty dates back the sixteenth and seventeenth centuries when the auditor was appointed by the sponsors of voyages of discovery as their 'own man on board' to record whatever the vessel gained through discovery or plunder.[5]

Whilst acting on behalf of members, the auditor will inevitably form relationships with directors and officers of the company. Suspicion can arise as to 'whose side' auditors are on, especially when they may provide non-audit fee-based consultancy, which may be considered to represent a conflict of interests.

However, in terms of regulatory matters, the auditor's duties are to undertake investigations that are relevant to enable him to form an opinion as to whether:

- the company has kept adequate accounting records;
- in respect of the parts of the business not visited by the auditor, adequate returns (in whatever form) are available, which enables the auditor to assess that they are in accordance with those records viewed by the auditor on other personal visits to parts of the company;
- the individual accounts of the company are in agreement with the accounting records and returns;
- for a quoted company, the auditable part of the directors' remuneration report is in agreement with the accounting records and returns.

If the auditor forms the opinion that any of the above is not the case, he or she has a duty to state this in his or her report. This duty to report includes the requirement to state whether the auditor is of the opinion that there has been a failure to obtain all the necessary information or explanations for the purpose of the audit.

Duties relating to directors' remuneration

A similar requirement applies to auditors of unquoted companies, in relation to the disclosure of directors' benefits such as remuneration, pensions and compensation for loss of office. Authors of quoted companies are required to provide the necessary information relating to the directors' remuneration report. If either of these requirements is not met, the auditor must include with his or her report a statement that includes the required particulars, so far as he or she is reasonably able to do so.

Duties relating to small companies

Where the directors of a small company have prepared their company's report and accounts in accordance with the small companies' regime, the auditor must state in his or her report whether in his or her opinion the directors were entitled to do so. As described earlier, this report – the 'special auditor's report' – must accompany the abbreviated accounts submitted to the Registrar of Companies. In the event that the full auditor's report is qualified in any respect, the 'special report' must set out that report in full, together with any other material necessary to fully understand the qualification.

Signing the auditor's report

On completion, the auditor's report must state the name of the auditor, who must sign and date it. Where the auditor is a firm rather than an individual, the report must be signed by the senior statutory auditor in his or her own name, on behalf of the auditor firm.[6] For quoted companies, the auditor must also sign with respect to his or her duties relating to the directors' remuneration report.

The senior statutory auditor is defined as the person identified by the firm as the senior auditor for the audit. The Act requires that only persons who are properly supervised and appropriately qualified are appointed as statutory auditors.

Who can be an auditor?

To be eligible for appointment as auditor, an individual must be a member of a recognised supervisory body, and be eligible for appointment under the rules of that supervisory body.

Such bodies are required to maintain and enforce rules concerning the eligibility of persons for such appointments and the conduct of statutory audit work. Further detail is available in s. 1219 of the Act referring to dates of eligibility – this is a fairly complex position and not easily summarised.

Members of the following organisations (or recognised supervisory bodies) are eligible to be company auditors:

- Institute of Chartered Accountants in England and Wales (ICAEW);
- Institute of Chartered Accountants in Scotland (ICAS);
- Institute of Chartered Accountants in Ireland (ICAI);
- Association of Chartered Certified Accountants (ACCA);
- Association of Authorised Public Accountants;
- Association of International Accountants.

An individual designated as senior statutory auditor is not liable to any civil liability in this role, other than that to which he would be subject in normal circumstances.

Auditor's signature

Every copy of an auditor's report published on behalf of a company must state the name of the auditor and the name of the person signing as senior statutory auditor. If a company publishes this report without including these names, the company and every officer who is in default will have committed an offence. If found guilty of such an offence, a person is liable under summary conviction to a fine not exceeding level three on the standard scale.

However, it is permissible to omit the names of the auditor and senior statutory auditor if it is believed that either party would be at serious risk of violence or intimidation if so named. This exception is designed to take account of activists who are carrying out a campaign against a company, as has been the case where animal rights activists have targeted officers of companies, as well as their advisors. However, to take advantage of this exemption requires a resolution to be made, notice of which must be given to the Secretary of State.

Auditor's rights

The duties described above would be arduous and probably impossible to achieve unless the auditor had balancing rights associated with these duties.

Access to records

To accomplish his or her duties, the auditor has the right of access to the company's books and accounts (in whatever form they are held) at all times. In addition, the auditor has the right to obtain any information or explanations that are deemed necessary by him or her to perform the duties of auditor of the company concerned.

Information and explanations can be requested from any officer or employee of the company, which includes any auditor of a subsidiary undertaking (as well as the subsidiary undertaking itself), if the company for which the auditor is undertaking the audit is incorporated within the United Kingdom.

In addition, the auditor can request information from:

- any person holding or accountable for any of the company's books or accounts;
- any person fulfilling the same duties for a subsidiary undertaking;
- companies providing outsourced facilities such as payroll or IT services;
- persons who fulfilled any of the above roles, during the period in which the auditor is undertaking the required audit;

- subsidiary undertakings not incorporated within the United Kingdom (however, the parent company is obliged to take all reasonable steps to obtain the information requested by the auditor, if this is necessary).

Offences relating to statements to auditors

The auditor is entitled to make a request for information from an individual. However, if that person makes a statement to an auditor, either in writing or face to face (knowingly or recklessly) that meets the request for information but is misleading, deceptive or false in any way, that person will be deemed to have committed an offence.

On conviction to indictment such person is liable to imprisonment for not more than 24 months, or a fine, or both. If the person is subject to summary conviction, and is found guilty, he or she is liable to imprisonment for not more than 12 months, or a fine, not exceeding the statutory maximum (or both).[7]

If a person fails to comply with the request for information without delay, that person is liable on summary conviction to a fine not exceeding level three on the standard scale.

It is important to note that unless a person is found guilty of an offence under the auditor's right to information, any statement made on an auditor's request may not be used in evidence under any other criminal proceedings.

In the case of an overseas subsidiary, if the parent company fails to comply with the requirement to take all reasonable steps to obtain the information, both the company and any officer who is in default are deemed to have committed an offence. Again, the penalty for this offence on summary conviction is a fine not exceeding level three on the standard scale.

If the auditor regards it as appropriate or necessary, he or she has the right to request an injunction to enforce his or her rights to obtain information.

If an auditor knowingly includes anything in the auditor's report that is misleading, false or deceptive, he or she commits an offence. An individual guilty of an offence is liable to a fine on conviction on indictment, or a fine not exceeding the statutory minimum, on summary conviction.

NOTES

1 Small companies are defined under the criteria described in Chapter 3. Where the financial year in question is less than a full calendar year, the revenue figures should be reduced proportionately.

2. Companies Act 2006, s. 478 defines the precise nature of companies meeting these definitions.
3. Abbreviated accounts are Companies Act accounts, including a balance sheet, but omitting the profit and loss account.
4. The requirement on the auditor in respect of the Business Review is different from that required for the OFR, when the auditor had to state that there was nothing that had been seen or uncovered at the time of completing the audit that was inconsistent with the information provided in the OFR. This was a far more stringent requirement on auditors and one that would probably have proved unworkable in practice.
5. Research paper 0462 on the Companies (Audit Investigation and Community Enterprise) Bill, by Timothy Edmonds of the House of Commons Library; available at www.parliament.uk/commons/lib/research/rp2004/rp04-062.pdf.
6. This is a marked shift from previous requirements, where the auditor's report was signed by the firm in question.
7. This penalty for summary conviction applies only in England and Wales. If the offence is committed in Scotland or Ireland, imprisonment is for a maximum of six months.

CHAPTER 5

Codes of Governance

KEY ISSUES

- Combined Code of Corporate Governance (July 2003)
- Key principles relating to corporate reporting
  - Financial reporting
  - Internal controls
  - Audit committee and auditors
- Disclosure of corporate governance arrangements
- Audit committee – reporting requirements
  - Responsibilities
  - Expertise and experience
  - Agenda
  - Report

- Responsibility towards risk management
- Remuneration committee – reporting requirements
  - Responsibilities
  - Total shareholder return benchmarking
  - Report
- Nomination committee – reporting requirements
  - Role and responsibilities
  - Membership
  - Board performance evaluation
  - Report

Chapters 1–4 discussed various legally based regulations as well as accounting principles that form much of the basis for the statutory aspects of corporate reporting. In this chapter the Codes of Governance will be considered; and how they impact on both the content and the manner of corporate reporting will be reviewed. Discussion will include the roles of the three board committees – audit, remuneration and nomination.

Much of what is described in this chapter is related to listed companies, as the Combined Code is a part of the Listing Rules. However, non-quoted companies may find that the discussion reflects best practice guidance and, as such, is relevant, especially for companies considering moving into the quoted or listed arena.

Combined Code of Corporate Governance (July 2003)

The first Code of Governance was published as a result of the Cadbury Report on aspects of corporate governance in 1992, which in particular raised the profile of the role of non-executive directors. This was followed by the Greenbury Report in 1995, focusing principally on executive remuneration (in the aftermath of the public debate about 'fat cats').

Subsequently, the two Codes produced by the Cadbury and Greenbury Committees were revisited by the Hampel Committee in 1998, which consolidated its reports and those of the previous two committees into a 'Combined Code'. This was intended to provide guidance on good governance standards for listed companies. As such it was annexed to the Listing Rules (which are issued by the Financial Services Authority as the UK Listing Authority, having taken over that role from the London Stock Exchange).

In 2003, the Higgs Report took the question of the role and effectiveness of non-executive company directors further than had been touched upon by the Cadbury Report. At around the same time, the Financial Reporting Council set up a committee to consider guidance principles for companies' audit committees. The culmination was the Smith Report. The findings of the Higgs and Smith Reports were combined with the existing Code of Governance and a revised Combined Code was produced in July 2003.

It is important to note that unlike the Listing Rules, which describe mandatory disclosures for companies that form part of the Official List of securities, compliance with the Combined Code is voluntary, although the 'comply or explain' requirement (see below) for listed companies is stronger than a purely voluntary approach.

The revised Code contains both main and supporting principles and provisions. These are included at Appendix 3 of this book. In addition, there are three schedules and various levels of guidance for various directors and officers.[1]

Listed companies are required to make a disclosure statement in two parts: the first part requires the company to report on how it applies both the main and the supporting principles of the Code; the second requires companies to confirm that they comply with the provisions, or, if not, to provide an explanation – described as 'comply or explain'.

Key principles relating to corporate reporting

The key principle of corporate reporting in the Code is accountability and audit. Section C of the Code consists of three parts: C.1 Financial Reporting; C.2 Internal Control; and C.3 Audit Committee and Auditors.

Financial reporting

The main principle in C.1 states: 'The board should present a balanced and understandable assessment of the company's position and prospects'.

The supporting principle states that 'the board's responsibility to present a balanced and understandable assessment extends to interim and other price sensitive public reports and reports to regulators as well as to information required to be presented by statutory requirements'.

There are two provisions relating to this section.

Provision C.1.1 requires the directors to state in their annual report that they have the responsibility for preparing the accounts, together with a statement by the auditors about their reporting responsibilities.

Provision C.1.2 requires the directors to report that the business is a going concern, with supporting assumptions or qualifications as necessary. This provision has greater implication than may be considered on first reading, since it requires directors to describe the nature of the business, as well as its prospects.

Internal controls

The main principle in C.2 states: 'The board should maintain a sound system of internal control to safeguard shareholders' investment and the company's assets'.

There is no supporting principle. Instead, the single provision requires the board to conduct a review, at least annually, of the effectiveness of the company's system of internal controls and report to the shareholders that they have done so. This review should include all material controls and risk management systems.

The Turnbull Guidance[2] provides the mechanism whereby the board can develop and maintain 'a sound system of internal control'. The Guidance emphasises that to be effective, a company's internal control and risk management systems must be embedded in a company's day-to-day business processes, led by the directors and extend beyond quantifiable financial and physical risks. The revised guidance, produced in 2005, added (amongst other things) that the board should be encouraged to communicate effectively on its management of risk.

Audit committee and auditors

The main principle in C.3 states: 'The board should establish formal and transparent arrangements for considering how they should apply the financial reporting and internal control principles and for maintaining an appropriate relationship with the company's auditors'.

There is no supporting principle. Instead, there are seven provisions. The first requires the board to establish an audit committee, comprising at least three[3] members, all of whom should be non-executive directors.

The second provision defines the main role and responsibilities of the audit committee (of which more will be discussed later).

The third provision requires that the terms of reference of the audit committee should be made available, and that the annual report should include a separate section that describes the work of the committee in respect of its main role and responsibilities.

The fourth provision provides the audit committee with the responsibility of reviewing the means by which staff can, in confidence, raise concerns about possible matters of impropriety. This covers both financial reporting and other matters. In some companies, this provision is met by the establishment of an ethics committee. However, in these circumstances, even though this may involve officers of the company as its members, it is most likely that the ethics committee will be a sub-committee of the audit committee, and report to it on a confidential basis.

The fifth provision requires the audit committee to monitor the effectiveness of the internal audit activities, including reviewing annually whether the company should establish an internal audit function. In the absence of such a function, the audit committee should make a statement in the annual report explaining the reasons for its absence.

The penultimate provision requires the committee to have the primary responsibility for the appointment, reappointment and removal of external auditors. If the board decides not to accept any recommendations made by the audit committee in this respect, a statement from the audit committee must be included in the annual report, stating the original recommendations and the reasons why the board has taken a different position.

The last provision requires the audit committee to explain in the annual report how auditor objectivity and independence are safeguarded where the auditor provides non-audit services.

Disclosure of corporate governance arrangements

Schedule C to the Combined Code, on disclosure of corporate governance arrangements, encapsulates all the disclosure requirements established under the Code, including the requirements laid down in sections other than those on accountability and auditing. It identifies what is expected to be included in an annual report and sets out what the annual report should record.

The board and its committees:

- a statement on how the board operates, including a high-level statement describing decisions taken by the board and decisions delegated to management;
- names of the chairman, the deputy chairman (if one is in position), the chief executive, the senior independent director, and the chairman and members of the nomination, remuneration and audits committees;
- numbers of meetings of the board and its three committees, together with a statement of the relevant directors' personal attendance record;
- names of non-executive directors determined to be independent (with explanations if required);
- other significant commitments of the chairman and how these have changed over the year in question;
- how the performance of the board, its committees and its directors has been evaluated;
- steps taken by the board (and, in particular, the non-executive directors) to understand the views of major shareholders about the company.

Board reporting:

- separate sections describing the work of the nomination and remuneration committees;
- an explanation from the directors of their responsibility for preparing the accounts and a statement from the auditors about their reporting responsibilities;
- a statement from the board that the business is a going concern with supporting assumptions or qualifications as necessary;
- a report that the board has conducted a review of the effectiveness of the company's internal control system;
- a separate section describing the work of the remuneration committee, including a statement describing the reason for the absence of an internal control function (if relevant), together with a statement for the board not accepting

the committee's recommendation regarding the auditor (if relevant) and an explanation as to how the auditor's objectivity and independence is safeguarded in the event of his or her undertaking non-audit services.

Other information (either on request or via the company's website):

- terms of reference of the three committees – audit, nomination and remuneration;
- terms and conditions of appointment of non-executive directors;
- where remuneration consultants are appointed, a statement of whether they have any other connections with the company.

Papers to be sent with the annual report:

- regarding a resolution to elect or re-elect a member of the board – sufficient biographical details, the reason why he or she should be elected to a non-executive role and, if to be re-elected, confirmation from the chairman that formal performance evaluation has demonstrated that the individual's performance continues to be effective and committed;
- regarding the appointment or reappointment of an external auditor, if the board does not accept the audit committee's recommendation – the sending of a statement from that committee explaining its recommendation and from the board setting out reasons why it has taken a different position.

Audit committee – reporting requirements [4]

Whilst a company's management has the responsibility for the preparation and completion of accurate financial statements and disclosures in accordance with both the relevant accounting standards and appropriate rules and regulations, it is the audit committee that works with the external auditors to ensure that they are satisfied with the accounting practices adopted by management, including the workings of the internal audit system.

Thus, the audit committee has two principal responsibilities – to oversee the company's financial reporting process and to oversee the company's financial risk and internal control process. The Smith Guidance recommends no fewer than three meetings per year, and, as such, it should be clear that much of the committee's work is dependent upon the input of the various officers in the company with responsibility for these two areas, as well as input from the senior external auditor.

The audit committee is appointed by the board; the Combined Code (Principle A.3) states 'no one other than the committee chairman and the members is entitled to be present at a meeting of the ... audit committee, but others may attend at the invitation of the committee'. The Smith Guidance[5] (which forms part of the Combined Code) is that 'appointments should be for up to three years' and that 'all members of the committee should be non executive directors. The chairman of the company should not be an audit committee member'.

Responsibilities

The responsibilities of the audit committee are defined by the Combined Code and are summarised as follows:

- to monitor the integrity of the company's financial statements;
- to review the company's internal control and risk management systems;[6]
- to monitor a company's internal audit function;
- to make recommendations to the board in respect of the appointment of external auditors;
- to review the external auditor's independence and objectivity;
- to develop and implement policy on the use of the auditor for non-audit services.

The Smith Guidance suggests that the audit committee has a particular role 'acting independently of the executive, to ensure that the interests of the shareholders are properly protected in relation to financial reporting and internal control'.

Expertise and experience

In terms of the level of expertise that should be expected of members of the audit committee, the Smith Guidance states:

> All audit committee members would normally be expected to have experience of financial matters, and at least one member should have recent and relevant financial experience. It is desirable that the member with recent and relevant financial experience should have a professional qualification from one of the professional accountancy bodies.

In this respect, the value of this experience lies in setting the questions regarding audit matters to be answered in advance by the finance director and the internal and external auditors. These individuals may be invited to attend regularly at the committee meetings as well as providing papers for their agenda items. The range of individuals invited to attend could be extended to cover those responsible for risk and compliance matters in relation to these matters. The chairman and the chief executive may be invited to attend, but it is essential that they do not dominate or lead the committee. It is the role of the committee's chairman to ensure that this does not occur.

Agenda

It is important that there is good and open dialogue with external auditors, particularly so that serious concerns may be brought swiftly to the committee's attention, without causing any problems in the relationship. In addition, the Smith Guidance states that the audit committee 'should meet, at least annually, with the external and internal auditors, without management, to discuss matters relating to its remit and any issues arising form the audit'.

In this respect, setting the committee's terms of reference is a key task, and one that the Smith Guidance suggests should be reviewed annually – by the committee itself. In addition, the Guidance suggests that the board should also 'review the audit committee's effectiveness annually'.

The nature of the subjects to be covered by the audit committee during its meetings is likely to include the following:

- **Risk management process and control** – particularly in relation to risks referred to within the Business Review, as well as industry and market updates, financial community expectations, technology changes, regulatory changes and emerging risk issues.
- **Reviewing the company's control processes** – compliance with code of ethics, control policies and procedures (including aspects such as fraud), internal and external auditor internal control observations and recommendations, and compliance with regulatory requirements.
- **Overseeing financial reporting** – reviewing financial statements and earnings releases and recommending their approval to the board, periodic reports and filings, management overview of quarterly financial results, review of accounting policies (including ensuring that they meet current accounting standards), reviewing accounting estimates (e.g. for interim statements), and reviewing latest developments in auditing, accounting, reporting, and tax matters and their application to the company.
- **Evaluating the internal and external audit processes** – co-ordinating internal and external audit activities and responsibilities, reviewing external auditor's performance and effectiveness, reviewing internal audit's performance and effectiveness.

- **Audit committee structure** – reviewing terms of reference and conducting self-assessment of committee's own performance.

These meetings are usually formal, with minutes being prepared. However, it may be necessary for the committee to have more time to consider key matters, so that informal meetings may be held to allow the audit committee chairman to keep in touch with key individuals such as the audit partner and the finance director. This will be particularly relevant in terms of final and interim results. Interim results will require more discussion, since estimates and adjustments may be used based on a degree of insight, which is not backed up by the benefit of a full external audit review.

In terms of final results it is essential that there is discussion between the chairman and the auditors (internal and external) and the finance director to address any areas of possible contention before the final accounts are submitted to the committee. The Smith Guidance states that 'The audit committee should review the significant financial reporting issues and judgements made in connection with the reparation of the financial statements, interim reports, preliminary announcements and related formal statements'.

A key issue is that cognisance should be taken of the need to manage investor (and especially analysts') expectations, and audit committees should consider current and emerging issues within the company's performance and advise on their reporting in a judicious manner.

For both interim and final results, it is important that the committee reviews the communications that will be made to the public, e.g. earnings releases, financial statements, and other information presented with the financial statements. This to ensure that the board meets the Smith Guidance recommendation:

> The audit committee should review related information presented with the financial statements, including the operating and financial review and corporate governance statements relating to the audit and to risk management. Similarly where board approval is required for other statements containing financial information, whenever practicable, the audit committee should review such statements first.

By undertaking this review, the audit committee will ensure that any communications are consistent with the decisions made by the committee. This is especially relevant when considering issues such as accounting policies and any provisions or key issues, such as revenue recognition, capitalisation and deferral of expenses, and application of the accounting standards.

Report

The following should be included in the audit committee's report (although, clearly, if there have been issues such as profit warnings during the year, these should also be referred to, as is relevant):

- membership of the audit committee, including the identification of the member with relevant financial experience;
- individuals invited to attend meetings – typically the external and internal auditors, the head of risk and the finance director, and other members of the board, if appropriate;
- a summary of the committee's responsibilities (together with a reference as to where these can be found on the company's website);
- the number of meetings held during the year, and a summary of the subjects covered at each meeting;
- a statement on the appointment of external auditors, and the provisions in place to ensure that they are independent.

There should also be commentary on the way in which the committee has proceeded in its deliberations to consider whether to recommend the reappointment of the auditor. If the board has declined to accept this recommendation, a full explanation of the committee's recommendation and the reasons why the board declined it should be included. In addition, there should be commentary on the areas considered in terms of evaluating the auditor's independence, as well as a statement on the company's policy regarding the provision of non-audit services by the auditor.

In the event that the company does not have an internal audit function, the committee's report should explain the reasons for this position.

Responsibility towards risk management

In addition to the committee's report, the annual report and accounts will also incorporate a report on the committee's risk management. Just as the committee has a responsibility for working with the external auditors for the purpose of reviewing the preparation of the financial statements, so too should the audit committee be reviewing the internal risk process (assuming that the board had included this within its terms of reference). Its objective should be to satisfy itself that the risk management report reflects a true and fair view of the risks facing the company.

The nature of this overseeing will depend upon the exact terms of reference for the committee, as is demonstrated by the Smith Guidance's recommendation:

> Except where the board or a risk committee is expressly responsible for reviewing the effectiveness of the internal control and risk management systems, the audit committee should receive reports from management on the effectiveness of the systems they have established and the conclusions of any testing carried out by internal or external auditors.

Remuneration committee – reporting requirements[7]

The duties of the remuneration committee are defined in the Combined Code (or, more correctly, by the Higgs Report, which is subsumed within the Code). The Code gives the shareholders the right to vote on the report of the remuneration committee, and requires that their approval is sought for all new long-term incentive plans.

Responsibilities

The purpose of the Code is to strengthen the effectiveness of the remuneration committee, to clarify its overseeing role and to enhance its accountability for the setting of the (largely) executive remuneration process. These duties are summarised as follows:

- To propose to the board the framework for the remuneration of the chief executive, the chairman and any other executives that it is requested to consider. Typically, this would include all executive directors and the company secretary (for the purposes of maintaining independence). Non-executives' remuneration is the responsibility of the chairman and the chief executive.
- To determine targets for any performance-related pay schemes.
- Within these policies, to determine individual executive directors' remuneration packages, including bonuses, incentives and share options.
- To agree the policy for authorising expense claims made by the chairman or the chief executive.
- To determine the policy and scope of pension arrangements for executive directors.
- To ensure that termination arrangements are fair for both the individual and the company. In this respect, there is a responsibility to ensure that failure is not recognised, together with the duty to mitigate loss.
- To advise upon any major changes in employee benefit structures within the company.

These are minimum guidelines, and some companies expect their remuneration committees to extend their remit to cover other issues such as remuneration schemes for all executives at or above certain levels, regardless of whether they are board directors.

In addition, the committee must take account of guidance and regulations such as the Combined Code, the Listing Rules and the Directors' Remuneration Report Regulations 2002.

As with the audit committee, only non-executive directors were permitted to be members of the remuneration committee; however, they are permitted to hire remuneration consultants as advisers to the committee. The Code permits the chairman to sit on the remuneration committee for financial years beginning on or after 1 November 2006. In this respect, the committee is solely responsible for setting the selection criteria and terms of reference for any adviser they choose to appoint.

Within these responsibilities lie the requirements to report on committee meetings and the attendance by members of the committee, as well as to publish the committee's terms of reference (which, like the audit committee, are set initially by the board, but reviewed annually by the committee). The numbers of members in the committee are defined on the same basis as for the audit committee. The experience of the members of the committee is expected to encapsulate knowledge and skills relating to:

- market statistical data;
- performance management;
- financial matters relating to stock options;
- pensions;
- trust and employment laws;
- tax matters.

The remuneration committee may invite others to attend its meetings – typically, these may include the chairman, chief executive and human resources director, as well as any appointed remuneration consultants. However, the chairman of the committee has the responsibility to manage and control the discussions.

The number of meetings is not defined by the Code (unlike the audit committee) but the ICSA recommends at least two meetings each year, the last of which will include approving the report of the remuneration committee in the annual report and accounts. The committee is expected to have a work plan, which it must follow. Topics include items such as the review of long-term incentive plans, a market practice review, and an update on current external remuneration issues, as well as more internal tasks such as the review of the committee's terms of reference, self-assessment of its performance and a review of the remuneration consultant's advice.

The remuneration committee is implicitly required to have a dialogue on remuneration matters, as set out in the Combined Code (Principle B.2): 'The chairman of the board should ensure that the company maintains contact as required with its principal shareholders about remuneration in the same way as for other matters'.

For this purpose, the committee is expected actively to participate in the development of the policy that delegates responsibility for this communication – typically to the chairman of the remuneration committee.

As with the audit committee, the board is expected to review the performance of the remuneration committee annually, and the committee itself is expected to undertake its own self-assessment of its effectiveness.

Total shareholder return benchmarking

Within the remit of the committee lies the setting of benchmarks for comparison purposes. Whilst much of this will be undertaken confidentially by the remuneration consultants on a remuneration package basis, it also includes setting the sample of companies to be included within the total shareholder return (TSR) comparison. For this purpose the calculation for TSR assumes that all benefits, cash dividend or otherwise, are reinvested in the constituent company at time of receipt. Apart from offering the potential to base executive directors' long-tem performance incentives on TSR, the TSR graph enables a ready comparison for shareholders against a bundle of similar companies.

As a result, TSR is a useful tool on which to judge the performance of company (and the board) over the long term. The choice of the constituent members of the TSR is typically within the remit of the remuneration committee, and it is important to ensure that the constituent companies are relevant and reflective. Key issues the committee needs to consider include changing the constituents of the TSR if mergers or takeovers occur that change the nature of the constituent companies, as well as ensuring that the constituent companies are of a similar size and scope for comparison purposes. The ICSA remuneration committee guide provides a series of criteria for the benchmarking process: market capitalisation, turnover, enterprise value (a proxy for takeover value) and employees. The ranges suggested are wide (for example, from 50–200% of the market capitalisation of the source company). As importantly, it includes both business sector and geographic spread. The latter is a critical example, because it will determine the cyclicality of the comparator companies.

In one example reviewed, in 2005, a retail company divested itself of some of its manufacturing subsidiaries, leaving itself as a predominantly UK-based retailer. In the following year, it merged with a largely European-based competitor. The new company now comprised retail in the United Kingdom and distribution companies across the EU – a vastly different animal from its 2005 predecessor, for which its TSR constituents comprised seven retailers and two manufacturers. Subsequently, of these nine companies, two have changed status through merger or demerger, and one has delisted and subsequently relisted in another format. Yet, because of the changes in the company's business portfolio, some of the TSR retailers are probably now far less relevant for comparison purposes than they were in 2004/05. Changes of this nature make it an imperative to review the TSR constituents regularly. However, executive remuneration is often tied to the TSR, and, as a consequence, such changes cannot be made without having due regard to these considerations. Perhaps unsurprisingly, some companies take a less-focused approach when considering the TSR constituents, and have as the benchmark constituents the entire FTSE100 index (or the FTSE250, if more appropriate).

Report

The Directors' Remuneration Report Regulations 2002 (DRR) lay down the reporting requirements of the remuneration committee. It is expected that the DRR will form the basis for any relevant Companies Act 2006 statutory instruments. The DRR require that the remuneration report in the annual report and accounts should include information on four areas, which are not subject to audit:

- **The means by which the committee assesses directors' remuneration.** This includes the names of the members of the committee, together with those who provided advice.
- **A statement of the directors' remuneration policy for the following year.** This includes detailed summary of performance conditions of share options and long-term incentive plans, the criteria for performance assessment, and a summary of the policy regarding contract length and the nature of termination payments under such contracts.
- **A TSR performance graph.** This is based on the constituents of the TSR, and a default period of fives years is set, unless, of course, the company is newly listed.
- **Information regarding each director's contract for services.** This includes dates of each contact, the unexpired term and the provisions for early termination.

In addition, the remuneration report should include the following audited information:

- **emoluments** for each director (and any compensations received);
- **number of share options** held by each director at the year end, including exercise price, vesting and expiry dates and any performance criteria;
- **details of any long-term incentive schemes** allocated to each director;
- **details of any pension scheme** held by each director, including details of any changes over the year and the transfer value of such schemes;
- **excess retirement benefits** of directors and past directors;
- **compensation paid** for past directors;
- **sums paid to third parties** for a director's services.

Again, these should be assumed to be minimum guidelines, and the remuneration committee should consider what other forms of information could be provided that would usefully serve the interests of the shareholders.

In this respect, it is important to consider those bodies that have a public view on what is included within companies' remuneration reports. These include the National Association of Pension Funds (NAPF), which has its own voting guidelines[8] that include requirements that the vesting of incentive awards should take account of the extent to which performance conditions have been met, as well as recommending a vote against the remuneration report of any company that has not removed re-testing from existing incentive schemes.

In a similar manner, the Association of British Insurers (ABI) has published its own guidelines[9] – these do not include voting recommendations, but the ABI advises its members of breaches of provisions by companies. In addition, it represents the latest thinking on key policy issues, such as its stance against the early vesting of sharing incentives in the event of a change of control.

The ABI expects remuneration committees to consider the principle of pro rata share awards vesting, and wishes to see more detail in the remuneration report on the extent to which previous year's incentive targets have been met. It also requires that any increase in the maximum annual bonus potential on a year-by-year basis should be fully justified by the remuneration committee of the board.

Whilst both the ABI and NAPF have investment clout behind them and are public in their pronouncements, the Pension Investment Research Consultants (PIRC) works on behalf of its clients, many of whom may be charities or church-based investment funds. Its advice on voting is exclusively for the purpose of these clients. Nevertheless, it can be very effective in its commentary on remuneration policies, and companies must consider its views in the preparation of their remuneration reports – even if the decision amounts to a 'take no action' approach.

In addition, the remuneration committee must take into account legislation, of which the most recent was the EU Prospectus Directive, effective under UK law from July 2005. Under this Directive, all awards for director and employee share schemes have to comply with its requirements. In this respect, the remuneration report will need to confirm that any such plans, either in force or proposed, meet the requirements of the Directive (not just for the group company, but also for any of its EU subsidiaries).

Nomination committee – reporting requirements

Ultimately, the chairman has the responsibility for the performance evaluation of the board. However, the nomination committee supports the chairman in this activity, and makes recommendations to the board on matters of succession, reappointment and appointment of executive directors.

Role and responsibilities

The role of the nomination committee is defined in the Combined Code (as a result of the input provided by the Higgs Report). Its main duties are summarised as follows:

- identifying and nominating candidates to fill board vacancies, for approval by the board;
- prior to making an appointment, evaluating the balance of skill, knowledge and experience within the board, so as to prepare a description of the person specification to fit that appointment;
- reviewing the time required of a non-executive, with performance evaluation to assess how well a non-executive is fulfilling his or her duties;
- considering succession planning for members of the board, taking a forward-looking view of the needs and challenges within the company;
- reviewing the structure and composition of the board and making recommendations as to any possible changes;
- reviewing the leadership needs of the organisation, both executive and non-executive;
- providing newly appointed non-executives with a formal letter of appointment, which sets out the expectations in their role on the board.

In addition, the committee is expected to ensure that its terms of reference are available, and that it reports in the annual report on its activities, processes and use of external advisers, such as head-hunters (if appropriate). In addition it should declare its membership and the number of meetings attended by members over the course of the year.

Membership

As with the other main board committees, the nomination committee consists of non-executive directors, although here it is expected that there will be other appropriate executive directors, with non-executives being in the majority. The chairman is either the board chairman or an independent non-executive director. In the event that the board's chairman is also chairman of the committee, he or she is expected to relinquish his or her chairmanship during discussion relating to succession to the chairmanship of the board. Nevertheless, the requirement that the majority of the committee are non-executives is designed to ensure that even in matters relating to directors other than the chairman, the committee is not dominated by the thoughts and wishes of the chairman.

Board performance evaluation

Given its stated requirement in the Combined Code, the committee's responsibility to carry out performance evaluation of both the processes of the board and its committees, and the performance of the individuals within the board and each committee, is very important. In addition, the chairman is evaluated to ensure that the appropriate level of leadership is being provided. Non-executive directors are specifically reviewed to ensure that they are prepared for and attend those meetings at which their presence is required. In particular, the evaluation attempts to assess their objectivity and willingness to probe issues. Typically, evaluations will be undertaken with the support of external consultants, and the committee is expected to report on the process used.

Report

The nomination committee's report should include the following:

- membership of the committee and their attendance at committee meetings;
- names of any external advisers used, or an explanation if such consultants have not been used;
- process of the appointment-making system;

- performance-evaluation process;
- nature of the topics discussed during each of the meetings held during a financial year.

NOTES

1 A copy of the full revised Combined Code of Governance is available on the FSA website at www.fsa.gov.uk/pubs/ukla/lr_comcode2003.pdf.
2 'Internal Control: Guidance for Directors on the Combined Code' (1999) can be purchased via the ICAEW website at www1.icaew.co.uk, and 'Revised guidelines on internal controls' (2005) is available on the Financial Reporting Council website at www.frc.org.uk.
3 For smaller companies, this requirement is reduced to a minimum of two. Smaller companies are those that were below the FTSE350 for the year immediately prior to the reporting year.
4 A more detailed review of the practical issues facing an audit committee is available in Timothy Copnell, *ICSA Audit Committee Guide* (ICSA Publishing, 2005).
5 A copy of the Smith Guidance report can be found on the Financial Reporting Council website at www.frc.org.uk/images/uploaded/documents/ACReport.pdf.
6 This responsibility for risk management does not apply if there is either a risk committee made up of independent directors, or if risk is reviewed by the board as a whole.
7 A more detailed review of the practical issues facing a remuneration committee is available in Sean O'Hare, *ICSA Remuneration Committee Guide* (ICSA Publishing, 2006).
8 A copy of the detailed voting guidelines can be obtained as a pdf from the NAPF bookshop at www.napf.co.uk/publications/publicationsaction.cfm?PubsCategory=*PF&PubsSortBy=Title&SubmitPubs=Submit&keywords=*.
9 These guidelines were revised in November 2006, and the latest version can be found on the ABI website at http://www.ivis.co.uk/pages/gdsc2_1.pdf.

CHAPTER **6**

Stock Exchange rules

KEY ISSUES

- Listing Rules
  - Financial Services Authority
  - Listing Rules on annual reports
  - Continuing obligations for corporate communications
  - Listing Rules and prospectuses
  - Shareholder communications
  - Listing Rules and circulars
- Alternative Investments Market – corporate reporting requirements
  - Annual reports
  - Prospectuses
  - Other announcements – notifications
  - Nominated advisers (Nomads)
- Introduction of Transparency Directive
  - Periodic reporting
  - Dissemination of regulated information

Listing Rules

The Listing Rules form part of the Financial Services Authority Handbook.[1] This is a very extensive book, available via the web. Its size had led one commentator in the FSA to suggest that if all the pages in the Handbook were to be printed and stacked in a single column, it would be taller than the current Chief Executive of the FSA! The Handbook covers all aspects necessary for regulation of the financial markets; its sections include:

- a glossary
- high-level standards;
- prudential standards;
- business standards;
- regulatory processes;

- redress;
- specialist sourcebooks;
- listing, prospectus and disclosure;
- handbook guides;
- regulatory guides.

Financial Services Authority

The Financial Services Authority[2] (FSA) is an independent non-governmental body, with statutory powers under the Financial Services and Markets Act 2000. Although it is financed by the financial services industry, the Treasury appoints the FSA Board, and it is accountable to the Treasury, and thus to Parliament. However, it is regarded as independent because of the Act's regulatory aims. This gives it four statutory objectives: market confidence, public awareness, consumer protection and reduction of financial crime, encapsulated in its stated overall aim, which is 'To promote efficient, orderly and fair markets and to help retail consumers achieve a fair deal'.

The aim of the FSA is designed to support and promote a free and fair financial services market. Its stated regulatory approach includes the following:

> In all our work we believe in the principles of a risk-based approach; the desirability of regulation working with the grain of the market rather than against it; the restriction of regulation to those circumstances where the market does not provide adequate answers and where regulation has the prospect of doing so at reasonable cost; and an acceptance that a regulatory system neither can nor should aim at avoiding all failures.

Within this regulatory approach, the FSA has responsibility for regulating stock exchanges by setting the required standards and taking action against companies that fail to meet the required standards. It is within this context that the Listing Rules affect companies that make corporate reporting statements. Breaches of the Listing Rules by a company, or its directors (or, in the case of senior employees, regarded as insiders for the purposes of dealing[3]) will create significant regulatory issues for a company, even though the Listing Rules do not form part of a statutory framework. Nevertheless, as the FSA's position stands currently, a breach of the Listing Rules will not automatically result in a delisting, unlike the position adopted in the United States, where the SEC's audit committee regulations require a company in breach to be delisted.

The Listing Rules do not apply to exchanges not regulated by the FSA, such as the AIM, and details of the listing requirements for companies contemplating or already traded on the AIM will be given later.

The Handbook also contains the Prospectus Rules and the Disclosure Rules, which are published under the FSA's role as the UK Listing Authority. These rules cover three areas of corporate reporting: annual reports, prospectuses (relating to new issues of shares on regulated exchanges, and the subsequent requirement for information relating to these shares), and circulars (documents sent to shareholders outlining important matters to be discussed at general meetings – annual or otherwise).

Listing Rules on annual reports

Adherence to Combined Code

The Listing Rules require UK listed companies to include a statement within their annual reports that describes their compliance with the Combined Code. This should include both a statement of how a company has applied the Code's principles (providing sufficient explanation to enable shareholders to confirm this to their satisfaction) and a statement that the Code's principles have been applied throughout the accounting period.

Specifically, Schedule C to the Combined Code defines the requirements for the disclosure of corporate governance arrangements within the annual report. The details have already been covered in Chapter 5, but in essence, the requirements cover the following:

- composition of the board and its committees;
- method of operation of the board and its performance evaluation;
- reports of the nomination committee, remuneration committee and audit committee;
- report from the auditors;
- relevant resolutions for election or re-election of directors.

In the event that a company has not complied with all or some of the Code's principles, or has done so for only part of the accounting period, it must specify with what part of the Code's principles it has been in compliance, and over what period, and provide its reasons for non-compliance with regard to the other principles (based on the 'comply or explain' approach).

Continuing obligations for corporate communications

There are specific rules relating to the nature of communication of corporate information that are listed under the 'continuing obligations' section of the Listing Rules and relate to the preliminary statement of annual results and dividends, the publication of the annual report and accounts and the publication of half-yearly reports.

Preliminary statement

A listed company is required to publish its preliminary statement of annual results as soon as possible after approval and within 120 days of the end of the period to which it relates. The company must notify a regulatory information service (RIS) after the board has approved the preliminary statement. This statement must have been agreed with the auditors and must show the figures in a tabular form consistent with the presentation of the annual accounts. In addition, if the auditors' report is likely to be modified, the preliminary statement must give details of the nature of the modification. It should also provide a form of explanation, if required, to assess the results. Where a dividend is payable (or withheld), the preliminary statement must include the exact net amount payable per share, its payment date, the record date (where applicable) and any foreign income dividend election, together with any income tax treated as paid at the lower rate and not repayable.

Annual report

The Listing Rules changed as a result of the implementation of the Transparency Directive (effective for all financial years starting on or after 20 January 2007). However, since there may be readers of this book whose company is still operating under the old Listing Rules (for example, those companies with year ends on 31 December 2006) a summary of the relevant Listing Rule is described below (full details are available in Listing Rule 9.8).

A listed company must publish its annual report and accounts as soon as possible after they have been approved, and within six months of the end of its financial year. The report must have been prepared in accordance with the company's national law and with national accounting standards or International Accounting Standards (IAS). It must have been independently audited and reported and be in consolidated form if the company has subsidiary undertakings.

The annual report and accounts must include:

- a statement of the amount of interest capitalised;
- details of any small related party transaction;

- details of any long-term incentive schemes;
- details of any arrangements under which a director of the company has waived or agreed to waive any emoluments;
- details of any allotments made of equity securities;
- details of any contract of significance existing during the period under review;
- details of any contract for the provision of services to the listed company or any of its subsidiary undertakings by a controlling shareholder;
- details of any arrangement to waive dividends.

In addition, there are further requirements relating to the declaration of directors regarding beneficial and non-beneficial shareholdings, a statement from the directors that the business is a going concern, a statement of the application of the principles of the Combined Code, and a statement regarding any purchases of the company's own shares. The annual report must also include a report to the shareholders by the board that contains details of the company's policy on executive directors' remuneration, together with details of this remuneration in tabular form (including information on long-term incentive schemes and share schemes), and details of the directors service contracts and pension benefits. The Listing Rules require that the auditors review the above disclosures and state whether they believe that there are areas of non-compliance (with details of any non-compliance).

This information is additional to the information required by law – such as the provisions of a Business Review.

If a company publishes a summary financial statement it must disclose the earnings per share and the information legally required for summary financial statements.

Half-yearly reports

As with the annual report and accounts, the Listing Rules changed as a result of the implementation of the Transparency Directive. Again, for readers whose company is still operating under the old Listing Rules for one more year, a summary of the relevant Listing Rule is described below (full details are available in Listing Rule 9.9).

A listed company must prepare a report, on a group basis where relevant, on its activities and profit or loss for the first six months of each financial year, for which the accounting policies and presentation must be consistent with the latest published annual accounts.

The company must publish its report as soon as possible after the report has been approved, and within 90 days of the end of the half-year period. It must notify an

RIS of its half-yearly report after board approval. The report must be published either by sending it out to holders of the company's listed securities or by the insertion of the report as a paid advertisement in a national newspaper.

The report must contain a balance sheet, a cash flow statement, an income statement (comprising net turnover, finance income, operating profit or loss, finance costs, profit or loss before taxation, profit or loss, minority interests, profit or loss attributable to equity holders, rates of dividend to be paid, taxation on profits showing UK and overseas taxation, and earnings per share). This financial information must include prior year comparisons. In addition there must be a statement of any changes in equity and an explanatory statement that enables investors to make an informed assessment of the company's activities and profit or loss. If the financial figures have been audited or reviewed by auditors the report of the auditors must be reproduced in full in the half-yearly report.

Full details of the changes in corporate reporting as a result of the Transparency Directive are included at the end of this chapter.

Listing Rules on prospectuses

Prospectuses comprise listing particulars that have to be submitted to the FSA before a company can be approved for listing. These particulars are submitted by the issuer and its sponsor (typically, the corporate finance department of a bank). The purpose of these particulars is to enable investors to make an informed assessment of the assets and liabilities, the financial position, and the profits and losses and prospects of the issuer of the securities in question.

For a company to satisfy the requirements for listing, it must have published audited accounts that:

- cover at least three previous years;
- are the latest accounts for a period (which has ended not more than six months before the date of the prospectus);
- are consolidated accounts for the company and its subsidiaries;
- have been independently audited, without modification by the auditors.

In addition, the company must be able to show that at least 75% of its business is supported by a historic earnings record that covers the three-year minimum period and that it controls the majority of its assets and has done so for those three years. The purpose of these requirements is to avoid circumstances where the company is seeking listing based on its future prospects, which may be significantly different from those that have gone before. As such, the intention is that the information contained in the particulars should be sufficient to enable investors to make a reasonable assessment of the future prospects of the business.

However, there are two important 'corporate sector' exceptions to this requirement. These relate to mineral companies (such as oil or mining companies, whose prospects may be based on the future extraction of resources that have been geologically proven) and scientific research-based companies (such as bio tech companies, where they may have undergone limited drug testing). However, minimum requirements relate to a scientific research-based company regarding the amounts of capital intended to be raised, as well as a requirement to demonstrate a three-year record of laboratory-based research and development, which includes providing details of patents granted and the successful completion of relevant product testing.

In addition to the requirement for financial records covering three years, a company seeking listing must also be able to demonstrate that it has sufficient working capital to sustain the next 12 months' trading requirements.

In approaching listing, directors must be able to ensure that their company can meet the requirements of the six listing principles:

- Directors should understand their responsibilities and obligations.
- The company should ensure that it establishes and maintains adequate procedures, systems and controls to enable it to comply with its obligations.
- It must act with integrity towards current and potential shareholders
- It must communicate information to current and potential shareholders in such a way as to avoid the creation of a false market.
- It must ensure that it treats all shareholders equally in respect of the rights attaching to their shareholdings.
- It must deal with the FSA in an open and co-operative manner.

The second principle requires that a company is able to report relevant information in a timely manner and that the directors have adequate time to consider it before it is communicated to shareholders. Essentially, this is setting the requirement for the management and publication of ongoing corporate reporting and aligns with the requirements set out in the Combined Code.

As part of the particulars submitted for approval by the FSA, there needs to be a summary set of information.[4] The purpose of the summary is that it sets out in a concise and non-technical manner, information that assists investors to understand the essential characteristics of, and risks associated with, the company making the issue and the securities to which the prospectus refers (as well as, if appropriate, to any guarantor of the issue).

The contents of the summary are defined under the Prospectus Directive, which was ratified by the UK Government in 2004 and became law in July 2005.[5] The issuer of the prospectus is free to determine for himself the content of the summary, but it must not exceed 2,500 words, and should be in the language in which the prospectus was drawn up. The summary should be accompanied by a note that warns that the summary should only be regarded as an introduction to the prospectus and that a decision to invest by an investor should be based on consideration of the prospectus as a whole.

In addition, the particulars must be in a prescribed format. The prospectus can be either a single document or a set of separate documents, in which case it must be divided into the registration document, the securities note and the summary. Again, the format is prescribed by the Prospectus Directive and must be composed in the following order:

- a clear and detailed table of contents;
- the summary;
- the risk factors linked to the issuer and the type of security covered by the issue;
- other information included in the schedules.

The prospectus is expected to have a minimum set of information included within it. Again, this is determined by reference to the Prospectus Directive, which introduced common standards throughout the EU for the publication of prospectuses. There are a total of 21 articles within the Directive that define the minimum information. These include pro forma financial information, information relating to any guarantees, information relating to the security being issued and its rights for investors in that security, and information for securities that are asset backed.

However, information can be incorporated within the particulars by reference to other documents. In these circumstances, such documents need to have been filed with the FSA, and can include one or more of the following:

- annual and interim financial information;
- documents prepared on the occasion of a specific transaction such as a merger or demerger;
- audit reports and financial statements;
- memorandum and articles of association;
- earlier approved and published prospectuses;
- regulated information;
- circulars to security holders.

The language in which the prospectus is written must be English if the security is to be listed only in the United Kingdom. However, if listings are sought in other European Economic Area states,[6] the prospectus must be in English and made available either in the language of the state or states in which additional listings are being sought, or in a language 'customary in the sphere of international finance', at the discretion of the issuer of the security. The same approach applies to the summary document.

The Prospectus Rules require that a company issuing transferable securities must prepare a document at least annually, described as an annual information update. This update is to contain all information that has been published or made available to the public over the previous 12 months. Such information includes information made available under the Companies Act – in effect the annual report and accounts – together with any information published under the rules of the EEA states. The update must be filed with the FSA.

Shareholder communications

The FSA requires that companies publish their communications to shareholders in whatever manner is appropriate to protect the interests of shareholders and to ensure the smooth operation of the market. In respect of the latter, the FSA has identified RIS, which include the following:

- Business Wire Regulatory Disclosure provided by Business Wire;
- FirstSight provided by Romeike;
- Announce provided by Hugin ASA;
- News Release Express provided by CCNMatthews UK Limited;
- PR Newswire Disclose provided by PRNewswire;
- RNS provided by the London Stock Exchange.

If company news is published at any time when the information service is not open for business, the alternative required by the FSA is that the information must be distributed via at least two national newspapers (UK-based), two news-wire services operating in the United Kingdom, and a release to be distributed as soon as the chosen RIS is open for business.

Information to be covered by such publication includes the release of financial statements, together with information on transactions undertaken on their own behalf by individuals discharging managerial responsibilities (i.e. directors) in the company concerned.

Listing Rules on circulars

A listed company is not permitted to publish a circular to its shareholders (as well as other holders of its transferable securities) without first gaining the approval of the FSA. Such circulars can comprise those concerning purchase of the company's own share capital, particulars about mergers or acquisitions, or other resolutions requiring approval by shareholders at a general meeting.

Every circular must follow a prescribed format for the content of the circulars, covering:

- a clear explanation of the subject matter of the circular, drawing attention to its characteristics, benefits and risks;
- an explanation as to why the shareholder is being asked to vote (or, if the shareholder is not required to vote, why the circular has been sent to the shareholder);
- sufficient information to enable a considered decision to be made, should a vote be required;
- a recommendation from the board as to the voting action the shareholders should take, in the event of a vote being required;
- a statement that the circular should be passed on to the relevant persons, if the addressed shareholder had sold the relevant shares;
- in the event of new shares being issued in substitution for ones already in existence, a statement describing the position regarding existing title documents;
- if appropriate, a statement describing how the rights of new shares will change, including the date on which this is expected to take effect.

Class 1 circular

UK listed companies must comply with the Listing Rules and the Disclosure Rules when they acquire a business or assets, or they dispose of part of their own business or assets. There are three levels of transactions:

- class 3 transactions – where the percentage ratios of the transaction relative to those of the listed company are all less than 5%;
- class 2 transactions – where any percentage ratio of the transaction relative to those of the listed company is more than 5% but each is less than 25%;
- class 1 transactions – where the percentage ratios of the transaction relative to those of the listed company are all more than 25%.

In addition reverse takeovers may be treated as a class 1 transaction if all of a series of conditions are satisfied.

STOCK EXCHANGE RULES   **93**

Class 3 transactions require the listed company to notify the RIS as soon as the terms of the transaction are agreed. Class 2 transactions similarly require the notification of the transaction to the RIS, but require a greater level of detail to be communicated. Class 1 transactions require both the communication to the RIS in line with the requirement for a Class 2 transaction, and in addition require that the company produces an explanatory circular (a class 1 circular) and that any agreement relating to the transaction is conditional upon the approval of the shareholders being obtained.

The contents of the class 1 circular must include the following information and statements:

- Information contained in the RIS notification:
    - details of the transaction;
    - description of the business that is the subject of the transaction;
    - consideration and its manner of being satisfied (or, in the case of a disposal, the application of the sales proceeds);
    - gross assets involved in the transaction and attributable profits;
    - effect of the transaction on the listed company, including the benefits of the transaction;
    - details of any service contracts of any proposed directors in the listed company;
    - details of key individuals in the company that is the subject of the transaction.
- Additional information, including:
    - risks factors;
    - trend information;
    - service contracts;
    - directors' interests in shares;
    - major interests in shares;
    - related party transactions;
    - litigation;
    - significant corporate changes;
    - material contracts;
    - working capital.
- Financial information (if the transaction would result in consolidation of the new company within the listed company as a result of an acquisition,

or deconsolidation in the event of a disposal). In this case, the financial information must:

- be consistent with the accounting policies adopted in the listed company's latest annual report's consolidated accounts;
- indicate, as appropriate, whether the information provided is based on historical financial information, or on forecasted financial information;
- where such information has not been drawn from audited accounts, contain a statement to that effect identifying the underlying assumptions behind the provision of this information;
- if the information provided is in summary form, contain a statement of where the full financial information can be obtained;
- contain a financial information table that includes information covering the past three accounting periods. This table must cover both parties involved in the transaction and contain a balance sheet, the income statement, a cash flow statement, a statement showing changes in equity, the accounting policies and all necessary explanatory notes. Since this financial information table relates to previous financial years, the table is required to be accompanied by an accountant's opinion stating that the table provides a true and fair view of the financial matters contained within it. This opinion is not required where the company the subject of the transaction is itself listed (and hence will comply with the Listing Rules) or the listed company is making a disposal of one its subsidiaries.

As the reader will appreciate from the extensive list of information required for a class 1 circular, not only does it cover information required to be provided within the annual report and accounts, but in some instances goes far beyond it.

Related party circulars

Related party circulars arise where a related party has been party to a transaction with the company. A related party will usually be a director or shadow director of the listed company, but could also be a director of a subsidiary, a joint venture (50:50) company, or a person who exercises significant influence.

The contents of a related party circular must include:

- details of major shareholders;
- significant corporate changes;
- material contracts (if these are relevant to the circumstances of the related party);

- for a related party who was a director or a shadow director during the 12 months previous to the transaction, details of service contracts, interests in shares and related party transactions;
- details of the transaction (together with a statement that shareholders are being asked to vote on the transaction because it is a related transaction);
- an independent valuation in the event of the acquisition or disposal of an asset where any percentage ratio is 25% or more;
- a statement from the board that the transaction is fair and reasonable from the perspective of the shareholders (including a statement that the related party has not taken part in the board's deliberation of the transaction).

Circulars on the purchase of a company's own equity

These circulars form the basis for a resolution to be put to shareholders to allow a company to seek the authority to acquire its own shares. In addition to this statement, a circular must include:

- a statement of the directors' intention about using such authority;
- the method to be used for acquiring shares, and the number to be acquired (if known);
- a statement of whether the company intends to cancel the shares or hold them in treasury;
- a statement of the names of specific individuals from whom the shares are to be purchased (if this is to be the case);
- details of the price to be paid;
- a statement of the total numbers of warrants and share options that are outstanding before the circular is to be published, and the proportion of the share capital they represent both before and after buyback of shares.

In the event that the intention is to buy back more than 25% of the issued share capital, the circular must also include information relating to:

- risk factors;
- trend information;
- directors' interests in shares;
- major interest in shares;
- significant corporate changes;
- working capital.

Other forms of circulars

In addition to the three major uses of circulars by companies, other forms are as a means of gaining shareholders' approval through the placing of resolutions to be voted upon. These include:

- authority to allot shares;
- disapplying of pre-emption rights (i.e. offers to shareholders on a pre-emptive basis);
- increases in authorised share capital (if a company retains this until its articles are amended as a result of the abolition of authorised share capital under the Companies Act 2006);
- reduction of capital;
- capitalisation or bonus issue;
- scrip dividend alternative and mandate schemes or dividend reinvestment schemes;
- notices of meetings;
- amendments to constitution;
- employees share schemes, including discounted option schemes;[7]
- reminders of conversion rights.

The contents of all of these various forms of circular are prescribed by the Listing Rules.

Alternative Investment Market – corporate reporting requirements

The Alternative Investment Market[8] (AIM) was established in 1995. It was specifically designed for smaller companies for whom the listed market may require more rigorous compliance than they could afford at this stage in their development.

The AIM is regulated by the London Stock Exchange (rather than the UK Listing Authority). As a result, the requirements for companies traded on the AIM market are less rigorous than those traded on the Official List. Unlike listed companies, AIM companies have nominated advisers ('Nomads') rather than sponsors. The relevance of this difference will be discussed later in this section.

The requirements set for AIM companies are set out below. To provide some useful sense of comparison for the reader, they have been laid out in broadly the same structure as that used in the previous section for listed companies. As a consequence, they cover three areas – annual reports, prospectuses and other announcements.

Annual reports

An AIM company is required to publish annual audited accounts not less than six months after its financial year end. This report is required to be circulated to its shareholders. AIM companies incorporated within the EEA are required to prepare and present their reports in line with IAS. If the company is not incorporated within the EEA, the accepting principles applicable are extended to include the IAS, US GAAP, Canadian GAAP or the Australian International Financial Reporting Standards.

An AIM company must prepare half-yearly reports, which must include at least a balance sheet, an income statement, and a cash flow statement with comparative prior year figures. The half-yearly statement must be presented in the same format as that adopted in the company's annual accounts.

Transactions with related parties must be disclosed in the annual report if any of the ratios exceed 0.25%. Details of these transactions should include the name of the related party and the consideration made for the transaction.

Prospectuses

A company seeking to be quoted on AIM must submit a series of announcement documents, rather than a prospectus as such. The first is a *pre-announcement document*, which must be provided to the Stock Exchange 10 days before the expected date of admission. This document must include the following information:

- a brief description of the business;
- names and functions of the directors, together with any person holding more than 3% of the equity;
- expected admission date;
- anticipated accounting reference date.

If the company seeking admission is a quoted company already traded on an AIM Designated Market,[9] the deadline is 20 days before admission, and, in addition to the above, the company must provide the following information:

- the AIM Designated Market on which its shares have been traded;
- confirmation that it has adhered to relevant legal and regulatory requirements;
- an address (or website) where any documents made public over the past two years are available;

- details of its intended strategy following admission;
- a description of any significant corporate changes since the publication of the last set of audited accounts;
- confirmation that working capital is available sufficient to support the company for 12 months following its admission;
- a website address on which investors can obtain details of the rights pertaining to the securities being admitted and the latest published annual report and accounts (which must be not more than nine months old prior to admission).

If a company applying to be admitted to an AIM is an investing company, a condition of its admission is that its intention is to raise a minimum of £3 million in cash (via equity fundraising), immediately on or before its admission.

Subsequently, the AIM company must produce an **admission document**, which must be made available to the public for at least one month after admission – although a previously quoted company need not necessarily do so. The information to be covered in the admission document includes the following:

- selected financial information;
- operating and financial review;
- capital resources;
- research and development (if appropriate);
- profit forecasts or estimates;
- management details;
- remuneration and benefits;
- working capital;
- capitalisation and indebtedness;
- relevant information about each director;
- details of any person who has received fees, securities or benefits in excess of £10,000 from the AIM company.

An important requirement for newly admitted AIM companies is that if they have not been independent and earning revenue for more than two years, all related parties and applicable employees are required to agree not to dispose of any of their interests in the company's securities for a period of 12 months following the admission to the AIM.

Other announcements – notifications

The AIM Rules require companies to issue **notifications of any developments relating to price sensitive information** that may lead to substantial share price movements if the public were aware of them.

These developments can include any or all of the following:

- changes in the company's financial condition;
- changes in the nature of its business activity;
- changes in the nature of its business performance;
- changes in the expectations of its future performance.

Similarly, an AIM company must issue a **notification of any substantial transactions**. These are defined as those that exceed 10% in what is described as the 'class tests'. These cover ratios relating to:

- gross assets;
- profits;
- turnover;
- considerations for the transaction;
- gross capital.

However, this excludes any transactions that are of a revenue nature and would be part of the normal course of business. If the latter could be described as a significant development (see above) then a notification would be required for this purpose.

Further, an AIM company must issue a notification if the company is subject to a reverse takeover (defined as exceeding 100% in any of the class tests or which results in a fundamental change in the nature of the business). In this case the company must issue a notification covering the following information:

- particulars of the transaction, including a description of the business;
- financial information relating to the transaction – profits, asset value, consideration and its method of satisfaction (or application of proceeds in the event of a sale);
- the impact of the transaction on the AIM company;
- details of any service contracts of proposed directors.

In addition, an AIM company must issue **a notification for a related party transaction**. This applies if any transaction with a related party exceeds 5% in any of the class tests. The information to be provided includes the following:

- particulars of the transaction, including a description of the business;
- financial information relating to the transaction – profits, asset value, consideration and its method of satisfaction (or application of proceeds in the event of a sale);
- the impact of the transaction on the AIM company;
- details of any service contracts of proposed directors.

The company must also publish an admission document for the revised and enlarged entity, which would have to be put to the London Stock Exchange for approval for admission.

Similarly, if the AIM company makes a disposal which results in **a fundamental change of business**, it must issue a notification. In this respect, a disposal resulting in a fundamental change of business is defined as one that exceeds 75% of any of the class tests. The information required to be included in this circular is the same as that for a reverse takeover. In such circumstances, the nature of the classification of the AIM company will change upon the divestment of all or most of its trading assets; it will be treated as an investment company and is required to publish its investment strategy as a consequence. It will then have to acquire assets within the next 12 months to enable it to regain its original status.

An AIM company must also issue **a notification for a related party transaction**. This applies if any transaction with a related party exceeds 5% in any of the class tests. The information to be provided includes that described above for a reverse takeover plus the following:

- the name of the related party and its interest in the transaction;
- a statement that the directors have consulted with the company's nominated advisers and are satisfied that the terms of the transaction are fair and reasonable from the perspective of the shareholders.

Notifications are also required in respect of *miscellaneous corporate information*, including:

- deals by its directors;
- relevant changes to significant shareholders;
- changes in the directors (resignations, dismissals, appointments);
- changes in accounting reference dates, registered office, legal name;
- material changes in financial information contained in its admission document (trading performance, financial condition, profit forecast);
- payments relating to its AIM securities (dividends, etc.);

- application for admission or cancellation of any AIM securities – and the reasons behind these decisions;
- shares taken into or out of Treasury;
- changes in its nominated adviser (resignation, dismissal or appointment).

AIM companies also have a responsibility to make any documents that have been provided to their shareholders (such as notifications, admission documents, annual and half-yearly reports) available to the public for at least one month after publication. This availability relies on the documents being available at an address, but, of course, this address may be that of a website.

In this respect, in February 2007 the London Stock Exchange announced enhanced disclosure requirements for AIM companies, including mandating all AIM companies to maintain a website and to display core management and financial information, including admission documents, on it.

Nominated advisers (Nomads)

Nomads are a unique concept to the AIM and in many respects have been integral to the market. Each company applying to the AIM must appoint a Nomad to guide it through the admission process and its subsequent life as a publicly quoted company. Nomads cover a wide range, including specialist departments in banks, investment banks, security houses and firms of accountants.

The London Stock Exchange sets strict criteria for becoming an AIM Nomad. Its intention is that they become one of the means by which the market's integrity is safeguarded. If an AIM company fails to have a Nomad, the Stock Exchange will suspend its securities.

The role of the Nomad is not only to support the AIM company in its application for admittance to AIM (including advising that the company is suitable for admission to the AIM), but also to advise and guide the directors of the company at all times in respect of their obligations with regard to the AIM rules. In addition, the Nomad has a responsibility to review the company's actual trading and financial performance against those included within the **admission document**, in order to advise whether a notification should be issued to shareholders (see above on notifications).

If the Stock Exchange considers that a Nomad has contravened the relevant AIM rules, it can fine or censure it, or remove it from the Nomad register, and publish the details of the action it has taken and the reasons behind such actions.

However, recently there have been suggestions[10] that Nomads have been less effective than was expected in terms of maintaining the integrity of the AIM market. In February 2007, the Stock Exchange introduced new regulations[11] to make it easier to take disciplinary action against Nomads which brought unsuccessful companies for admission to the AIM. The issues raised included the number of companies performing poorly or failing, especially in areas such as minerals extraction and oil and gas. Furthermore, it is being questioned whether Nomads are doing enough to ensure proper scrutiny of overseas companies being admitted to the AIM. Amongst additional measures expected to be introduced are a more careful check of the backgrounds of companies and directors, together with visits to overseas production facilities, if appropriate.

Introduction of the Transparency Directive

The Transparency Directive is an EU Directive that emanates from the EU's Financial Services Action Plan. Its purpose is to promote a single European capital market by ensuring that the issuers of capital provide transparency for investors by ensuring the disclosure of appropriate information. It is a minimum harmonisation Directive – which means that Member States can impose more stringent regulations if they feel that this is appropriate for their own purposes. The Directive came into law in the United Kingdom on 20 January 2007, as a result of the publication by the FSA of its rules in December 2006.

The requirements of the Directive cover a pan-European approach for periodic reporting, the dissemination of regulated information and the disclosure of major shareholdings. For the purpose of this book, the focus will be on the first two areas, which only affect listed companies.

Periodic reporting

With the exception of certain exemptions, issuers of listed securities (which will exclude AIM companies) and whose 'home state' is the United Kingdom (generally speaking, those companies incorporated under the Companies Act 1985) are required to comply with the rules of the FSA. The date on which these rules take effect is for all reporting periods starting on or after 20 January 2007. These rules replace the existing rules on periodic financial reporting – Listing Rules 9.8 and 9.9.

Annual reports

The new rules require companies to publish their annual report within four months of the end of their financial year. This compares with the current UK requirement of six months. In addition to requirements of the existing Listing Rules, the new rules state that the annual report must include:

- audited financial statements prepared in accordance with the applicable accounting standards;
- a management report giving a fair review of the company's business and describing the principal risks and uncertainties a company faces;
- a responsibility statement made by persons responsible to the company for the report.

The FSA has indicated that the responsibility statement will generally be given by the directors, and must state that the financial statements give a true and fair view and that the management report includes a fair review of the development and performance of the business.

The introduction of the responsibility statement means that there is a new statutory liability regime that rests solely with the issuer rather than the directors. This gives protection to investors who suffer loss due to errors or omissions in any of the periodic financial statements covered by the responsibility statements. However, for an investor to claim compensation, there has to be both an untrue or misleading statement, and a director or senior executive within the issuer must have known that the statement was untrue or misleading, or was reckless as to whether the statement was untrue or misleading. For compensation to be paid, the investor must be able to demonstrate that he or she relied on the information at a time when it was reasonable to so rely.

In addition to the above changes, companies are no longer required to produce a preliminary statement of their annual results. However, companies that elect to continue doing so will be bound by the existing Listing Rules relating to these statements.

Half-yearly financial reports

Half-yearly reports (often known as interims) must be published within two months of the end of the first six months of the financial year (compared with the current UK requirement of 90 days).

The new rules state that the half-yearly report must include:

- a condensed set of financial statements prepared in accordance with the applicable accounting standards;
- an interim management report;
- a responsibility statement.

Whilst there had been some concern about the ability to confirm a 'true and fair view' with condensed accounts, particularly given that they may be unaudited, the

FSA has said that issuers complying with the IFRS should prepare the condensed set of financial statements in accordance with IAS34.

Currently, a company must either send the half-yearly report to shareholders or insert the report in national newspapers. This requirement no longer applies.

Both the annual and half-yearly reporting requirements are applicable to issuers of debt securities, although the FSA has exempted issuers of wholesale debt securities (with denominations of €50,000 or more) in respect of the half-yearly report.

Interim management statements

Unless a company already publishes quarterly financial reports (for example, where it is dual listed with the United States), there is a new requirement for a company to publish an interim management statement (IMS) during each six-month period of its financial year. The IMS must be published in a period commencing 10 weeks after the commencement and six weeks before the end of the relevant six-monthly financial periods.

The IMS must contain:

- an explanation of the material events and transactions that have taken place during the period in question;
- a commentary of their impact on the company's financial position;
- a description of the financial position and performance of the company during that time.

A company may meet these requirements with trading statements or other reports, provided the requirements above are included.

There is no requirement for the inclusion of financial numerical data (unless the company chooses to do so) provided a meaningful narrative description is supplied.

Whilst the changes in the timing of the publication of the annual and half-yearly reports will necessitate changes in the definition of the relevant 'close periods', the FSA has indicated that, for the present, it does not propose a formal close period before the issuing of an IMS.

Guidance

The FSA has decided to adopt a light-touch approach and is not intending to publish any guidance – by 'copying out' the Directive as much as possible. The intention behind this approach is to avoid a box-ticking or checklist approach by issuers.

However, the FSA has indicated that it will take a risk-based approach to enforcing these new requirements and that a market practice review will take place between 18 and 24 months after their introduction.

Dissemination of regulated information

In essence the new rules will pose relatively few new requirements for UK companies. As with the periodic information, the rules apply to all companies listed on a regulated market and incorporated within the United Kingdom. Some of the key new requirements include the following:

- Companies proposing to amend their constitution must communicate the draft amendment to the FSA as well as the regulated market by the date of the calling of the general meeting.
- Companies using electronic communications with their shareholders must have this approved at a general meeting, write to shareholders to request consent, and make electronic communication available to shareholders wherever they are located. This means that companies must avoid the use of electronic communications for any mailing that needs to be restricted – for example, with regard to US securities laws.
- Companies must disclose any variation in the rights pertaining to certain classes of shares.

NOTES

1 Access to all parts of the Handbook can be found on the Handbook website at www.fsahandbook.info/FSA/select-handbook/focus-on.
2 Permission to quote from the Handbook has been granted by the FSA, and all material quoted is subject to its copyright.
3 Directors and designated employees are treated as 'insiders' for the purposes of the FSA's 'Model Code'. This places restrictions on share dealings that go beyond those required under legislation, such as insider trading legislation. The FSA expects that listed companies will enforce a code of conduct that is at least as stringent as the restrictions included within the Model Code.
4 The requirement for a summary is not applicable for 'specialist securities', i.e. securities limited in terms of the numbers available for issue and traded by individuals considered to be professionally knowledgeable in investment matters.
5 Prospectus Directive Regulation No. 2004/809/EC.

6   The EEA incorporates all EU states plus Norway, Liechtenstein, Iceland and Switzerland.
7   All awards under director and employee share plans need to comply with the Prospectus Directive Regulation.
8   Details of the AIM rules can be found on the London Stock Exchange website at www.londonstockexchange.com/en-gb/products/companyservices/ourmarkets/aim_new/.
9   The designated markets currently include the Australian Stock Exchange, Deutsche Börse, Euronext, Johannesburg Stock Exchange, NASDAQ, New York Stock Exchange, Stockholmbörsen, Swiss Exchange, Toronto and the UK Official List.
10 Martin Waller, 'Exchange to tighten quality controls for AIM Listing', *The Times*, 2 January 2007.
11 AIM Rules for Nominated Advisers can be accessed via www.londonstockexchange.com.

SECTION 2

MANAGING THE PROCESS

CHAPTER 7

Developing the annual report – traditional processes

KEY ISSUES

- Opportunities provided by publishing a company's report and accounts
- Processes
- Delivering audited accounts on time
- Producing other relevant board committee reports
- Producing designs for annual reports and delivering them on time

Opportunities provided by publishing a company's report and accounts

The publication of a company's report and accounts provides it with a significant communications opportunity. It enables shareholders to evaluate progress within their company and potential investors to assess the prospects for the company. It also enables employees to understand 'the bigger picture' concerning their company, which can motivate (or demotivate) employees, and appraise potential employees of the strength and stature of a company to which they may consider applying for a job.

The annual report and accounts may be the only source of information for other stakeholders, including government, as the basis for research as part of regulatory development. In addition, for other stakeholders – customers, suppliers and, potentially, NGOs – these documents may be one of the main sources of information on which to make decisions regarding the company, its performance and behaviour.

As such, ensuring a timely and effective process is an essential part of delivering the annual report and accounts. In this chapter, the various activities that have to be managed are considered.

Processes

Within the development of the annual report and accounts, traditionally several elements require managing:

- delivering the audited accounts on time;
- producing the other relevant board committee reports;
- producing the designs for the annual reports, and delivering them on time;
- producing the statements from the chairman and chief executive.

As a result of the addition of narrative reporting, it is also necessary to manage the production of the directors' report, incorporating the Business Review. The first three elements above will be dealt with in this chapter, whilst Chapter 8 will address the issue of the Business Review, together with the issue of how the statements and letter from the chairman and chief executive should be dealt with in conjunction with the Business Review.

Each element is likely to have different individuals responsible for its production. As such, the delivery of the annual report and accounts requires a significant amount of co-ordination. No company wants to have to delay its report because of administrative difficulties. In many respects, such difficulties may create as bad an impression as would the need to delay reporting because of the discovery of financial errors.

There are several good checklists available for preparation of the annual accounts, one of which, the Company Secretary Checklist, produced by Addleshaw Goddard, is presented as a summary in Appendix 4 to this book. This summary covers only the elements involved in preparing for the annual report. The full checklist also includes procedures for notice of general meetings. Like all good checklists, Addleshaw Goddard updates its version annually to take account of the latest rules and regulations. It is important for those using such checklists to use the most up-to-date version.

Delivering audited accounts on time

Most modern-day accounts are significantly different from those prepared as little as 20 years ago. The Financial Reporting Council's discussion paper, 'Promoting Audit Quality',[1] highlights that:

- The way business is transacted has become more complex. The use of financial instruments has become commonplace.
- The number of transactions involved has increased exponentially. Processing

of transactions is now automated (and virtually instantaneous). Increasingly, there is less underlying physical documentation.

- The carrying amount of an increasing number of assets and liabilities at fair value may be difficult to measure.

As such, the view in the discussion paper is that because:

> the high number of transactions has reduced the effectiveness of obtaining audit evidence by testing the authenticity of transactions ... auditing has become more "risk based" and increased reliance is placed on the auditor's assessment of the client's control environment.

Consequently, in managing this element, the key issue is ensuring that the audit committee's management of the audit process and auditors is both timely and effective.

The planning of audit committee meetings to line up with the schedule of the production of the annual report and accounts is therefore critical, as are the interim financial statements. For this purpose, the tasks of the audit committee have been split into five categories: audit committee management, ongoing risk and internal audit process management, assessing the auditors, policy and control review, and producing financial statements.

Tasks that should be phased as appropriate throughout the financial year away from key dates for review of financial statements are as follows:

- **Audit committee management:**
  - reviewing the committee's terms of reference;
  - assessing the skills and experience of the committee members;
  - updating on key topical financial issues;
  - performing assessment of the performance of the committee;
  - reviewing director and officer expenses;
  - reviewing related party transactions.
- **Ongoing risk and internal audit process management:**
  - developing audit plans for the external and internal auditors;
  - considering the risk control process;
  - considering the code of conduct and whistleblowing arrangements.
- **Assessing the auditors in terms of their performance and appointment:**
  - reviewing the performance of external and internal auditors;

- approving audit fees and terms of engagement;
- considering the objectivity and independence of external auditors;
- establishing policy with regard to non-audit services;
- for the internal audit function, reviewing the performance of that function and the appointment of the head of that function if appropriate.

Tasks that should occur in the first meeting before the end of the financial year are as follows:

- **Policy and control review:**
  - discussing the appropriateness of the accounting policies;
  - discussing the effectiveness of the risk control environment, including taking on board the views of the external auditors.

Tasks that should occur in the first meeting after the end of the relevant financial reporting period are as follows:

- **Producing the financial statements:**
  - reviewing the results of the external and internal audit;
  - reviewing and recommending the approval of financial statements – annual, half-year or quarterly (if appropriate);
  - holding discussions with the internal and external auditors in the absence of executive directors;
  - reviewing the committee's report to shareholders on its role, activities and responsibilities.

As will be clear from the above, the ability to complete the report of the audit committee is dependent on work that occurs throughout the year, including any special investigations initiated during the year. The need to provide assurance to shareholders of the well-being of the company's risk control system and the quality of the auditors (both external and internal) should not be left until the year end.

Similarly, the requirement to sign off the audited accounts (and the interim financial statement) is dependent on the audit committee having progressed work throughout the year. Ideally, at the conclusion of the year, the need to meet with auditors to discuss any issues that have arisen during the audit should not produce any significant surprises. Naturally, there will always be discussions about differing opinions on issues such as approaches towards policies, and accounting treatments, as well as discussions about the accuracy of any estimates that have been included in the accounts.

To help ensure that an unqualified set of accounts is achieved, an efficient audit committee will start work from month one after the end of the previous financial year. In delivering an annual report and accounts, the key consideration is planning the tasks with the end objective in mind. It is important therefore to ensure that tasks that are not time dependent, such as reviewing the code of conduct and the whistleblowing arrangements, are phased into the planned tasks for the committee in such a way that they do not interfere with tasks that are time dependent, such as reviewing the results of the external and internal audit.

All of this assumes that the financial control processes of the company are effective and efficient. This may not always be the case, and will depend on the quantity and quality of the meetings held, as well as on the availability of sufficient internal resources. It is likely to be particularly relevant regarding risk management, which is still only at the development stage in some companies.

The ability to achieve quality audited accounts on time depends both on the effectiveness of the audit committee and its agenda planning, the quality of the external auditors, and, more importantly, the quality of the internal audit function. The three elements are like the components of a jigsaw – if any are missing or inadequate, it will be difficult to establish a complete picture of the company's financial processes.

Producing other relevant board committee reports

Planning the process of the audit committee report should be carried out on a full-year basis, given that the committee will have at least three meetings throughout the year – although the Smith Guidance is that the committee should meet as often as is required.

The remuneration committee is likely to have a similar number of meetings. The tasks of the remuneration committee have been split into five categories: remuneration committee management, ongoing remuneration policy assessment, assessing external consultants, policy and control review, and producing the committee's documents for inclusion with the financial statements.

Tasks that should be phased as appropriate throughout the financial year away from key dates for production of the report for inclusion with the financial statements are as follows:

- **Remuneration committee management:**
  - reviewing the committee's terms of reference and code of conduct;
  - assessing the skills and experience of the committee members;
  - updating on key issues relating to remuneration matters;

- undertaking a self-assessment of the performance of the committee;
- reviewing the policy on chairman and chief executive expenses.

- **Ongoing remuneration policy assessment:**
    - undertaking a review of market practice for remuneration matters;
    - reviewing key shareholders' reactions to the previous remuneration report;
    - reviewing the appropriateness of the remuneration policy;
    - undertaking a bonus plan review;
    - undertaking a review of short- and long-term incentive plans.

- **Assessing external consultants in terms of their performance and appointment:**
    - reviewing the performance of external remuneration consultants;
    - approving their fees and terms of engagement;
    - considering their independence (including reviewing any other links with the company).

Tasks that should occur at the first meeting before the end of the financial year are as follows:

- **Policy and control review:**
    - reviewing the draft remuneration committee report;
    - developing and recommending to the board any resolutions relating to remuneration matters to be put before the shareholders;
    - reviewing the current status on bonus and incentive programmes;
    - conducting a pay review – based on a brief set and researched upon previously;
    - reviewing the relevance of the current total shareholder return reference points.

Tasks that should occur at the first meeting after the end of the relevant financial reporting period are as follows:

- **Producing the committee's documents for inclusion with the financial statements:**
    - reviewing and agreeing any payments due under short-term incentive plans;
    - finalising targets for the next round of annual bonus plans;
    - finalising any resolutions relating to remuneration matters for submission to shareholders;
    - reviewing and recommending to the board the committee's report to shareholders on its role, activities and responsibilities.

Clearly, to produce a meaningful remuneration committee report requires considerable planning of the activities involved on an ongoing basis. The report itself should report on the activities undertaken during the year, as well as providing the opinion of the committee on the effectiveness and appropriateness of the remuneration policy for executive directors and company senior management.

In contrast to the audit and remuneration committees, the nomination committee has a less tightly defined agenda. The Combined Code states that the nomination committee should adopt a strategic role in assisting in the determination of the board's progressive development – especially in terms of planning for succession and reviewing leadership requirements. The ICSA's guidance is that the committee should meet at least once a year, prior to the end of the financial year, in which it should review the positions of directors retiring by rotation or approaching a predetermined age. The result of this review should be put forward in the form of a recommendation for appointment as a resolution for voting upon at the next annual general meeting.

Whilst this represents the formally defined element of the role of the nomination committee, the more important role is gathering nominations at a time when a board vacancy occurs. Under these circumstances, it is important that the committee is able to move with some degree of speed, especially if the vacancy is unexpected because of illness.

It is important, therefore, that the nomination committee held meetings during the year when it planned for various board departures. These meetings should investigate the possible routes available to fill such vacancies, which may include considering individuals known to members of the committee. However, it is important that the committee also consider options such as the use of head-hunter consultancies. In this respect, it is advisable that the nomination committee should meet favoured consultancies regularly, on a more informal basis, with a view to employing them when the occasion requires. Such meetings should include advice on the state of the market for non-executive directors, and the availability of individuals of the required calibre.

Producing designs for annual reports, and delivering them on time

The design for the annual report is something that is taken very seriously within the corporate headquarters of a listed company. This is not surprising given the very significant amounts that may be spent on the design, production and distribution of the report, which will vary from around £100,000 to almost £1 million.

The design cost will depend on the numbers of shareholders on the register. Privatised industries have a very large number of retail investors, who still require a printed copy of either the full annual report or a summary report. The cost of producing and posting these reports is probably far in excess of the value gained from this communications exercise. In addition, the design cost will vary by the complexity of the company – the greater the numbers of divisions, the greater the length of the report, and hence both the cost of design and the cost of production.

The changes introduced by the Companies Act 2006 regarding electronic communications will change the spend on production and distribution, with the opportunity for a company to send shareholders a copy of the annual report (or a summary) if they have agreed – either generally or specifically.[2] In addition, quoted companies are expected to put their annual report on their website and to leave it in place until the following year when the subsequent annual report is loaded onto the website.[3] Shareholders who have agreed to receive electronic communication of the company's annual report will probably receive an email announcing the availability of the report, with a link to the company's website on which the report is available in either html or pdf versions.

In some of the interviews described in Chapter 13, views were expressed as to the likely effect of these changes. One company acting as share registrar had suggested that only 10–15% of shareholders would request a hard copy version of the annual report, whilst one company secretary suggested it could be as low as 5%. The actual amount will vary by company, depending on the numbers of shareholders, and the percentage of retail shareholders represented in the shareholder profile.

Shareholders may still request a hard copy version of the annual report, but its nature will change. If the percentage of shareholders requiring a hard-copy version is very low, the marginal cost of producing each copy for a small number of shareholders may be excessive. If so, one possibility is that the company will offer its annual report in a desk top publishing version rather than incurring the full cost of printing the report in the traditional fashion.

However, these changes will only affect the end part of the annual report design process – i.e. the production and distribution of the report. The design of the report is likely to remain the same. The process will be managed by either the head of investor relations or the corporate affairs director, and will cover the following steps:

- initial agreement on the tone of the report and its key message;
- agreement on requirements for photography, and undertaking the photography;
- layout of page iteration;
- production of draft concepts for page layouts;

- preparation of page layouts for insertion of copy from internal providers of the various sections;
- production of finished proofs for proofreading and checking by relevant company officers, together with review by auditors and legal advisors;
- production of the final version of report for loading onto the website and for printing as hard copy.

In addition to the above, the company may use a professional copy writer to take the internal versions of the various report sections and convert them into a more readable form. This is especially valuable if the content sections are technical. Typically, the sections involved would describe the company and its activities in the Business Review, but the use of a copy writer could extend beyond these sections, with the caveat that the individual should have knowledge of relevant legal and regulatory issues in areas such as the audit committee report or the notes to the accounts.

Whilst setting down the timetable in the manner described above is relatively simple, the reality is usually very different and can be complex.

The challenges and frustrations that will arise include the following:

- Gaining initial agreement on the tone and key message can be difficult as generally this will be required about three months before the end of the financial year, and the company may be experiencing changes.
- Photography will be of two types: photographs that represent images of the company at work, for example, in a store, factory, or with customers, and photographs of the company's senior executives. The latter are likely to prove the more challenging, both because of the difficulty of individuals finding the time, and because they may have particular preferences for how they are photographed, which may not fit in with the desired style of image established for the overall report format. It is suggested that photographic shoots of executive personnel should coincide with company events, such as a senior managers' conference or a board away day, where more time is available and executives are more relaxed.
- The page iteration and draft concepts and preparation of page layouts will be challenging from the point of view that they are discussed in advance of copy being written and whilst the outcome of the financial year may be still unclear. The writers of each section should work to a word length specified by the designers of the report. However, where internal writers do not have the full range of writing skills necessary, the services of a professional copy writer may be necessary.

- The annual report will be proofread by experts looking for words or punctuation that could leave the company open to criticism, or, even worse, legal liability. It is also the stage after the end of the financial year when the company's directors are thinking of how their strategy will be implemented over the coming year. They will not wish to be hoist by their own petard by including statements about actions they already know may be carried out differently over the following months. As a consequence, they should ensure that their comments on strategic developments reflect the very latest thinking. This is the stage when the midnight oil burns and often runs out!

Once all of these issues have been ironed out, the annual report can be put to press, and consideration then give to preparation of the interim statement and, provisionally, the following year's annual report. At this stage, it is good practice to review the response from shareholders and key investors to the annual report and decide how the following year's annual report could be improved.

However, the Business Review has now introduced a fundamental change to the development and production of the annual report, and this will be addressed in Chapter 8.

NOTES

1 Financial Reporting Council discussion paper, *Promoting Audit Quality* (November 2006).
2 Companies Act 2006, Sch. 5, Pt 3.
3 Ibid., Ch. 7, s. 430.

CHAPTER 8

Developing the annual report – Business Review

KEY ISSUES

- Producing the directors' report and incorporating the Business Review
- Required elements of Business Review – and what each means
- Additional requirements of Companies Act 2006 and Business Review
- A practical approach to develop Business Review
    - Strategic goals and objectives
    - Business impact areas
    - Risks and opportunities
    - Material and robust KPIs
    - Assessing strategic impacts
    - Internal establishment of risks and opportunities

- Developing the audit path
- Policies and effectiveness
- Alternative approaches to producing Business Review
    - Storyboard approach
    - Accountancy practices' approaches
    - Quoted Companies Alliance approach
    - IPA approach
- Producing statements from chairman and chief executive
    - Role of statements
    - Writing statements
    - Planning for statements
- Key steps to assess progress in planning

Producing the directors' report and incorporating the Business Review

The Business Review is a relatively innovative development in comparison with the reports traditionally produced by the three board committees, and is likely to be more challenging at the present time because its direction and focus is not one that has been associated with annual reports and accounts in the past.

The Business Review has been developed from two routes:

The 2005 Business Review was developed by the Government as a statutory instrument under the auspices of the Companies Act 1985[1] and implementing the European Accounts Modernisation Directive,[2] which required companies to produce an enhanced directors' report as part of the company's annual report.

The 2006 Business Review (developed as an additional set of requirements for quoted companies) draws its pedigree from the Operating and Financial Review (OFR). The OFR was introduced (albeit briefly) into the Companies Act 1985 to implement part of the company law reform consultation, and became a statutory requirement for quoted companies alongside the 2005 Business Review for financial years beginning on or after 1 April 2005. These provisions were repealed in January 2006[3] following the change announced by Gordon Brown in his role as Chancellor of the Exchequer, leaving the OFR as a voluntary reporting approach supported by the Accounting Standards Board's Reporting Statement. The Companies Act 2006 reintroduced some of the OFR's requirements as a statutory requirement.

Required elements of Business Review – and what each means

All UK companies,[4] except those meeting the statutory definition of a small company, must include a Business Review in their directors' report. A medium-sized company is required to produce a Business Review, but there is no requirement to provide information about key non-financial performance indicators, although this may be done on a voluntary basis. However, a small or medium company cannot take advantage of the exemption if it is a public company, it has permission under Pt 4 of the Financial Services and Markets Act 2000 to carry on one or more regulated activities, or if it carries on an insurance market activity (expanded under the Companies Act 2006).

The definition of 'UK companies' includes private and public companies, listed and unlisted quoted companies, and foreign-owned subsidiaries registered in the United Kingdom.

Within a group, all companies (except small companies) must also produce their own Business Review; there is no group exemption. A parent company must produce a group directors' report, covering the parent and any consolidated subsidiaries.

The provisions specifying the requirements for the Business Review[5] are not prescriptive as to its content. Instead, they lay out broad guidelines, with the content in each being left to the directors. As a consequence there are some vague areas that can be interpreted in several different ways.

The requirement is that the directors' report for a financial year must contain a fair review of the business of the company and a description of the principal risks and uncertainties facing the company. The following describes the underlying intention behind each of the requirements for the 2005 Business Review, with comments on differing interpretations:

- **Business Review identified as part of directors' report:** It is essential that the Business Review is contained within the directors' report. It must therefore have as a heading 'Business Review' (and may also refer to the relevant sections of the Companies Act). It must also identify the pages in the annual report the directors regard as being incorporated by cross-reference into the Business Review. In looking at previously published Business Reviews (see Chapter 9 for examples), significantly different approaches have been taken. Some have included the statements of the chairman and chief executive, together with the report on corporate social responsibility. Others have included a specific Business Review. Some larger companies have produced an OFR as part of the annual report. In each case, there must be a cross-reference paragraph within the directors' report indicating clearly which sections relate to the Business Review, with a statement such as the following: 'The information that fulfils the requirements of the Business Review can be found in the OFR on pages x to y, which are incorporated in this report by reference'. In most instances, the OFR is treated as fulfilling all the requirements of the Business Review and is included in its entirety, although this may change over time.

- **Fair review of the business of the company:** This may include what would have been produced in previous annual reports in the form of reports by the chief executive and the finance director, together with information on the performance of different business divisions. The ASB, in its recent report on narrative reporting,[6] indicated that it interpreted this requirement by reference to its Reporting Statement – namely that 'the directors should include a description of the business and the external environment in which it operates'. The ASB goes further to describe the nature of this description by referring to the Reporting Statement's recommendation that the directors should also discuss the objectives of the business and the strategies to achieve those objectives, on the basis that the Government has stated that the 'central requirements of the Business Review are largely identical to those of the statutory OFR'. In this respect, it would be reasonable to include information down to a geographic or product business unit level, which would include financial performance, its geographic/product split, and a description of the business environment.

- **The review should be a balanced and comprehensive analysis of the development and performance of the business of the company during the financial year and the position of the company's business at the end of that year, consistent with the size and complexity of the business:** This is vague – what does 'a balanced and comprehensive analysis' really mean? The ASB's report acknowledges that there is an overlap between 'fair review' and 'balanced and comprehensive analysis'. In its report, the ASB has interpreted this as 'being the requirements for the backward-looking part of the Business Review'. As a consequence, its assessment of compliance with this requirement is linked to the Reporting Statement's recommendations covering the current development and performance of the company and its financial position. However, this could be considered a limiting recommendation, given the requirement to describe the position of the company at the year end. It would be prudent to include a review of the strategies and the future outlook for each business area.

- **Description of the principal risks and uncertainties facing the company:** Again, this is a vague requirement – what amounts to 'a description'? There is no guidance, but a common sense approach is that the company identifies each area of risk, and establishes what may be the impact if the risk were to arise. The risk areas should relate to the company's strategy and demonstrate where it may or may not be affected. The list of risks should include both financial and non-financial risks, such as reputation, regulatory impacts, customer attitudes, etc. The key word is 'principal'. This requirement is not interpreted by the ASB as requiring the company to provide a long list of risks and opportunities – only those that may impact on the company's ability to perform against its strategic objectives. Again, a prudent board will ensure not only that the principal risks and uncertainties are described, but also that there is a statement of the extent to which the company has developed mitigation controls to ensure that in the instance of any risk being realised, its impact is managed in the most effective manner.

- **The review must, to the extent necessary for an understanding of the development, performance and position of the business, include analysis using financial key performance indicators (KPIs):** There has been uncertainty about what would be regarded as KPIs. For the purposes of assessing compliance against the Business Review requirements, the ASB referred to its Reporting Statement. In this context, the selection of financial KPIs is those used by the directors 'to assess progress against their stated objectives'. These should be KPIs 'that the directors judge are effective in measuring the delivery of their strategies and managing their business'. These words imply that the indicators should be those that measure progress – such as improvements in gross profit percentages, rather than outcomes – such as gross profit in value for the financial year. There is nothing wrong in producing extensive financial data, but it is important that the directors identify which elements of the data they regard as a **key** indicator. The ASB, in drawing up the original OFR approach, indicated that it expected quality rather than quantity in terms of the overall approach. This sentiment applies well to the selection of KPIs – too many and the shareholders will consider that their board will find it difficult to see the wood for the trees. It is important that the KPIs selected should demonstrate a close alignment with the strategy, be capable of demonstrating its success or otherwise, and be consistently comparable over time.

- **The review must, to the extent necessary for an understanding of the development, performance and position of the business, include, where appropriate, analysis using other KPIs, including information relating to environmental and employee matters:** This requirement has not been described in any detail. The ASB takes the view that the selection should be effective in measuring the delivery of the company's strategies and of managing its business. However, in this respect, even this is not sufficiently clear. The company must consider what its principal business drivers are, and how non-financial measures relate to them. Clearly, for a company in the support services sector, one of its principal business drivers will be the performance of its employees. As such, it would be reasonable to include indicators that relate to its employees' performance – such as data on health and safety, employee retention and employee satisfaction. For those companies in the retail sector, where regular visits by customers are a main revenue driver, indicators of customer attitudes would be appropriate – such as customer satisfaction or levels of customer complaints. In a business where innovation of new products is a critical determinant of future strategic success, indicators that demonstrate the quality of its new product pipeline would be relevant to communicate to the shareholders. Environment is included as one of the areas that directors may consider it appropriate to comment upon. In this case, one of the key questions is to understand the extent of the company's environmental impact, and how this affects the delivery of the company's strategy. With climate change having grown in recognition as an economic issue, it would be surprising if most companies did not at least consider how their business may be affected. As an example, telecommunications may not be a sector that immediately springs to mind when considering climate change, but maintaining its landline network for its customer base means that BT is one of the biggest users of electricity in the United Kingdom. If climate change were to dramatically change the energy price structure, this would impact to some extent on the cost of running the network. It is important at this point to reflect upon the wording 'to the extent necessary', which is included in the reference to both financial and non-financial KPIs. It is for the board to decide on which indicators they choose to report; their choice will be influenced by the relevance of the indicators to their strategy and not in response to demands from external stakeholders such as non-governmental organisations or lobby groups. If companies choose to comply with the ASB's Reporting Statement, they will be expected to link their reporting very closely to their strategy.

- **The review must, where appropriate, include references to, and additional explanations of, amounts included in the annual accounts of the company:** This is intended to allow the Business Review to become the means whereby areas of change in the financial statements can be expanded upon, and their relevance to the business's prospects made more relevant. Again, in terms of giving clear guidance to directors as to what should be considered, this requirement is vague. For listed companies, it is fair, but it may be too taxing for other companies. The ASB refers to its Reporting Statement for guidance, which suggests that companies include a financial analysis referring to events that have impacted on the company's financial position during the year and events that may have longer-term financial effects. In addition, the Reporting Statement suggests the inclusion of information about the company's capital structure, treasury policies and objectives and cash generation position (together with its current and prospective liquidity). It also suggests that the company should comment upon the accounting policies referred to in the notes to the accounts, and discuss those critical to enabling a shareholder to reach an understanding of the financial performance of the company.

- **As part of the duty to prepare such a report, the directors' report shall contain an indication of likely future developments in the business of the company:** This is an area that may have raised concerns amongst companies when providing forward-looking information because of fears of potential liability. However, all that is required under the 2005 Business Review Regulations is that companies provide 'an indication' of likely future developments. It is important that when forward-looking information is provided in the Business Review, the annual report also includes some caveats relating to this provision. Wording along the following lines could be considered:

> This Annual Report and Accounts contains certain forward-looking statements. These statements and forecasts involve risk and uncertainty because they relate to events and depend upon circumstances that are likely to occur in the future. But, there may be a number of factors that could cause actual results or developments to differ materially from those expressed or implied by these forward-looking statements and forecasts.

However, some companies have produced much more extensive cautionary statements, taking into account possible consequences from legislative and regulatory authorities in other countries in which they operate. Clearly, this is an area where potential liabilities may exist and a company would be particularly wise to take legal advice on its approach to this matter.

Additional requirements of Companies Act 2006 and Business Review

The Companies Act 2006 provided a statutory purpose for the Business Review, which is described below. It should be noted that this purpose applies to all companies, not just quoted companies.

The 2006 Act imposed additional requirements for Business Reviews of quoted companies. These include additional or extended information in the following areas (to the extent necessary for an understanding of the development, performance or position of the company's business):

- the main trends and factors likely to affect the future development, performance and position of the company's business;
- information about:
  - environmental matters (including the impact of the company's business on the environment);
  - company's employees;
  - social and community issues,

  and information about any policies of the company in relation to those matters and the effectiveness of those policies;
- information about persons with whom the company has contractual or other arrangements that are essential to the business of the company.

If the company's Business Review does not contain information relating to the last two bullets points, the Review must state the information that it does not contain.

The implications of these additional requirements are as follows:

- **Main trends and factors:** This is much stronger wording than the requirement to give 'an indication of likely future developments'. As such, a quoted company's Business Review will be required to include far more detailed explanation of current trends and future developments. Directors have been provided with a 'safe harbour' protection against liability in the event that there are statements or omissions in (amongst other things) the directors' report, unless these statements were knowingly or recklessly untrue or misleading, or the omission amounted to dishonest concealment of a material fact. Even then, the liability of the directors is to the company and not to other persons who rely on information in the directors' report.

- **Information about environmental maters, employees, and social and community issues:** The board is required to provide information that it considers should be included 'to the extent necessary'. However, given that it will be necessary to specify information not included it seems unlikely that any board will omit to include environmental matters, employees, and social and community issues on the basis that it considered them to be unnecessary from the perspective of understanding the development and performance of the company's business.

   The requirement for the provision of analysis using other KPIs, including information relating to environmental and employee matters, remains as a separate requirement. However, whilst it is left to the directors' judgment, again it would seem unwise for a quoted company to provide information on the broader set of non-financial areas, and not include some data of a performance indicator nature. A company may decide to include such indicators for the purpose of communicating with other stakeholders, but emphasise that they are not deemed to be key for the purpose of understanding the progress of the company's strategies. A more challenging requirement is likely to be the need to comment on the policies pertaining to these three areas, and to assess their effectiveness. Assessing effectiveness will be difficult, especially for larger companies operating internationally; and it will be for companies to devise the most appropriate approach to determining the levels of effectiveness.

- **Information about persons with contractual arrangements:** This requirement is in the exact manner of the former OFR requirement and, as such, the argument in Parliament over its inclusion in the Act was surprising. Its scope is very wide-ranging, although the board must determine that the relevant contract or arrangement is essential to the business of the company. The potential persons who could be reported on include major customers – for whom it will be necessary to identify the categories of customer, for example split between public and private sectors, or national or international customers with contractual arrangements. This will also include suppliers of key components or services, which would include, for example, suppliers of call centre services to banks or outsourced distribution and logistics suppliers to retailers. In addition, companies are required to report on contractual activities such as major joint ventures. There is no requirement to include KPIs for this area, although the board may decide to do so. The disclosure requirement regarding certain persons can be omitted if such disclosure would 'be seriously prejudicial to that person and contrary to the public interest'. This was included because of concern about animal rights activists targeting key suppliers to pharmaceutical laboratories. Some form of protection should be provided by not publicising details about persons who have a significant contractual arrangement with a company that is being targeted in this manner.

- **Statutory purpose of the Business Review:** For the first time, the statutory purpose of the Business Review is defined, and is linked back to the new definition of directors' duties. The purpose is stated to be to inform members of the company (i.e. shareholders) and to help them assess how the directors have performed their duty to promote the success of the company. This duty includes a non-exhaustive list of factors and the purpose gives effect to the 'enlightened shareholder value' concept. The purpose applies to all Business Reviews, not just those of quoted companies, for which there are additional reporting requirements.

A practical approach to develop Business Review

The key issue to be established in the development of the Business Review is 'who is responsible for its overall approach?'. The following graphic presentation[7] shows how the Business Review should be developed:

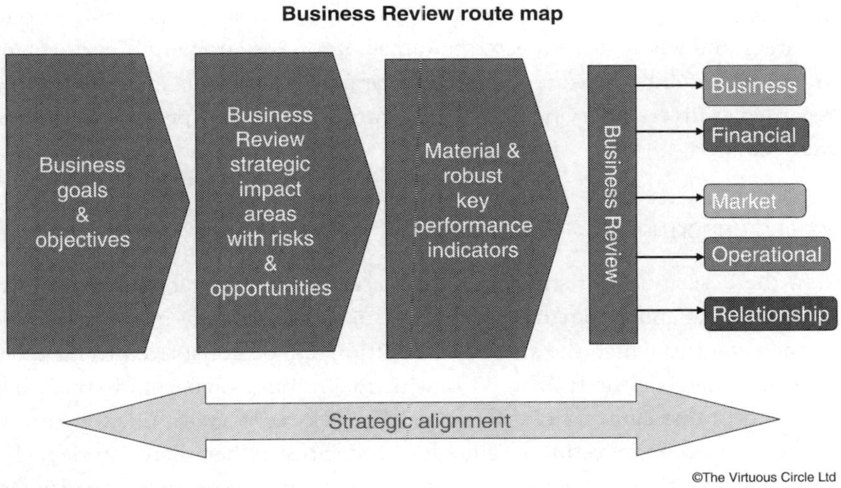

Business Review route map

[Diagram: Business goals & objectives → Business Review strategic impact areas with risks & opportunities → Material & robust key performance indicators → Business Review → Business, Financial, Market, Operational, Relationship. Strategic alignment spans across.]

©The Virtuous Circle Ltd

Figure 8.1

The Business Review offers the board an opportunity to present the company's strategic thinking in a coherent manner and to demonstrate the quality of implementation of this thinking. As such, it is important that those contributing towards the Business Review should appreciate that their input is a part of the whole, and not an individual item in its own right. The Business Review should demonstrate a flow of joined-up thinking, rather than a series of silo entities.

Strategic goals and objectives

The approach described in the graph above begins with the need to identify and define the strategic goals and objectives of the company. Ideally, these should be capable of being quantified, either directly, e.g. 'having the highest return on capital of any in our sector' (in which case the measure is easily determined by reference to the performance of others in the sector), or indirectly, e.g. 'being regarded as the leader of our sector' (in which case, some surrogate measures are required, such as the ROC determined previously, or market share percentages). These statements will communicate the nature and scope of the company's business strategy.

Business impact areas

Determining the objectives and underlying strategy should not be challenging (although there are examples where the strategy is more implicit than explicit and would require formalising for this purpose). Once this is done, the board must establish the key business impact areas and how they relate to the underlying strategy and its objectives. This requires a very precise description of the strategy and where it is expected to impact upon the company's performance. It will be important to ensure, therefore, that any superfluous material that may be regarded as diversionary from the main implementation aspects of the strategy is excluded.

Risks and opportunities

Within the description of strategic impact areas it is important to spell out the underlying risks and opportunities that relate to the strategy in order to determine the extent to which the strategy will ultimately be considered to have been a success. What is clear from talking with major fund managers is that shareholders accept that running a business can be a risky activity – if this were not the case, they would be investing in gilt-edged securities rather than equities. However, what shareholders do expect is that the company will be making endeavours to manage all the relevant risks on their behalf.

In many respects this aspect of the Business Review overlaps with what was regarded as part of the audit committee's report. However, whilst there remains a need for the audit committee to report on the process by which it governs the company's risk management process, there is also a need to put the identified risks in a strategic context within the Business Review.

There should be clear evidence that the company has identified the risks that may impact on the success of its strategy, should they arise. These risks can be described in the form of a list – which may be daunting to an investor. To overcome this, it is important that alongside each risk, the company describes the controls it has in place to mitigate their effects, should these risks arise. This is critical if the confidence of the shareholders in the company's ability to manage its risks is not to be destroyed. Too many risks and too few mitigation controls will lead shareholders to take a more risk-averse attitude towards retaining their shareholding (or investing in more shares). A list of risks with no mitigation controls will lead to a series of questions on the minds of the shareholders about the ability of their company's management to be able to manage the inherent risks in the company's strategy.

Material and robust KPIs

The selection of material and robust KPIs is critical as a means of building shareholder confidence in the quality of their company's management. The choice of indicators needs to reflect the means by which the company's management is assessing the performance of the company in achieving its strategic objectives.

A poor selection of indicators could be interpreted as meaning that management is not clear as to how it should be assessing the company's strategic performance, and lead to some doubts about how well the strategy is in fact being managed. In this respect there should be clear linkages between the risks that have been identified and the choice of performance indicators.

In the utilities sector, a common risk identified by management is the need to comply with the requirements of the regulators and to manage their expectations by performing well in the areas the regulators regard as being critical to fulfilling the responsibilities towards utilities' customers. As a consequence, performance indicators that relate to these responsibilities should be included within the selection of KPIs. One of the key areas of concern to utilities regulators is the amount of water leakage through the existing pipe network. Dealing with regulators about this problem is often quoted by water utility companies as one of their key risks. It is reasonable to expect that a KPI should measure leakage rate, since an adverse leakage rate may result in potential fines, as well as potential increases in maintenance costs to address current pipe failures and capital investment to correct more long-term issues – all factors that would affect the profit expectations of shareholders in a water utility.

In this respect, the board will need to review its selection of KPIs to ensure that they are both robust and material.

Establishing robust KPIs

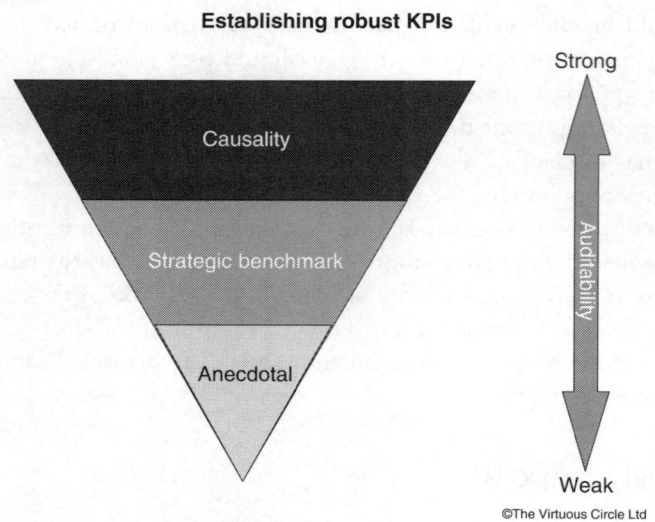

[Figure: Inverted triangle divided into three sections from top (widest) to bottom (narrowest): "Causality", "Strategic benchmark", "Anecdotal". Beside it, a vertical double-headed arrow labelled "Auditability" ranges from "Strong" (top) to "Weak" (bottom).]

©The Virtuous Circle Ltd

Figure 8.2

It is important that KPIs should be robust in so far as they can be regarded as being indicative of changes in the performance of a business area. Ideally, they should be seen as evidence of a high degree of causality – for example, 'numbers of customers', if increasing, are likely to be indicative of increased turnover over the medium and longer terms.

However, it is often difficult to demonstrate causality because there may be other factors that will impact upon a business area. The more likely form of robust indicator is a 'strategic benchmark' – one that relates to the strategic activities and demonstrates the achievement of milestones in the implementation of the strategy. For example, such a benchmark for a retail group would be 'the number of new store openings planned' and would be perceived as a better benchmark if supported by other indicators such as 'numbers achieved on time'.

An unacceptable indicator from the perspective of robustness would be one based on anecdotal or subjective data. For example, an unacceptable indicator for a company anticipating introducing a new product range would be the 'numbers of potential customers that expressed interest via a free phone number or in an opinion survey' since it is unlikely to be capable of being replicated, and it is also incapable of being audited.

The key criterion in selecting the range of key performance indicators is the materiality of the indicators. The graphic opposite shows how material indicators can be identified.

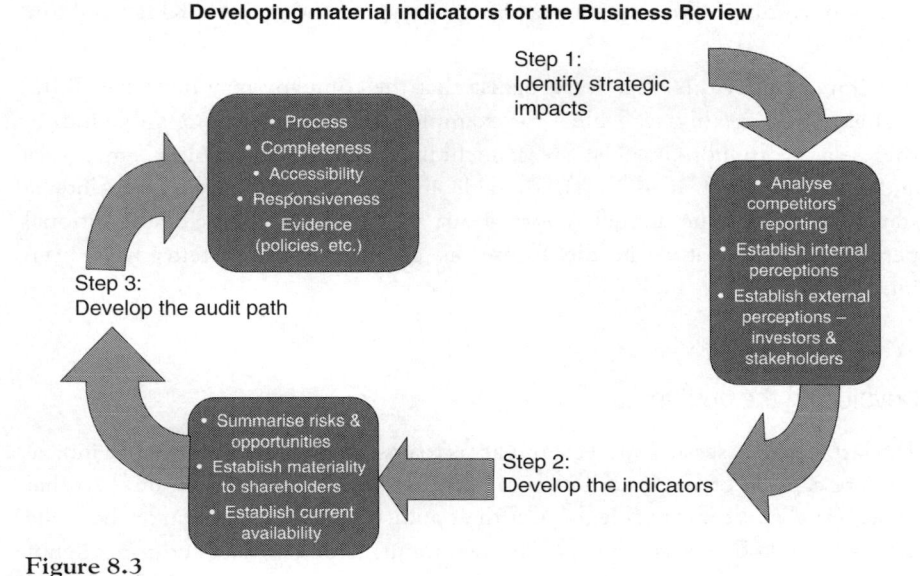

Developing material indicators for the Business Review

Step 1: Identify strategic impacts
- Process
- Completeness
- Accessibility
- Responsiveness
- Evidence (policies, etc.)

Step 3: Develop the audit path
- Analyse competitors' reporting
- Establish internal perceptions
- Establish external perceptions – investors & stakeholders

Step 2: Develop the indicators
- Summarise risks & opportunities
- Establish materiality to shareholders
- Establish current availability

Figure 8.3

Assessing strategic impacts

The first step in assessing strategic impacts includes the need to review and analyse competitors' reports. In our discussions with companies in the financial services sector about the development of the OFR, concerns were expressed about KPIs in two areas. First, companies identified the risk that shareholders would question their progress as identified by individual indicators. Secondly, they recognised that, over time, they anticipated investment analysts comparing the selection of indicators with companies in the same sector, and questioning companies about why they did not include indicators that were present in one or more of their competitors' Business Reviews. Further there is a need to assess the internal perceptions of the strategic impacts and the resulting range of possible performance indicators. Alongside this is the prudent move to enquire of investors and analysts what their perceptions are of the strategic impacts and their views of the relevant performance indicators.

Internal establishment of risks and opportunities

The second step in assessing strategic impacts is an internal establishment of the risks and opportunities relating to the strategy, and an assessment of what would be regarded as the views of shareholders towards the materiality of these risks and opportunities. From this assessment, a range of the possible KPIs would be developed.

It is important at this stage to recognise that the company may not have all the desirable KPIs readily available – for example when considering possible indicators relating to non-financial areas, including customers, supplies, employees and environmental areas. It is advisable in such circumstances to include a statement within the annual report about the intention to include additional performance indicators in the future, as data reporting systems have been introduced.

Developing the audit path

The last step in assessing strategic impact is to ensure that the performance indicators are capable of being audited – at least by the internal audit team – so that the external auditors are able to meet their auditing requirements under both the 2005 and 2006 Business Reviews. The requirements on external auditors are not as stringent as was envisaged under the original OFR regulations, which required auditors to review and comment upon any matters that came to their attention and that they regarded as being inconsistent with the information given in the OFR. Instead, the less arduous requirement is that auditors 'must state in their report whether in their opinion the information given in the directors' report for the financial year for which the annual accounts are prepared is consistent with those accounts'.

The audit needs to demonstrate the process by which the performance indicator data are gathered and calculated. It should also demonstrate that the performance indicators are complete in describing the performance relating to any strategic impact area.

A good illustration of the need for completeness is the question of how to demonstrate improving customer relationships. Many companies use 'the number of customer complaints' as a measure of the quality of customer relationships. However, experience shows that few customers are willing to complain, preferring instead to purchase elsewhere, or, in the case of subscription services, to cancel their subscriptions.

Performance indicators need to be easily accessible – to the extent that they can be produced for management review on a regular basis. Indicators presented only as part of the annual report cannot be regarded as 'key' from the perspective of the shareholders. In a similar manner, indicators selected to be 'key' should be seen to be responsive to changes in strategic direction or performance variability.

Policies and effectiveness

It is important that companies have in place policies that ensure the indicators are being managed, rather than just reported upon. Under the 2006 Business Review requirements this has a more significant impact on quoted companies. In relation to every aspect of environmental, employee or social or community issues commented upon in the Business Review the directors should discuss the related policies and comment on their effectiveness. In a large company, especially one that operates internationally, this is a major challenge. Too often, cultural differences can mean that the existence of **common** policies will be few and far between. International companies may develop umbrella statements under which their subsidiaries develop the policies that are appropriate for their own business environment and the relevant legislation of their own country of operation.

However, behind this challenge lies an even greater one – establishing the extent to which the policies are regarded as being effective. The Virtuous Circle established a five-point scale for one client to enable it to consider the extent to which it had indicators backed by effective policies:

1. No policy or evidence of best practice exists.
2. Evidence of best practice exists.
3. Policy exists.
4. Policy exists and all are aware.
5. Policy exists, all are aware and compliance is measured.

As can be seen, the existence of best practice is included. Best practice often depends on one or several individuals driving activity because of their own conviction in the correctness of the approach. Inevitably, this best practice can deteriorate if the individuals concerned leave the company for any reason. However, assuming best practice does exist, it is normally a very simple task to move from best practice to develop a policy that essentially regulates an existing method of operation. The real challenge in evaluating effectiveness of an individual policy is the extent to which managers and employees are aware of the policy, the extent to which they actively implement the policy, and that its compliance is being measured.

Alternative approaches to producing Business Review

Increasingly, many organisations are offering opinions as to how companies should produce Business Reviews. These range from a 'Storyboard' approach from Independent Audit Ltd, through templates by the major accountancy firms (particularly for non-listed companies, especially the subsidiaries of listed companies), to advice from the Quoted Company Alliance as to the format smaller quoted companies should consider. To ensure that this book covers a wide range of opinions, summaries and comments on these approaches are provided below.

Storyboard approach

Independent Audit Ltd is a consultancy set up with the aim to bring 'new thinking – and new solutions – into corporate performance, governance and narrative reporting'. Its Storyboard approach[8] was developed as a result of consultations with major companies, investment institutions and regulatory and other bodies. As such it represents views of individuals and organisations closely linked to major listed companies.

Its approach is for the Business Review to be a high-level document, setting out the strategic performance overview, describing the company's performance as seen through the eyes of the board and acting as a signpost for the rest of the report. An interesting perspective of this recommendation is that it is viewed as a very short document – the template example given on the Independent Audit's website[9] is only four pages long. This is because the intention is that the detail should be included within a voluntary OFR that is also incorporated within the annual report. As such, the overall length of the annual report is unlikely to be any shorter than if the Business Review were considered to be a more extensive version, without an OFR being included.

The recommended approach is more about how to get the message across to shareholders in a succinct manner, and it is worthy of consideration because of this intention. It is called a 'storyboard' because it is laid out in a sequential manner – similar to that of an advertising agency describing a television advert. Its contents are as follows:

- What are we aiming to achieve?
- What do we have to get right?
- How do we encourage strong performance?
- How do we know we are getting it right?
- How does this position us for the future?

The first section – what are we aiming to achieve? – aims to describe the board's objectives and priorities in the context of the market in which the company operates.

The second section – what do we have to get right? – addresses how the business is driven and managed, and how the value in the business is protected through its risk management process.

The third section – how do we encourage strong performance? – touches a vein that is not often considered within annual reports, namely how does the board motivate the company's managers to deliver the strategy, and hence the performance, they are following?

The fourth section – how do we know we are getting it right? – addresses the provision of KPIs. This section offers some additional insights, since it addresses both input and output indicators. Input indicators are described as those that help ensure that the company is being managed in a manner that enables the strategy to be implemented effectively. Examples include levels of employee satisfaction or turnover, and customer satisfaction or complaints. Output indicators are those that have implications for maintenance and improvement of shareholder value. Examples include financial indicators such as return in capital employed for each division, and free cash flow, as well as non-financial indicators like market share in relevant markets, and environmental impacts (which may damage the company's long-term sustainability).

The final section – how does this position us for the future? – provides the shareholders with a picture of progress so far against the strategic goals, and a view on how performance may develop in the future.

Whether or not this Storyboard approach will gain popular favour is yet to be seen (particularly as its recommendation is based on the inclusion of a voluntary OFR). But it deserves merit because it will encourage boards to think about the aspects of a company's business performance and management that its shareholders consider relevant. What is more important, it focuses the board's attention on the need to communicate these aspects to the shareholders in a readable and logical manner. At the very least, this stylised approach should be considered by companies, even if it provides them with only a summary for inclusion in their own broader and more comprehensive Business Review.

Accountancy practices' approaches

Most accountancy practices provide advice on how to prepare a Business Review since they are required to provide their opinion on its consistency with the information provided in the annual accounts. These recommendations will range from Deloitte's very helpful OFR Disclosure Checklist (for companies intending to produce OFRs in line with the ASB's Reporting Statement), to Pricewaterhouse-Cooper's (PwC) templates for Business Reviews depending on the nature of the company reporting. The latter is very useful because of its provision of guidance for non-listed companies, and this is considered below.

A major tenet of the company law reform was 'Think Small First'. Given the additional burden that smaller non-listed companies may consider is imposed by the need to produce a Business Review, it is worth considering first the views of the Government in its Regulatory Impact Assessment (RIA),[10] and to review some of the advice given by accountants on how to prepare Business Reviews.

The RIA shows that the Government expects that the changes to the narrative reporting provisions, resulting from the introduction of the 2006 Business Review, will add quality without imposing additional costs. However, it acknowledges that there are additional costs for companies in the original 2005 Business Review requirements. These were estimated at £107.9 million for implementing the Accounts Modernisation Directive and a non-assured statutory OFR for quoted companies (which is in effect the current position for the 2006 Business Review, particularly if the Reporting Statement is followed). The Government saw the benefits arising from improved corporate governance and the ability to provide a comprehensive analysis of 36,000 large and medium-sized UK registered companies, plus 1,290 UK registered quoted companies. For the latter, a significant benefit was perceived to be enhanced shareholder dialogue and engagement. If a straight average is taken, the costs to companies of implementing the Business Review into their corporate reporting amounts to approximately £3,000 per company, although clearly it will be greater the larger the company.

Given that there is some form of additional burden on companies, it is not surprising that some of the accountants have given guidance to companies that fall into the category of owner managed, or wholly owned subsidiaries, as well as AIM companies not required to complete their annual report to 2006 Business Review requirements.

PwC has published a range of illustrative examples[11] for such companies (for quoted companies, the advice is to complete a voluntary OFR complying with the Reporting Statement).

For this purpose, PwC offers two forms of Business Review. 'The standard Business Review' is for companies that have dispersed ownership – either privately owned or traded on exchanges such as the AIM – and covers the areas already discussed in this chapter. The second is 'the simple Business Review'. This is for companies that are owner managed, including wholly owned subsidiaries. PwC takes the view that members of these companies will already have a good understanding of the development, performance and position of the company. Its conclusion is that 'little information, simply the minimum required to comply with the legislation, is necessary to present a clear picture to members in the Business Review'. The 'simple Business Review' is intended to contain only high-level disclosures in the directors' report. The illustrative example given on the PwC website limits the descriptions to the bare minimum and uses the 'to the extent necessary' test to enable the directors to declare few, if any, KPIs.

The approach suggested by PwC is a realistic one, given the nature of the shareholders in such companies. However, care should be taken to avoid a minimalist approach, if the directors anticipate changing circumstances in the medium term. Such circumstances could include moving from privately owned to publicly quoted companies (most probably via the AIM), as well as seeking significant additional capital through debt finance. In such circumstances, it may be preferable to move to a more complete form of Business Review, so as to be able to answer the questions of potential investors or lenders with a track record of available information declared publicly via the annual report.

Quoted Companies Alliance approach

The Quoted Companies Alliance (QCA) produced a booklet[12] offering guidance for smaller quoted companies. It set out to reduce concern amongst these companies by emphasising that the Business Review differs little from what has been included traditionally in the chairman's statement and the reports of the CEO and finance director, although it does add that 'a little more is needed by way of concrete KPIs'.

The booklet emphasises that the Business Review should be written by board members or closely overseen by them. It suggests that the Business Reviews of companies that are members of QCA should not be extensive documents, recommending that 'five pages would be more than sufficient'. In terms of the content, the recommendation is that 'as the document should be a board level view of the company, it should encompass all issues which fall to be considered at board meetings and about which the board receives regular reports'. It also stresses the importance of discussing competitive advantage as a means of providing an overview understanding for shareholders to demonstrate how shareholder value will be maximised into the future.

The guidance recommends that 'the most useful [KPIs] will therefore be those which give a rounded view of the future of the company rather than reiterating the current future position'.

The booklet gives simple guidance, which is probably very valuable for smaller companies, and the way in which it presents its recommendations is reassuring rather than being scripture. It emphasises that its recommended approach should not result in additional cost burdens for reporting.

IPA approach

The Institute of Practitioners in Advertising (IPA), together with the Worshipful Company of Marketors, produced a checklist in September 2005 based on the OFR. This is being updated[13] in line with the Business Review requirements under the 2006 Act

The checklist addresses the reporting from a marketing perspective. The OFR checklist featured three sections – context, nature, objectives and strategy; drivers of development and performance; and financial position (analysis and explanations). The checklist offers a useful guide to the types of commercial content that should be considered for inclusion in a report, and takes as its standpoint 'How will the company generate, or at least preserve value over the longer term'? As a thought provoker, it is worth reviewing.

Producing statements from chairman and chief executive

Role of statements

One of the areas to be considered is the role of the chairman's letter in the light of the Business Review. Some companies are incorporating both the chairman's letter and the chief executive's report within their Business Review.

In its report (see above) Independent Audit Ltd suggests that the chairman's statement could be used as an introduction to the Business Review – and that the CEO's statement could become an introduction to the OFR. However, the underlying assumption behind these recommendations is that the Business Review is a short, succinct statement on the strategy and performance of the company, and is an overview – probably of four to 10 pages – whilst the OFR contains all of the detail. The problem therefore is how many companies will produce an OFR? – certainly it is likely that most smaller companies will not do so. In addition, based on the review of the first batch of Business Reviews (set out in Chapter 9), there is a tendency to make the Business Review a more detailed document than the short summary suggested. Indeed, one company tried to follow the approach of subsuming the chairman's letter within the Business Review, but initially, at least, found that this created practical difficulties.

Writing statements

Whichever route is taken it is necessary to add the personal note that is part and parcel of the chairman's letter. This will address some of the key issues facing the company but will also include comments on the value of employees, and offer a thank you to particular members of staff, as well as a statement of gratitude to directors retiring from the board.

These documents are typically written by one of the following three senior executives in the company – the head of investor relations, the corporate affairs or communications director, or the company secretary – for approval (and undoubtedly, modifying) by the chairman or the chief executive. A key requirement is that these personnel fully understand the thinking that has gone on within the board, and in particular to understand the views of the chairman and the chief executive on issues that have developed over the past year, and the strategy for the future.

Planning for statements

Planning for the statements should be part of an ongoing process. Reviewing the board minutes will not be sufficient, since these usually lack the rich texture of the direct discussions between chairman or chief executive and investors or analysts. This sense and depth of understanding is important to communicate to shareholders in the annual report.

Several alternatives can be considered in order to deliver this quality of communication.

The first is to meet with the chairman or chief executive and encourage them to speak freely about issues and future prospects. Where time constraints prevent this, an alternative is to sit in at several investor relations meetings and collate the formal responses given to investors or analysts, and establish how the informal responses to questions are handled. The latter is particularly important as a means for understanding the issues that investors may consider to be important, and to include these areas within the finished statement. The third alternative is to collect notes on the various occasions throughout the year when either the chairman or chief executive presents company progress in conferences and seminars to mangers and staff. Whilst this will not cover some of the issues that are particularly relevant to investors, it will provide a good basis. It can subsequently be bridged to the finished statement by reviewing the statements and articles that the chairman or chief executive make to journalists as part of the financial PR programme.

It should be clear that the planning of the delivery of these statements does not occur at the end of the financial year, but during the year as an ongoing data and comment collection exercise. Probably the most appropriate time to start doing this is at the end of the half year, when any changes in strategy will be communicated to investors and the media as part of the interim statement.

Key steps to assess progression in planning

Our experience with clients has identified some key steps to assess progression in planning for the current Business Review and the changes emanating from the Companies Act 2006. As a result we have identified 12 questions that help to establish progress – these are set out below for you to use with colleagues in your organisation. In the table below, Business Review has been abbreviated to BR.

Table 8.1

Activity	Already achieved	Underway	Not yet started
1. A multifunctional team has been established to consider the BR.			
2. The key issues facing the company as a result of the BR in its current form have been identified.			
3. The key issues facing the company as a result of the proposed BR under the CA 2006 have been identified.			
4. All qualifying subsidiaries have been notified of the need to produce a BR.			
5. For the financial areas of the BR, the following have been identified: –principal risks and uncertainties; –appropriate KPIs; –related policies.			
6. For the non-financial areas of the BR, the following have been identified: –principal risks and uncertainties; –appropriate KPIs; –related policies.			
7. A system to assess policy effectiveness has been established or already exists.			
8. Effectiveness of these policies has been assessed.			

9. A mock-up BR has been produced and reviewed with senior managers and directors.			
10. The board is aware of the statutory purpose of the BR and its link to the new codification of directors' duties and its implications.			
11. Plans have been established to explain the implications of the new role to group non-executive directors and directors of subsidiaries.			
12. The range of corporate reports has been reviewed, and plans are in place to consider how annual reports, CSR reporting and web-based reporting align.			

NOTES

1 SI 2005/1011.
2 Directive 2003/51/EC, amending Directives 78/660/EEC, 83/349/EEC, 86/635/EEC and 91/674/EEC.
3 SI 2005/3442.
4 Companies Act 2006 extended the provisions to Northern Ireland for the first time.
5 More detailed guidance on the 2005 Business Review can be found on the DTI website at www.dti.gov.uk/cld/docs/Businessreviewguidance.doc.
6 Accounting Standards Board, *A Review of Narrative Reporting by UK Listed Companies in 2006* (January 2007).
7 Reproduced with the agreement of The Virtuous Circle Limited.
8 Independent Audit Ltd, *Telling the story. . . through the eyes of the board – A framework for the Business Review* (October 2006).
9 'What a Business Review might look like'; available at www.independentaudit.com.
10 DTI, *Company Law Reform Bill – Regulatory Impact Assessment* (June 2006).
11 Available via PwC's 'OFR Now' website at www.ofr.pwc.com/uk/tls/ofr.

12 Copies of 'Guidance for Smaller Quoted Companies on preparing a Business Review' (August 2006) can be purchased via the QCA website at www.quotedcompaniesalliance.co.uk.

13 When available, this will be called 'A Framework for Reporting' and will be accessible via the IPA site at www.ipa.co.uk.

SECTION 3

BEST PRACTICE AND FUTURE DEVELOPMENTS

CHAPTER 9

The value of better quality reporting

KEY ISSUES

- Company law reform arguments
  - Enlightened shareholder value
  - OFR as part of corporate reporting
- Academic research
  - Greater transparency – lower cost of capital?
  - Greater institutional ownership – longer-term views?
- A practitioner's view – PricewaterhouseCoopers ValueReporting team
  - ValueReporting
  - Issue of intangibles
  - Does the quality of reporting affect investor valuation?
- Some conclusions on the value of better quality reporting

Introduction

This book began with a discussion about the regulatory requirements of corporate reporting. Underlying the increasing level of regulation is a presumption that the inclusion of narrative corporate reporting is of value, rather than being reporting for reporting's sake. In this section, we will review some of the thoughts behind better quality reporting – first with a discussion about the intent behind the corporate law reform process; secondly, with a view of some of the academic research underlying the move to more transparent reporting; and finally with the view of a practitioner – in this case, emanating from the PricewaterhouseCoopers ValueReporting team.

Company law reform arguments

The initial company law reform paper[1] made much play about the importance of company law providing the legal basis for all companies and being fundamental to 'our national competitiveness'. It focused on the sheer complexity of Britain's company law that was then in place.

It stated that the difficulties related to four key areas – over-formal language, excessive detail, over regulation and complex structure. Whilst it referred to the need to address the relationship between company law and corporate governance, it stressed the belief of the Government that the issues relating to codes of governance are best dealt with under codes of practice rather than legislation.

Enlightened shareholder value

When the brief for what was to become a prolonged company law reform process was initiated in March 1998 there was no explicit reference on the part of the Government to the need to improve the quality of corporate reporting. The first discussion on corporate reporting came with the reference to 'enlightened shareholder value' in the first consultation document[2] of the Company Law Reform Steering Group. As well as addressing the need to consider stakeholders as well as shareholders, it also discussed the issue of the directors' report. The document commented that the directors' report had proved to be a 'convenient peg on which to hang a range of statutory disclosure requirements'. As such, there had been criticism that such requirements did not 'seem to reflect any coherent philosophy and invite standard and meaningless statements', i.e. boiler plate statements.

Given the bland nature of some of the other comments on areas for change, this is fairly strong language. The consultation paper went further to comment on the growth of non-statutory reporting, including the early version of the Operating and Financial Review (OFR), which it described as being of real importance, but not recognised as such by law, with much of the information being non-financial and forward looking.

Particular mention was made of the growth of environmental and social reporting. It suggested that there was a market need for financial and non-financial reporting that the existing statutory requirements failed to reflect. It emphasised that this did not point to a need for increased statutory requirements, but it recognised that a fundamental consideration was to whom the directors should be accountable and in what respects. Importantly, it questioned whether accountability should extend beyond shareholders and creditors. It concluded by saying that voluntary reporting 'implies an inequality of information . . . and . . . the only disclosure of information which shows a company in a positive light . . . is it fair that companies that provide such information should be placed at a competitive advantage?'. Even at this early stage of the reform process it is clear that there were elements helping to shape the debate into one not solely about addressing the needs of one audience – namely the investors.

OFR as part of corporate reporting

In 2000 the Government published another consultation document[3] based on the responses received to the earlier consultations. This included specific reference to the OFR as a statutory part of corporate reporting within the United Kingdom.

Whilst this document acknowledged that some of the consultation responses suggested that the Government was not going far enough, it also highlighted that there were differences of opinion as to whether there should be a more flexible (or less mandatory) approach. Those in favour of mandating tended to represent the views typically of unions and NGOs and those in favour of non-mandating tended to represent the views of business and the professions.

The document stated that the OFR was regarded as a matter of fundamental importance, and that its production should be subject to standards to ensure that it was based on a materiality threshold. The conclusion was that the OFR was designed to address 'the need in a modern economy to account for and demonstrate stewardship of a wide range of relationships and resources, which are of vital significance to modern business but often do not register effectively or at all in traditional financial accounts'. The view of the Steering Group was that the OFR should be mandatory for private companies with more than £500 million turnover and for public companies with more than £5 million turnover – there was no differentiation (apart from size) for listed companies having a more rigorous reporting requirement.

With hindsight it seems clear in reviewing the archived documents that there was little consideration about the real benefits to shareholders of extended narrative reporting as part of the statutory requirements. In contrast, it appears that more consideration was given to meeting some of the pressures from third parties, such as the unions and NGOs, which were setting the agenda in terms of what information they expected companies to provide, in order to use it as part of their own dialogue with those companies. Whilst it may be understandable that these bodies were taking the opportunity of the consultation to position their arguments strongly, it is disappointing that more consideration was not given to how better quality reporting could give a better platform for investment decision-making. Fortunately, there are more research-based examples of how such reporting could improve the position of the investors.

Academic research

Greater transparency – lower cost of capital?

A recent paper[4] by Miles Glietzmann considered the trade-off between the benefit of greater transparency in lowering the cost of capital and the need to maintain commercial confidentiality, with the view that this could represent a virtuous circle with both investors and companies benefiting. This paper acknowledged that there is some concern that additional disclosures are associated with short-term increased share price volatility. However, its focus was to consider whether increased corporate disclosure correspondingly increased the stability of holdings by major institutional investors.

In this respect, the paper discusses the way in which investor relations managers identify and target institutional investors who will make efforts to relate to the company in a more positive manner and be supportive of it, in terms of both supporting resolutions at general meetings and acting as a friendly face at times of aggressive corporate actions.

Greater institutional ownership – longer-term views?

Other research[5] has already shown that greater institutional ownership (of the right type) can help corporate management take a medium- or long-term view of strategic objectives by allowing time for managers to achieve their strategic objectives. The key issue in this respect is to ensure that the company's senior management is more transparent in relation to areas of information on which their institutional investors focus. The view[6] is that companies that voluntarily disclose information are more likely to be considered to have a good reputation.

The conclusion of Glietzmann's paper (which was based on an econometric analysis) was described as initially positive – namely that major institutional investors maintain more stable patterns of ownership in companies that make timely and forward-looking discourse. In this respect, disclosures that are most likely to affect shares held by major institutional investors are those of a non-financial and non-routine nature.

This supports the view that narrative reporting is beneficial, but given the comment about the value of non-routine information, it does not as yet prove the value of better quality corporate reporting (as distinct from better quality regular communications). The question of course is how does more non-financial information affect the judgment of investors towards the company providing the information?

A practitioner's view – PricewaterhouseCoopers ValueReporting team

ValueReporting

PricewaterhouseCoopers set up its ValueReporting team approximately 10 years ago. One of its major outputs has been the development of its ValueReporting framework.[7] This is an approach to measuring and managing corporate performance, and links to the means by which communications about that performance are structured.

This work was based around the assumption that the traditional corporate reporting model was considered no longer effectively to meet the needs of companies in terms of reporting their performance to investors and other stakeholders. The view was that public trust in persons reporting corporate performance had been shaken, and that investors (and other stakeholders) were demanding greater transparency from corporations. It set as its goal the development of a framework that met investors' needs for more and better information.

Issue of intangibles

ValueReporting is intended to be a supplement to, rather than a substitute for, the traditional forms of financial reporting, with the benefit of having greater transparency of key non-financial elements, such as market opportunities, strategies, risks and intangible assets. It focuses on those elements that can be considered to be important non-financial drivers of shareholder value.

This is particular relevant given the increased importance of the intangible aspects of a company's business. The book value percentage of the market value of FTSE100 shares has fallen from 79% in 1975 to only 39% in 2003. Put another way, the value of a company's share that is based on intangible assets, and hence represented by its reputation (and its relative level of perceived risk), has risen threefold from 21% to 61% in that period. In this context, the value of non-financial information is considered to have become of much greater importance for an investor seeking to place a value on a company's shares.

The ValueReporting framework focuses on four areas – market overview, strategy, value-creating activities and financial performance. Each of these areas is then broken down into more detailed elements, as follows:

- **Market overview** – covering the company's competition and the industry dynamics, the regulatory environment in which it operates, and the macro economic nature of its markets.

- **Strategy** – detailing the company's goals and objectives, its organisational design to enable it to achieve those goals and objectives, and its methods of governance to ensure that the overall strategy is managed in line with the interests of the shareholders.
- **Value-creating activities** – covering the company's involvement with its customers, employees and financial performance, its approach to innovations and brand management, its relationship with supply chains and the extent of its impacts in the environmental, social and ethical areas.
- **Financial performance** – detailing its financial position, including its accounting policies and management of cash flow, its economic performance, including its segmental analysis, and its risk profile.

Given its commercial nature, it is remarkable how similar this framework is to that of the OFR. As part of its work for clients, the ValueReporting team publishes an annual review of corporate reporting against this framework, which is intended to offer practical guidance to companies, especially given the increasing burden of corporate reporting legalisation.

Does the quality of reporting affect investor valuation?

The 2005 review 'Trends 2005: Good Practices in Corporate Reporting'[8] commented on 42 examples of companies that it regarded as offering good practice in their communications of corporate performance. One company – Coloplast, a Danish company – is noted for its consistency in the quality of its corporate reporting, with a strong reputation for the levels of financial and non-financial information it provides. In the early 2000s Coloplast received an award from the Danish Association of State Authorised Public Accountants for the best intellectual capital reporting.

The PwC team decided to determine how the quality of a company's corporate information could affect investors' valuation of that company.[9] The question posed was to what extent corporate transparency in reporting made a difference to the information user.

For this purpose, the research took the 2001/2002 accounts of Coloplast. The PwC team dissected this set of accounts and produced two sets of accounts. One omitted the quantified non-financial data that Coloplast typically provides. The result was a report that was fully compliant with the relevant regulations, meeting the pure financial reporting requirements, together with the normal front-end narrative. The second report included all of this information, together with the extended range of non-financial data and narrative information that related Coloplast's operational performance to its strategic objectives and achieved outcomes.

THE VALUE OF BETTER QUALITY REPORTING 151

The PwC team took these two reports to the investment analyst team at Schroders. Each member of the analyst team was given one of the two versions of the report. They were asked to use the information provided to produce three outcomes: a forecast of revenue and earnings for the next two years, a recommendation for the stock (supported by their key reasons behind that recommendation) and an estimate of the beta value of the company relative to its peer group. The latter is an important aspect of investment decision-making since it is a measure of the risk related to the company's return compared with that of others in its sector.

The results showed that the average revenue and earnings forecast from those analysts with the complete set of financial and non-financial data was actually lower than those who made their forecast with just the financial data. This could be interpreted as unfavourable by advocates of greater transparency for shareholders and investors.

However, in sharp contrast, despite the lower forecast, those with the complete information set were overwhelmingly in favour of buying the stock. This was in contrast with those with only the financial data, for which their forecast of two-year revenue and earnings data was higher, and yet 80% of whom recommended selling the stock.

On investigating these findings, the research showed that those with the complete set of report information had produced financial estimates that represented a much tighter range than those with only the partial set of data. Similarly, those with the complete set of information took a more positive view of the company's risk, regarding it as being 'no more risky than its peers', whilst the view of those with the partial set of information was that the company represented an 'above average sector risk'.

The reasons for this variation showed that although the process underpinning decision-making in Schroders is built on projections of financial numbers, the confidence attached to the estimates developed is underpinned by any relevant non-financial data provided.

This level of confidence could be seen when the analysts provided reasons behind their buy/sell recommendations. Those with the more complete set of information based their recommendation on their confidence in the non-financial aspects of the company, such as market positioning, credible strategy and innovation cycle.

Without such incremental information, analysts were forced to gain confidence from the traditional front-end narrative of the report. In this area, there was much cynicism about the reporting of corporate performance. As will be seen later from the views of the users, those involved in investment and fund management are particularly critical of the quality of the chairman's letter and chief executive's statement, suggesting that these often add little additional value to the content of the financial reports.

The conclusion of the research was that those with the fuller set of corporate information, which put corporate performance into context, were able to be more confident of their forecasts. They were in a position to put a higher valuation on the shares and, as a result, were more confident to make a 'buy' recommendation. Those with only the financial information to hand felt more uncertainty about the future performance of the company and, as a result, were more questioning about the value of the company.

As the author of the report says: 'This case study reveals the magnitude of the economic benefits that can accrue to companies that offer a more comprehensive picture of corporate performance'.

Some conclusions on the value of better quality reporting

The initial approach of the company law reform process seemed to focus more on the benefit of greater transparency for other stakeholders than shareholders themselves. Yet the above discussion shows that there is very real benefit for a company to be more transparent in its reporting, in terms of both more positive analysts' recommendations and in maintaining longer-term fund management ownership.

The main message that comes out of these studies is the extent to which the reputation of a company (and, implicitly, shareholders' trust in it) is likely to be positively affected by the nature of its disclosures regarding its corporate performance and the extent to which these disclosures are transparent.

As the Coloplast study demonstrated, whilst the analysts may use valuation models that are financially driven, their confidence (or trust) in their valuation will be greatly determined by factors that are non-financial – and typically are communicated by the addition of contextual narrative. Inevitably, if such context is not provided to an investor or analyst, then, human nature being what it is, the likelihood is that even the most knowledgeable person will be inclined to assume the worst in terms of attempting to evaluate future performance. This will, as a consequence, place the valuation on the shares of the company in question.

However, as will be demonstrated in the two research studies in Chapter 10, it is the quality of information rather than the quantity of information that will persuade the observers of a company. This is particularly relevant when the information is portrayed in a coherent and consistent manner, rather than as a series of silo commentaries. The link between activity and strategy is an essential element that enhances the quality of narrative reporting and gives added relevance to financial reporting. In an era where the value of a company's intangible assets continues to rise as a percentage of its capitalisation, the value of combining effectively financial and non-financial reporting into a coherent and aligned communication will come through in terms of reduced share price volatility and increased shareholder value – there appears, indeed, to be a value to better quality reporting.

NOTES

1   DTI, *Modern Company Law for a Competitive Economy* (1998).
2   DTI, *Modern Company Law for a Competitive Economy – a strategic framework* (1999).
3   DTI, *Modern Company Law for a Competitive Economy – completing the structure* (2000).
4   Miles Glietzmann, 'Disclosure of timely and forward looking statements and strategic management of major institutional ownership' (2006) 39(4) *Long Range Planning* 409.
5   TB Bushee, 'The influence of institutional investors of myopic R & D investment behaviour' (1998) *Accounting Review* 73.
6   P Mazzola, D Ravasi and C Gabionetta, 'How to build reputation in financial markets' (2006) 39(4) *Long Range Planning* 385.
7   PwC has now renamed this approach as the Corporate Reporting framework
8   The online version of Trends 2006 can be found on the PwC website at www.pwc.com/extweb/pwcpublications.nsf/docid/4A1D17B722D5ACEB8025712A00567E49.
9   Alison Thomas, Director of Research of PwC's ValueReporting Team, 'A tale of two reports', published in European Business Forum online, Autumn 2003.

CHAPTER 10

Understanding how companies meet their Business Review corporate reporting requirements

KEY ISSUES

- Background
- Research findings
  - Research area
  - Background to research
  - How did these companies cope?
  - Results
  - Length
  - Explanation
  - Balanced and comprehensive analysis
  - Risks
  - KPIs
  - Overall
  - Report's concluding comment
- ASB's analysis
  - Business Review identified as part of directors' report
  - Fair review of business
  - Balanced and comprehensive analysis
  - Description of principal risks and uncertainties
  - Financial KPIs
  - Non-financial KPIs
  - Annual accounts: additional references and explanations
  - Forward-looking information
  - Description of business and external environment
  - Further development and performance
  - Resources
  - Principal risks and uncertainties
  - Capital structure and treasury; cash flows and liquidity
  - Environmental, employee and social issues and contractual arrangements/ relationships
  - KPI reporting – financial and non-financial
- Conclusions and ways forward from both reports

Background

Many company secretaries or finance directors producing Business Reviews will seek to gain guidance from other sources before putting their recommendations to the board. For these sources, they may consider their own advisors, or professional bodies.

Perhaps a more important resource is to understand how other companies have been reporting. It is likely that the development of the Business Review will take three to five years before it achieves a steady state. To an extent this is because of the impact of changes of the Companies Act that will take some time before coming fully into force. However, it is also a recognition that corporate reporting does not change overnight. Companies will move up a learning cycle, improving their own internal capabilities and listening and learning from others' experiences.

In this chapter, we will review the findings of the research undertaken by The Virtuous Circle (TVC) into the quality of narrative reporting in some of the first Business Reviews to be produced. In addition, we will consider the analysis undertaken by the Accounting Standards Board (ASB), and, in particular, review the thinking implicit in its findings. The latter included TVC's report as one of its five external sources, as well as its own internal research. The importance of the ASB's report is that it gives guidance as to what may be expected in terms of adjudication when the Financial Reporting Review Panel (FRRP) commences its assessment of company reporting – given the legal powers it has in this respect under the Companies Act 2006.

Research findings

TVC's study[1] was produced in late autumn 2006. Its purpose was to enable it to better advise corporate clients on best practice in narrative reporting, taking into account the European-wide reporting requirements (the new Business Review in the United Kingdom) and the new requirements to be introduced under the Companies Act 2006. TVC's interest started because of its professional work supporting clients with corporate social responsibility (CSR) reporting. In addition, it recognised that CSR and Business Review reporting is converging and utilises much of the same information.

Research area

TVC's research looked at the first batch of listed companies producing Business Reviews under the Business Review Regulations to understand how companies have coped with the Regulations and to assess the quality of their corporate reporting. In this respect it aimed to give an indication of the areas on which to focus to ensure that the requirements of the Companies Act are taken into account. The companies researched included the following:

- **FTSE30**
  BT
  National Grid
  SABMiller
  Vodafone
- **FTSE100**
  BA
  Boots
  British Land
  GUS
  ICAP
  Kelda
  Land Securities
  M&S
  Scottish & Southern
  Severn Trent
  Tate & Lyle
  Yell
- **FTSE200**
  Burberry
  Cable & Wireless
  Electro components
  EMAP
  EMI
  First Group
  Invensys
  Johnson Matthey
  Viridian

All the above companies had financial year endings of 31 March 2006 and, as such, were the first companies to present their Business Reviews. The FTSE categorisation of companies was based on the market capitalisation published in the *Sunday Times* of 13 August 2006. This does not necessarily indicate actual membership of the FTSE categories, but was considered to be a more realistic means of categorising the companies, given that the FTSE constituency can change over time.

A summary of this research was presented at the ICSA Conference on 5 October 2006.

Background to research

The research focused on the requirement for a statutory Business Review under the Business Review Regulations, which implemented the requirements of the European Accounts Modernisation Directive. It applies to all large and medium companies (quoted and unquoted), and includes all subsidiaries, as well as UK legal entity companies that are foreign-owned. The Business Review is part of the enhanced directors' report – intended to contain a fair review of the business of the company and a description of its principal risks and uncertainties.

In addition, in place is the voluntary OFR. The preparations for the OFR format of reporting of listed companies that had their financial years ending on 31 March had commenced before the Chancellor decided to rescind the statutory requirement for an OFR. This meant that these companies had to consider whether they would continue to prepare an OFR as their chosen route to meet the currently applicable Business Review requirements, or whether they would start again on a basis of the Business Review Regulations requirements. If they decided to continue to use the OFR, they would need to ensure that it complied with the ASB's Reporting Statement (RS) (which is the non-regulatory form of the previous Reporting Standard RS1). The RS was developed on the basis that it supported the OFR, whose objective was to assist members (or shareholders) to assess a company's strategies and the potential for these strategies to succeed.

Undoubtedly part of their thinking as to whether to follow the OFR format was what the latest iteration of (what was then) the Companies Bill meant for listed companies. At that time it was relatively clear that the future format of the Business Review would mirror, to all intents and purposes, the old OFR regulations. The latest requirements were expected to include information about environmental and employee matters, plus additional information (including KPIs) about social and community matters – with the requirement that if none were included in the Business Review, the company should explicitly state this and explain why they had been excluded. In addition, the Business Review should describe policies related to these matters and describe their effectiveness. At that time, the last-minute arrival of the requirement to report on 'persons with contractual arrangements' had not yet seen the light of day – although in introducing this clause, the Government almost completed the full circle back to the original OFR.

Added to these future Business Review Regulations was the fact that the new role for directors did much to provide the Business Review with a regulatory based purpose:

> to promote the success of the company for the benefit of its members as a whole. . . . In fulfilling the duty imposed . . . a director must (so far as reasonably practicable) have regard to the likely consequences of any decision in the long term:
> - the interests of the company's employees
> - the need to foster the company's business relationships with suppliers, customers and others
> - the impact of the company's operations on the community and the environment
> - the desirability of the company maintaining a reputation for high standards of business conduct
> - and the need to act fairly as between members of the company.

At the time of writing the report, TVC was aware that the International Accounting Standards Board (IASB) was still cogitating whether to lay down an international standard for the management commentary to be included in annual accounts – which to all intents and purposes would be the OFR.

How did these companies cope?

There is little or no guidance for Business Review reporting (except for companies producing an OFR), and TVC wanted to understand how companies had coped with developing their Business Review in the light of this lack of guidance. The 2006 annual reports of 25 listed companies reporting – 4 FTSE30, 12 FTSE100 and 9 FTSE200 – represented about 65% of FTSE200 companies with the 31 March year end date.

The study was based on these companies' compliance with the current statutory Business Review requirements, but it also assessed the extent to which they built an informed picture of the company for the shareholders and investors, as a means of developing a view of best practice narrative reporting.

Forty-eight per cent of the companies studied had produced an OFR. This figure rose to over 50% of companies that were part of the FTSE30 or FTSE100, and fell to around 40% for those in the FTSE200, suggesting that, ultimately, the numbers of OFRs amongst FTSE500 companies would be significantly lower. Furthermore, some companies had both a Business Review and an OFR, which showed some confusion.

As regards the quality of reporting, it was clear that the devil lay in the detail! In evaluating companies' reporting in terms of compliance against statutory Business Review requirements, the research focused on the main principles laid down in the Business Review Regulations:

- **Directors' report:** Business Review identified as part of the directors' report (CA 1985, s. 234(1)).
- **Relating to the annual accounts:** cross-references to other documents and additional explanations of amounts in the annual accounts.
- **Fair review:** a fair review of the business of the company (CA 1985, s. 234ZZB(1)(a)).
- **Balanced/comprehensive:** a balanced and comprehensive analysis of the development and performance of the business of the company during the financial year and the position of the company at the end of that year, consistent with the size and complexity of the business (CA 1985, s. 234ZZB(2)(a) and (b)).
- **Risks:** a description of the principal risks and uncertainties facing the company (CA 1985, s. 234ZZB(1)(b)).
- **Financial KPIs:** analysis using financial KPIs to the extent necessary for an understanding of the development, performance and position of the business (CA 1985, s. 234ZZB(3)(a)).
- **Other KPIs:** analysis using other KPIs, including information relating to environmental matters and employee matters, to the extent necessary for an understanding of the development, performance and position of the business, and where appropriate (CA 1985, s. 234ZZB(3)(b)).

In order to evaluate compliance with these requirements, TVC constructed an analysis framework that included a 10-point scoring system.

Results

As well as providing overall results for all the companies, TVC looked at the differences between the different categories of FTSE companies, i.e. FTSE30, FTSE100 and FTSE200. In addition, given the relatively small sample, it decided not to report on individual industrial sectors, but rather to group companies by their nature of operation. In this case, TVC grouped companies according to whether they were asset rich or people rich, as follows:

Table 10.1

Category	Industrial sectors
Asset rich	Utilities, electricity, food and drink, manufacturing, real estate, chemical manufacturing
People rich	Retail, telecom, media, travel, support services, electronic equipment distribution, financial

The findings that follow are sequential in terms of the compliance requirements outlined previously.

Length

The average length of the Business Review/OFR was 27 pages – but varied from 11 to 64 pages.

Within the FTSE sector there was a distinct difference in length of Reviews, with larger companies having longer reports, as can be seen in the following chart:

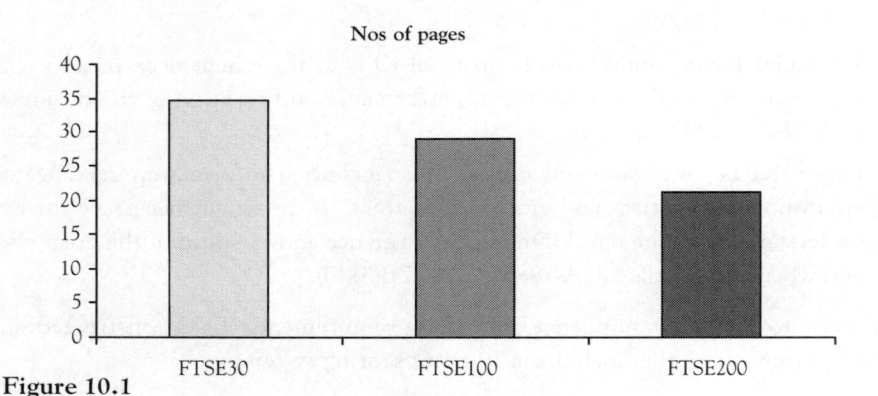

Figure 10.1

There was very little difference in the average length of Business Review between people-rich and asset-rich categories – both being around an average of 26.9 pages.

Explanations

Only about one-third of companies provided further explanation to the accounts.

However, there were some distinct differences of approach between the various FTSE sectors, as can be seen below:

References to, and additional explanations of, amounts in the annual accounts

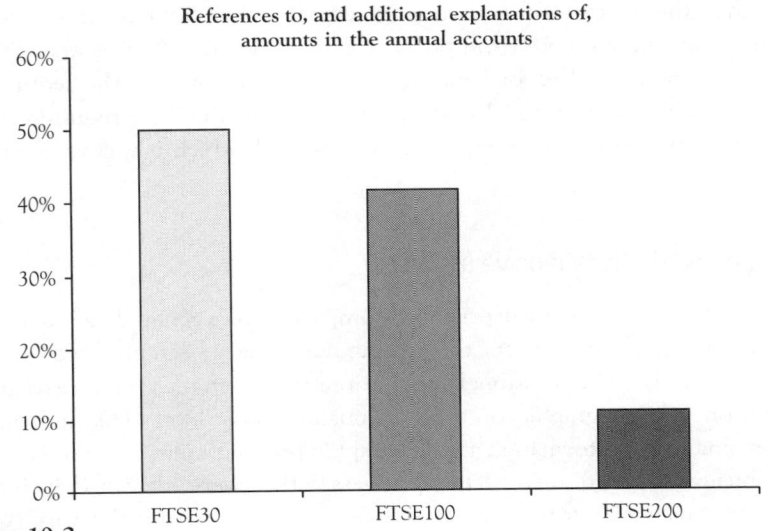

[Bar chart: FTSE30 ≈ 50%, FTSE100 ≈ 42%, FTSE200 ≈ 12%]

Figure 10.2

Whilst there was relatively extensive use of this facility by FTSE30 companies, there seems to be almost a reluctance to make further references in the reports produced by FTSE200 companies.

This variation was also seen between people-rich and asset-rich companies, with the latter providing more explanation, possibly because they are more familiar with the need to explain changes in their asset base:

References to, and additional explanations of, amounts in the annual accounts

[Bar chart: People rich ≈ 22%, Asset rich ≈ 46%]

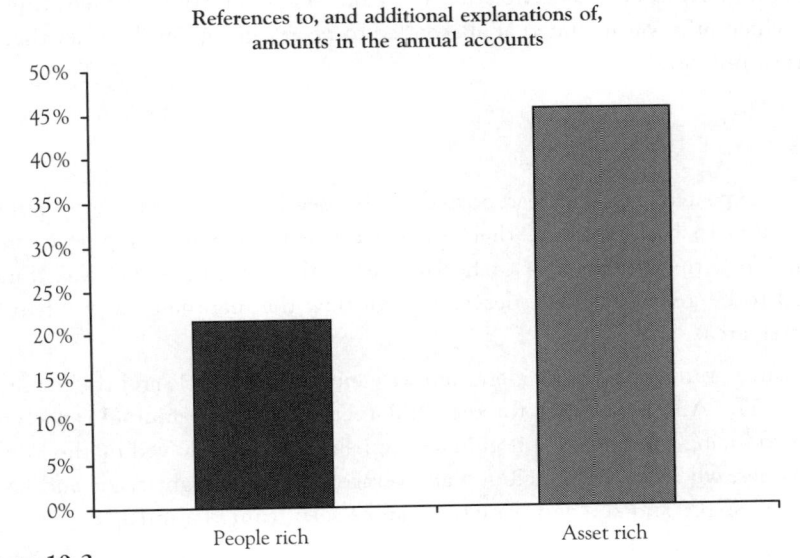

Figure 10.3

Given that the format of reporting is new to shareholders and investors, very little explanation about the purpose of the Business Review was given to investors in the annual report – although one company used the requirement to its competitive advantage by stating that it saw the new requirements as representing greater transparency for investors, with which it was very much in favour.

Balanced and comprehensive analysis

In general, and probably unsurprisingly, companies were generally good at giving 'a fair review'. In many respects, this is what would have been produced in previous annual reports. The additional expectations (based on the OFR) are to include information at a geographic or product business unit level. This information includes financial performance, the geographic/product split, and a description of the business environment. The weaknesses that were identified included a paucity of financial information at business unit or divisional levels. Where this was available, the information provided tended to be revenue and profit, but excluded capital employed or capital investment. In addition, there tended to be poor quality descriptions of the business environment faced at a business unit level.

For many companies, the more significant weaknesses lay in the 'balanced and comprehensive' analysis – with significantly much less attention being paid to the strategies and outlook for each business area. Where strategy was discussed, it tended to be at a group level rather than segmented into the relevant business units. Similarly, there was little attention paid to a description of the future outlook which, if it was included at all, tended to be at a group level, rather than at a business unit level.

Risks

As was expected, risks were reported on by nearly all the companies studied, but tended to be little more than a list. Very few companies reported on the mitigation actions related to each risk area, although where this was done, it tended to be a very effective description of how the management was handling each risk area.

The average number of risks identified was approximately 11, and the maximum was 33. The ASB's guidance for the OFR focuses on the **principal** risks, rather than producing a long list. This guidance appeared to be followed by the FTSE30 companies, whose reports included an average of around eight risks, and less so by the FTSE100 and 200 companies, as can be seen from Figure 10.4:

Average nos of risks

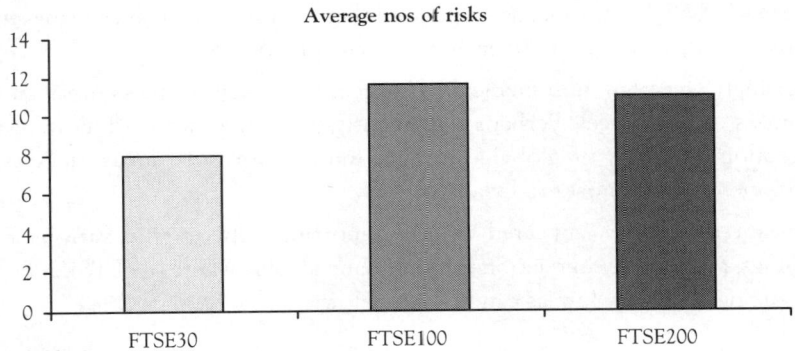

Figure 10.4

More surprising was that people-rich businesses identified more key risks and uncertainties than asset-rich businesses (which are likely to have more regulatory and environmental risks), as can be seen in Figure 10.5:

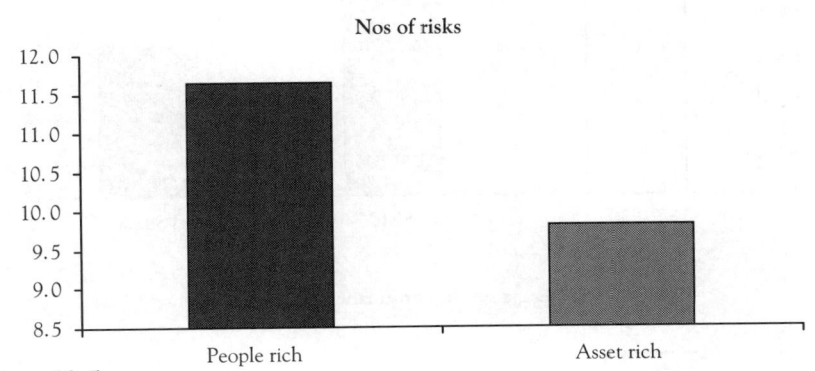

Nos of risks

Figure 10.5

KPIs

KPIs clearly caused companies problems. Too few companies appeared to be able to identify key measures that demonstrated how the board was managing performance. Indeed, some companies failed to identify either financial or non-financial KPIs. Even though there was often a surfeit of data, nothing could be described as an indicator of performance, with many of the indicators being an output figure, such as total sales revenue. Companies failed to identify which data represented the KPIs used to manage their business.

On average, two financial KPIs and nearly five non-financial KPIs were identified. Some companies specified no KPIs at all, whilst the maximum figure for non-financial KPIs was 33 – it could be questioned whether all 33 were key, and, more importantly, whether the management used them all for performance management purposes. The maximum number of financial KPIs was 14.

Surprisingly, very few non-financial KPIs related to key business areas such as customers or employees. Perhaps significantly, given the increased awareness of the economic effects of global warming, indirect (or soft) areas such as the environment were almost totally absent.

Significant differences appeared in KPI reporting between the various FTSE groupings, particularly in relation to non-financial KPIs where the FTSE200 levels of reporting were very low, as can be seen below:

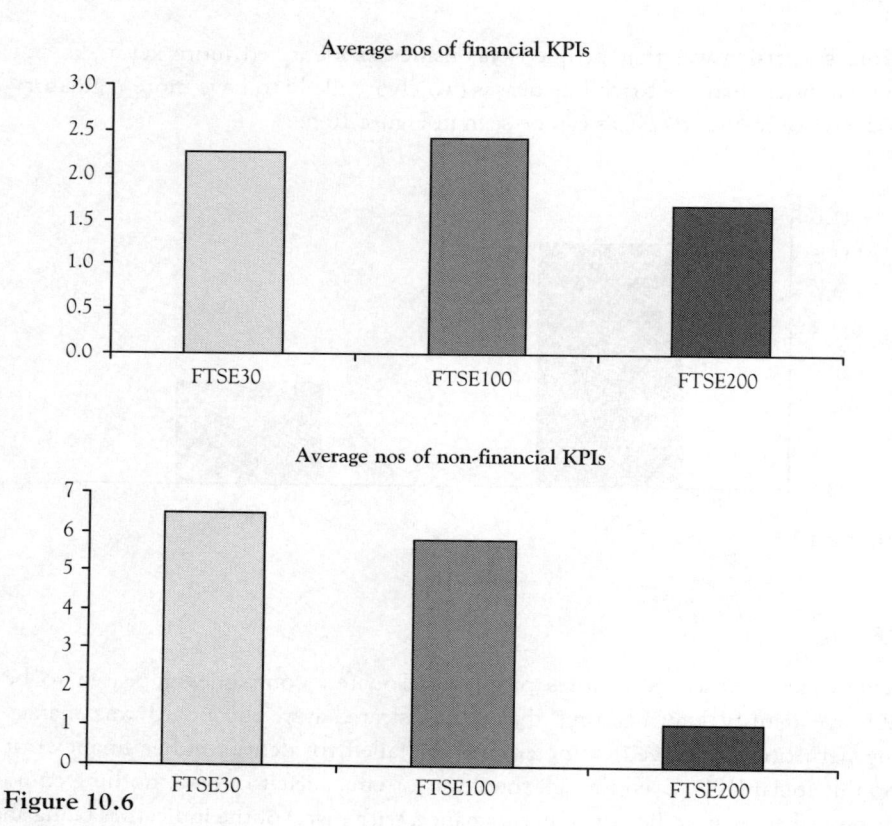

Average nos of financial KPIs

Average nos of non-financial KPIs

Figure 10.6

The differences were even more apparent when comparing people-rich businesses with asset-rich businesses. The latter are clearly more familiar with KPI reporting, particularly in relation to non-financial reporting, as can be seen in Figure 10.7:

Nos of financial KPIs

[Bar chart: People rich ≈ 1.0; Asset rich ≈ 3.5]

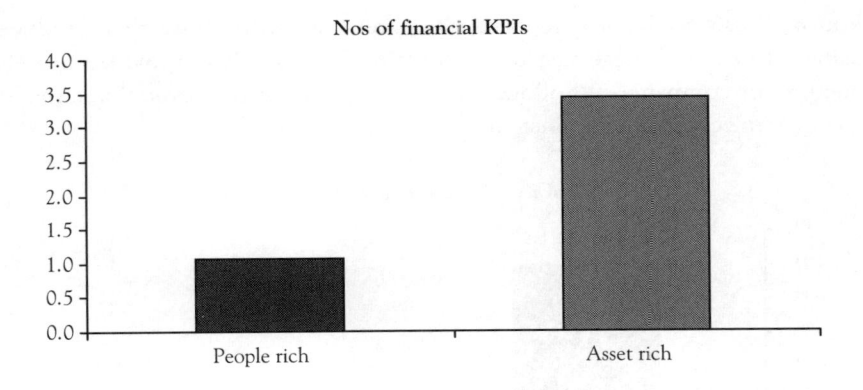

Nos of non-financial KPIs

[Bar chart: People rich ≈ 2.5; Asset rich ≈ 6.7]

Figure 10.7

Levels of non-financial reporting in the people-rich sectors are surprising, especially since it would be expected that there would be some employee-related KPIs for this category of business.

In terms of the quality of KPIs reported, very few companies reported more than two years' data, leading to the question of whether this is sufficient to help investors judge the quality of a company's performance.

Overall

The impression is that the Business Review was drawn together from a series of silo functions – there was inadequate alignment between description of the business segments, the strategy and outlook, the risks and the KPIs used to manage the business.

In terms of how well companies produced compliant reports, companies that produced OFRs were more likely to have better complied with the underlying statutory Business Review reporting requirements than those that produced Business Reviews – suggesting that Reporting Standard RS1 provided a useful structure for companies to follow. This is shown best by the overall compliance scoring of the companies against current BR requirements:

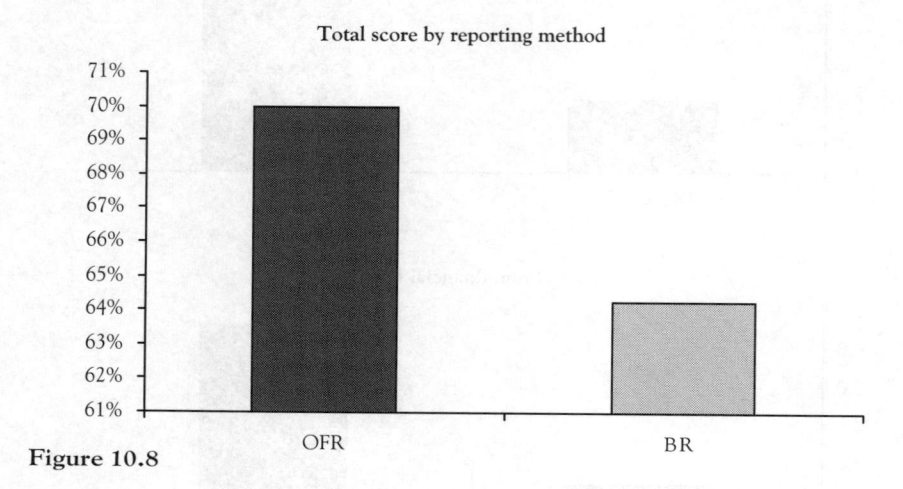

Total score by reporting method

Figure 10.8

In terms of how well companies demonstrated best practice reporting, FTSE30 companies were more complete in their reporting against Business Review requirements than their FTSE100 counterparts, and similarly against their FTSE200 counterparts in the sample, as can be seen from the following chart:

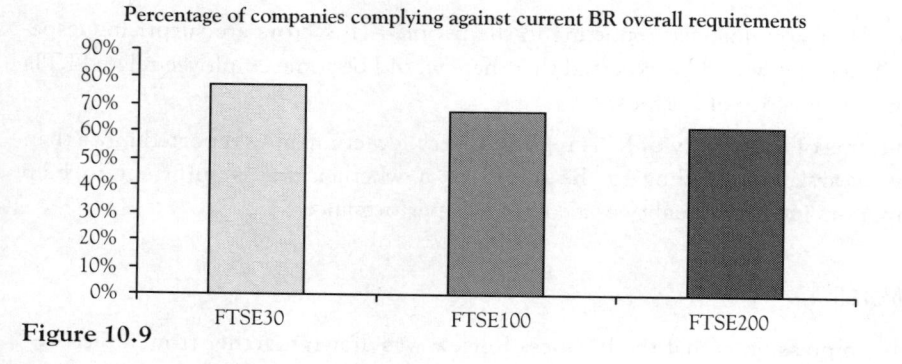

Percentage of companies complying against current BR overall requirements

Figure 10.9

Report's concluding comment

There is no doubt that the obligation to produce a comprehensive Business Review as part of the annual report will place a new responsibility and workload on those directly and indirectly involved in its production and preparation. However, it is equally true that analysts and investors will rely increasingly on Business Reviews to supplement the mainly financial information that has been provided in the past.

The questions a company should consider when preparing its Business Review are whether the Review helps investors and shareholders gain a more informed view of the company and, consequently, whether it helps improve the reputation of the business and the board's strategic thinking and implementation.

The Business Review offers the opportunity for company executives to give a full and fair portrayal of the company's strategy and performance. It is likely, in time, to become a very significant tool in investor relations, to ensure that a true appreciation of shareholder value is achieved.

In addition, its emphasis on KPIs will focus the minds of management on key business drivers and their success in utilising these drivers to achieve company performance improvements. Perhaps, as a result, the Business Review will help ensure a far more holistic approach to corporate management that should be more than worth the effort involved in its compilation.

ASB's analysis

The ASB's purpose in producing a survey of narrative financial reporting was 'to highlight strengths and weaknesses of current reporting in the interests of the widespread adoption of best practice ... provide some useful guidance to companies ... encourage them to move their reporting beyond compliance and towards best practice'. It indicated that it would continue to review narrative reporting as practice develops.

Its report[2] had two objectives: assessing compliance with the Business Review 2005 requirements and assessing best practice by reference to the ASB's Reporting Statement on the OFR. The first objective is relevant because the role of the ASB is to give guidance to the FRRP when it assumes its legal powers in relationship to reviewing the compliance of the directors' report for all financial years starting on or after 1 April 2006. The second objective is interesting because it suggests that the Financial Reporting Council expects listed companies to change over time to reporting using the OFR as a basis.

The ASB's survey covered 23 companies (one having a financial year end of 30 June 2006, the remainder having 31 March 2006 year ends). In addition, it drew on five other independent research surveys – those of Black Sun, Radley Yeldar, Deloitte, PricewaterhouseCoopers and TVC.

The ASB's evaluation of compliance was particularly helpful in terms of providing explanations of some of the terms of the Business Review Regulations that are especially vague and open to various levels of interpretation.

Business Review identified as part of directors' report

The Business Review must be identified as part of the directors' report, but it is acceptable to cross-refer in the Business Review section of the directors' report to information contained elsewhere in the annual report. The ASB found that nearly all companies were complying with this requirement, but that one company had not complied because of a failure to cross-reference or inaccuracy in drafting cross-references – for example a description of the principal risks and uncertainties were included in the annual report but not defined as within the Business Review.

Equally, the ASB found that companies were not including statements in the Business Review that could have been useful in satisfying the Business Review requirements – for example, 12 companies excluded the chairman's report, three excluded the chief executive's report, four excluded information on strategy and one excluded a section entitled 'Business Review'.

Fair review of the business

The ASB acknowledged that neither the Regulations nor the guidance from the DTI elaborates on the meaning of the term 'a fair review', and that there is an overlap between this and the 'balanced and comprehensive analysis'.

The ASB assessed the 'fair review' legal requirement against the Reporting Statement recommendation that directors should include a description of the business and the external environment in which it operates. Implicitly it suggested that directors should also discuss the objectives of the business and the strategies to achieve those objectives. These are not explicit legal requirements for the Business Review, but are included within the OFR. On this basis, the ASB found that all the companies included within its sample complied with this requirement.

Balanced and comprehensive analysis

The requirement for 'a balanced and comprehensive analysis of the development and performance of the business of the company during the financial year and the position of the company at the end of that year, consistent with the size and complexity of the business' was interpreted by the ASB as the requirements for the backward-looking part of the Business Review. It used the recommendations in the Reporting Statement on the current development and performance of the company and the financial position as the basis for assessing compliance.

This backward-looking interpretation is interesting, given the words at the end of the requirement to discuss 'the position of the company at the end of that year'. Nevertheless, given the regulatory position of the ASB's parent, it is helpful to have clarification of what these two important terms mean in the Business Review. However, even with this clarification, the ASB admitted that the term still posed some difficulties when interpreting the requirement from a regulatory position. In particular, it described the term 'balance' to be a difficult area to assess from an external perspective, since it would require 'a very good knowledge of the development and performance of the company during the period covered by the Business Review' to deliver an effective assessment. In this context, the ASB commented on some instances where companies in its sample had faced some high-profile and well-publicised challenges, which, although occurring during their financial year, could have had greater prominence within their reporting. Clearly, whilst this demonstrated strict compliance with the requirements of the Business Review, the ASB questioned whether the level of balance had been adequate with regard to these challenges.

Description of principal risks and uncertainties

The description of principal risks and uncertainties is noted by the ASB as less than that required under the OFR. Whilst the ASB found that one company had not discussed risks and uncertainties as part of its directors' report, the ASB was content with the improvement of reporting in this area. However, it was critical over the numbers of risks that were reported, and emphasised that the statement calls for a description of the **principal** risks and uncertainties.

Financial KPIs

Whilst recognising the qualification 'to the extent necessary' in the Regulations, the ASB found that only 52% of the companies disclosed what they termed financial KPIs. It went on to note that this was purely on the basis of compliance, and not on quality of information. The ASB went further to suggest that 'the lack of inclusion of financial KPIs in a Business Review in the future will provide the FRRP with a possible indicator that the Review may not be compliant with the law'.

Non-financial KPIs

Like TVC, the ASB found that companies had difficulty complying with the requirement to include non-financial KPIs. The FRC found that only 39% of the companies surveyed disclosed what they termed non-financial KPIs. As with financial KPIs, the ASB suggested that because of this 'lack of inclusion of non financial KPIs . . . the Review may not be compliant with the law'.

Annual accounts: additional references and explanations

The ASB found that the requirement to include additional references and explanations was not well covered – with only 30% of companies achieving a good or best practice score.

Forward-looking information

The ASB stated that the requirement that the directors' report should contain an 'indication' of likely future developments actually stemmed from requirements found much earlier in Sch. 7 to the Companies Act 1985. The ASB evaluated companies' ability to conform to the (then) forthcoming requirements under the 2006 Business Review. It found that there was 'better disclosure relating to companies' strategies and developments than specifying future developments', but noted that the 1985 Act required only an 'indication'.

However, the ASB report flagged a warning to companies with its final comment that 'for quoted companies, the legal hurdle will increase when the Companies Act 2006 comes into force'.

The ABS made an explicit comparison between companies' reporting against best practice and its Reporting Statement. Its comments in this respect are useful in guiding companies to areas where they should consider improving their reporting.

Description of business and external environment

In general, the ASB found that companies were performing effectively in this area, but that information provided on companies' external environment was less prevalent – and more exaggerated the smaller the company's market capitalisation.

Further development and performance

The requirement to report details of further development and performance requires a forward-looking orientation, and the ASB commented that this had the lowest average score for all areas investigated.

Resources

The Reporting Statement expects a description of resources available to the company and a description of how they are managed – identifying the key strengths and weaknesses – including intangible resources that are not reflected on the balance sheet. Again, details provided were poor, and the ASB's report quoted that of Deloitte's:[3] 'There were few examples of a cohesive approach to this area'.

Principal risks and uncertainties

The reporting of details of principal risks and uncertainties was seen as less than satisfactory, but the ASB commented further, noting (as did TVC) that there was little explanation of potential mitigation or how the risks could affect the company's strategy.

Capital structure and treasury; cash flows and liquidity

The reporting of capital structure and treasury is not specifically required under the Business Review, although it is a requirement of the Reporting Statement. However, overall both were assessed as being one of the best performing areas. This may be because both are areas with which companies are familiar.

Environmental, employee, social issues and contractual arrangements/relationships

The reporting of environmental, employee, social issues and contractual arrangements/relationships is a specific requirement of the 2006 Business Review. The ASB noted that most companies were able to satisfy the best practice requirements with the inclusion of their CSR reports as part of the annual report. However, it also noted that 'very few companies discussed information concerning persons who the company has contractual arrangements with, such as significant customers or suppliers'.

KPI reporting – financial and non-financial

The Reporting Statement requires the provision of KPIs and an explanation of their calculation, future targets and purpose. For both financial and non-financial KPIs the ASB found very little explanation as to why companies considered the KPIs they had included were 'key'. In addition, it found that whilst the provision of financial KPIs was generally fair, companies had difficulty in providing details of non-financial KPIs – a difficulty that increased the smaller the company's market capitalisation.

Conclusions and ways forward from both reports

The reports of the TVC and ASB offer a range of different perspectives. The TVC report looks at the issues from the angle of communication with investors, whilst the ASB report considers both the legal compliance and the 'best practice' aspects – the latter being based around the OFR, which some observers had criticised as being overly demanding.

Their conclusions tend to point in the same direction:

- **Principal risks and uncertainties:** the quality of reporting in this area was mentioned in both reports. The issues included the company identifying what were the 'principal' risks – with the ASB commenting that where one company had reported on 33 risks, 'we question whether a company really can have 33 principal risks and uncertainties'. TVC's report commented on the need for companies to discuss the mitigation controls in place to reduce the impact of risks should they occur. The need to reassure shareholders that the company is in control is never more appropriate than when considering potential risks. Providing only a list of risks is of little benefit to shareholders.
- **KPIs:** the need for companies to consider what is **key** was subject much comment. Both reports highlighted the need for KPIs to relate to strategic objectives. Neither the 2005 nor 2006 Business Reviews require the statement of targets, but the ASB's report relied on its Reporting Statement to reinforce the need for companies to consider reporting on this requirement – at least as a means of demonstrating that the strategy is being managed in a meaningful manner.
- **Balanced and comprehensive:** as a means of ensuring a balanced analysis the ASB's report referred to the need for companies to include comments on 'bad news' that occurred during their financial year. This is clearly an issue of judgment for the directors, but a measure of assessment would be the amount of media coverage the 'bad news' had attracted to the company. For example, the Baker Report on BP's explosion in Texas, and BA's industrial relations record – the strike at Gate Gourmet, disputes with its catering suppliers, where the strike was estimated to cost BA around £45 million, and the ongoing negotiations with its cabin crew in early 2007 – would all be deserving of featuring in the Business Review.
- **Resources:** this is not a requirement in either the 2005 or 2006 Business Review Regulations, but the ASB's report makes a valid point about the need for a better description of resources available to the company – especially intangible resources, such as company brands and the quality of its employees. In reality, these areas should be covered as part of the discussion of risks and non-financial KPIs – if they are regarded as significant to the company's performance – but highlighting the subject, as the ASB has done, is a useful

reminder to companies preparing their Business Review. In a similar manner, TVC commented on the silo approach to Business Review reporting, and checklisting resources would help avoid this silo approach to communications.

- **Forward-looking information:** whilst this requirement applies with more rigour under the 2006 Business Review, the ASB commented on the difficulty of companies in providing forward-looking information, and suggested that the availability of 'safe harbour' provisions in the 2006 Act may make it easier for them to do so. However, companies may have the same problems even with 'safe harbour' provisions, and may find it easier to discuss the scenarios, and possible options, rather than making definite decisions on future solutions.
- **Guidance:** TVC's report discusses the improved quality of reporting resulting from companies using the OFR as their Business Review reporting format. It recommended that companies should at the very least use the OFR as a checklist. Guidance is clearly necessary, and it is not surprising that the ASB used its own Reporting Statement as the basis for determining best practice.
- **Preparation:** TVC's report emphasised the need for companies to make advanced preparations for the introduction of the 2006 Business Review, including:
    - developing a multi-functional approach;
    - identifying the key issues facing the company;
    - ensuring that all qualifying subsidiaries have a consistency of approach towards Business Review reporting;
    - ensuring that there is a system in place to assess policy effectiveness;
    - ensuring that the board is aware of the new role of directors (including group non-executives and the directors of subsidiaries) in reviewing the range of corporate reporting in the light of the Business Review and the opportunity to streamline reporting within the annual report.

As this book is being written, the first Business Reviews to be published by companies with 31 December financial year ends are in the process of being produced. No doubt, they will have reviewed commentary from these reports and others, and will be building some of the lessons addressed above within their own first Business Reviews – or at least, that is to be hoped!

NOTES

1 The Virtuous Circle, *Preparedness for new corporate reporting requirements – A study of FTSE200 Business Reviews and a consideration of their readiness for the new Companies Act* (November 2006).

2 Accounting Standards Board, *A review of narrative repairing by UK listed companies in 2006* (January 2007).

3 Deloitte, *Wrote to reason: Surveying OFRs and narrative reporting in annual reports* (October 2006).

CHAPTER **11**

Corporate reporting – current developments

KEY ISSUES

- Developments in the United States
- Output from Big Six summit in November 2006
- Convergence in accounting standards and the management commentary
- New version of ABI Guidelines
- Development of ISAE3000
- Report Leadership initiative
  - Discussions on private equity firms' disclosure
- Conclusion

This chapter will review the activities currently under discussion or underway in relation to corporate reporting, and some indication of their likely application will be discussed. However, like all future gazing, this discussion cannot cover every eventuality and, as will have become clear from the previous chapters, readers should bear in mind that corporate reporting is an ever-changing environment.

Developments in the United States

Whilst this book has focused on the corporate reporting circumstances of the United Kingdom, it is also important to consider the possible impact of developments in the United States, given that the capital markets are global in both their trading and direction.

First, we will give a brief overview of developments regarding the 2002 Sarbanes Oxley Act (SOX). The US Treasury Secretary, Hank Paulson, commented[1] on the need to review financial market rules. He suggested that SOX did not require any changes, but that the way in which the law was enforced should be improved. Since Mr Paulson was head of Goldman Sachs before becoming Treasury Secretary, his comments come from a perspective of industry experience as well as government legislator. He suggested that the changes should ensure that 'the right regulatory balance should marry high standards of integrity and accountability with a strong foundation for innovation, growth and competitiveness'. His focus was that the regulatory balance should be more 'agile . . . and responsive to changes in today's marketplace'.

This concern related to more than just corporate governance. Irwin Stelzer, in his *Sunday Times* Business News column, suggested that 'London has become a capital market of choice for more and more companies'.[2] He suggested that New York investment bankers point as a reason for this to the regulatory environment that is more onerous in the United States than in Britain, thanks to SOX, with the cost of compliance being much higher than in Britain.

The result of such comments has led Chris Cox, Chairman of the Securities and Exchange Commission (SEC), to review Britain's principles-based securities regulation under the FSA and compare it with the rules-based regulatory system under the SEC.

How quickly will these developments result in changes? The answer is definitely 'not overnight'. Paulson suggested that the US Government would meet in early 2007 to review capital markets and effectiveness, but more importantly, the Chair of the SEC is a political appointment and, with an election at the end of 2008, there are unlikely to be many changes before then.

If changes do come about, however, how may this affect corporate reporting? Under the SEC approach, the annual report is a compliance document. Observers suggest that this means that there has been less innovation by companies compared with the United Kingdom, where the FSA encourages best practice, meeting the needs of analysts who expect to see information in context.

If the United States were to move closer to adopting the UK system, this may be a positive move, provided convergence does not result in the risk of introducing US rules-based standards. Companies who are dual listed have stated that UK/US conciliation of their annual reports is a nuisance, but not necessarily difficult, and it would be worse if they had to comply with US standards.

The hope is that by 2009 there will be mutual recognition between the US and UK markets. This is achievable, but, as described earlier, politics play their part. The long-term objective would be a seamless, single set of global standards, but this is unlikely because there are many deep-seated differences. Instead, from the perspective of the EU securities regulation, there may evolve an equivalence of standards, enabling investors to make the same investment decision using both sets of standards. The challenge will arise if, in a give-and-take scenario, UK or EU regulators give up part of the principles-based approach to encourage the SEC to move away from rules-based standards – in which case, the possibility of a form of SOX-style legislation may not be unrealistic.

Alongside the move to modify the regulatory system in the United States, there are also moves to consider greater corporate democracy. Barney Frank,[3] a Democrat who chairs the House Financial Services Committee, wants to enact legislation that will empower 'fairly responsible people with a lot at stake' to ensure that corporate managers operate in the interests of their shareholders. In a similar move Paul Kanjorski, Chair of the House Sub-committee on Capital Markets, wants to increase shareholder rights because 'if we had better shareholder rights we wouldn't have as much litigation'. If this is carried through to changes such as electronic voting for shareholders in the United States, it would be difficult for UK regulators to resist considering similar changes.

However, it should not be assumed that all shareholders would move in a seemingly rational manner. In February 2007, Action Fund Management, a US hedge fund, responded to concerns from activists such as the Free Enterprise Action Fund that the adoption by General Electric (GE) of a green approach and its development of green innovation products may hurt GE's profits. As a result Action Fund Management proposed a shareholder resolution to force GE to take account of the effect on its investors of its green campaigns. GE tried to regain control by striking out the proposed resolution, but activists complained to the SEC, and won its support. The jury is still out on the result at the time of writing!

As a last point, the stock options scandal at Apple, in which Steve Jobs, its chief executive, had his stock options backdated to a more advantageous point, is likely to have some considerable impact if it is proven that the company was at fault. The SEC is currently reviewing the position. The outcome could have an impact on the work of remuneration committees, and would be felt not only in the United States. There are already suggestions amongst leading company secretaries that remuneration reports may change over the next five years because of the US's more stringent regulations.

Output from Big Six summit in November 2006

The accounting world has been subject to criticism recently, beginning perhaps with the peremptory abandonment of the statutory Operating and Financial Review (OFR), which left many companies in a state of uncertainty. In February 2006, presenting BP's annual results, Lord Browne, its Chief Executive, commented that:

> some would argue that IFRS neither produces a record of the accountability of management, nor a measure of the changes in

the economic value of assets and liabilities. I would agree with them. What IFRS actually does is make our results more difficult to understand.

In early November 2006, the International Governance Network articulated its worries about accounting. Subsequently, on 8 November 2006, the CEOs of the Big Six in the accounting world – PricewaterhouseCoopers, Deloitte, KPMG International, Ernst and Young, Grant Thornton and BDO – held a summit in Paris. Their purpose was to unveil a new model of corporate reporting to press regulators and policymakers into action. One journalist suggested that their ideas, if implemented, could consign twentieth-century accounting into the dustbin. This reasoning is reflected in the statement made by Mike Rake, Chairman of KPMG International, in which he declared that 'we all believe the current model is broken. We're not in a very happy situation'.

The most interesting proposal was that annual and quarterly reporting should be superseded by real time internet-based reporting, enabling investors to get whatever information they want, whenever they want it. The proposal wanted investors to have the same degree of choice as consumers purchasing goods over the internet.

The view was that investors would have to accept that more frequent levels of disclosure would be balanced against different levels of assurance to which they are accustomed currently. The benefit is that investors would get dynamic information on which to base their decisions – either through the preliminaries (published about two months after the year end) or the annual report (published over three months after the close of the period to which it relates).

This received some criticism. The Lombard column in the *Financial Times*[4] suggested that:

> to a certain degree, the accountants' vision is self-interested . . . they want to base their work on flexible broad principles rather than restrictive rules, and make more money from non-audit operations. For that to happen, they need regulators and governments to lift national restrictions and offer the firms protection against crippling litigation.

More comments on real time reporting are included in Chapter 14.

However, a second part of the proposals caused less concern and received less attention. This was to move corporate reporting away from purely financial information to include a wider set of information that could provide greater insight into a company's performance and prospects. In essence, this already exists in the United Kingdom with the Business Review and OFR, but the importance of this proposal is that it should apply internationally and provide a common set of standards for companies and their auditors to follow. This would link in closely to the development of better forms of internet-based investment decision-making systems such as XBRL,[5] which provides for tagging of various components of an annual report, enabling them to be downloaded directly into an investor's spreadsheet.

The summit also included urging for the move to convergence of International Accounting Standards. In addition, it raised concerns about the limited usefulness of historical costs, given the significance of intangible assets within companies' market capitalisation.

Like all changes, the results will take time. The Big Six have thrown a pebble into a pond, and what will develop over the next few years is a debate about the issues and the way forward. Things will not change overnight, but the Big Six have started the debate and have invited views on where corporate reporting should go for the future.

Convergence in accounting standards and the management commentary

One aspect of the proposals developed by the Big Six was a proposal for the convergence processes to be completed to benefit the global financial markets and their stakeholders.

These convergence processes include the need to minimise national differences in the overseeing of auditors, and the enforcement of relevant audit standards – which may best be described as assisting accounting firms to develop more generic or common approaches across all countries in which they operate. The Big Six also sought a convergence of national audit standards.

However, the most significant proposal was to encourage the completion of the efforts of the IASB and the US Financial Accounting Standards Board (FASB) to harmonise the differences between international (IFRS) and US reporting standards (US GAAP). They recommended that complex rules should be resisted and withdrawn and that the standards need to be principles-based. Their concerns were that current rules produce financial statements that virtually no one understands.

The work is being undertaken under a work plan published by the Committee of European Securities Regulators (CESR) and the SEC. In addition to convergence, the work plan included consideration of a modernisation of financial reporting and disclosure information technology, together with regulatory platforms for risk management. The comments of Chris Cox, the SEC Chairman, that 'the intention of CSER and SEC ... is to take practical steps to encourage high quality and consistent application of IFRS' suggest that this is one area where international co-operation will happen.

The IASB and FASB have developed proposals for a new joint conceptual framework. One key issue is who is the audience for financial reports – all stakeholders in capital markets, or a narrower group such as investors? Another issue is stewardship and the role of financial statements in supporting good corporate governance and accountability for past invested capital. Some members of the accounting profession consider that the term 'stewardship' is not well understood in the United States. Even so, the likely timescale means that there is unlikely to be an emergence of relevant conclusions until 2008 or 2009 at the earliest. The outcome will be a new framework, which should provide a foundation for developing future accounting standards that are principles-based, internally consistent and internationally converged.

Companies that will benefit from the introduction of such standards will be those with international operations, with easier and more consistent accounting. Investors will benefit from a set of global standards that will enable greater comparability of company accounts and, as a result, more effective investment decision-making.

However, there will be changes even within the current standards. The most likely will be the introduction of the Management Commentary by the IASB, which is in essence the same as the OFR. The real benefit will be that narrative reporting could become a standard for companies' annual accounts, regardless of which country's legislation applies. The question is whether the Management Commentary will be regarded as mandatory or voluntary. If it is mandatory, governments such as the EU will introduce legislation across all Member States. If it is voluntary, companies will be able to opt in if they choose, and it will then be up to investors to place pressure to encourage them to adopt the Management Commentary.

The IASB put the concept of the Management Commentary out for consultation and received very positive responses. A draft proposal will be reviewed by the IASB in mid-2007, and the likelihood is that an exposure draft will be issued for consultation in 2008 – what happens after that depends on how many IASB members get on board the idea.

In the meantime, the IASB has attempted to make a play for the use of IFRS by small companies (as well as emerging markets around the world). In February 2007, it published a 320-page draft standard for small and medium-size enterprises (compared with its full rule book, which is over 2,500 pages long). It is suggested that the final version of the standard, once adopted by national governments (if directed to do so by the EU) would transform the accounting of small and medium enterprises and private equity-owned companies.

If implemented, the standard will be used to simplify and harmonise accounting, but the EU has already stated that the standard would only be beneficial if it contributes to simplifying the accounting rules for the small and medium enterprises. Inevitably, therefore, there will be some further discussions before it sees the light of day.

New version of ABI Guidelines

The Association of British Insurers (ABI) first published its *Responsible Investment Disclosure Guidelines* in 2001.[6] In November 2006, it developed a position paper following the Royal Assent of the Companies Act 2006, which reviewed narrative reporting and what the ABI and its members (leading insurance companies in the United Kingdom) would expect to see in narrative reports. Peter Montagnon, Director of Investment Affairs, Association of British Insurers, stated that they expected to 'see forward looking discussion . . . and a greater use of key performance indicators'. His concluding remarks emphasised the importance of prioritising information provided to investors:

> We don't want to see everything in this. We just want to know what matters. What we also don't want is everything lumped into a CSR report as a PR venture. What we want to know is where the risks are and how companies are dealing with them.

As a result, at the end of January 2007 the ABI produced revised guidelines. In his letter accompanying these new guidelines, Peter Montagnon commented that he considers that the guidelines dovetail with the Business Review. It was his opinion that the previous guidelines worked so well that the updated version involved only modest change. He commented that the focus was on issues significant to the business, and introduced what for many was new terminology – environmental, social and governance reporting (ESG).

The aim of the guidelines[7] is to highlight aspects of responsibility reporting on which shareholders place particular value. This was described as narrative reporting which:

- sets ESG risks in the context of the whole range of risks and opportunities facing the company;
- contains a forward-looking perspective;

- describes the actions of the board in mitigating these risks.

The guidelines recommend that the board should make a statement regarding ESG risks and matters in its annual report. With regard to policies, procedures and verification, the report should:

- include information on ESG risks and opportunities;
- describe the possible impact on short- and long-term values that arise from ESG matters;
- include information (including KPIs) about the company's procedures for dealing with ESG matters;
- describe measures the board has put in place when ESG performance has fallen short of its objectives;
- describe the procedure for verification of ESG procedures, to a reasonable level of credibility.

In addition, the remuneration committee should state whether it included corporate performance on ESG matters when setting the executive directors' remuneration and whether the incentive structure for senior management raised the ESG risk by inadvertently motivating irresponsible behaviour.

Much of what is described above could be considered good practice for companies in the development of Business Reviews, especially companies following the ASB's Reporting Statement. However, two areas caused some surprise. The first was the recommendation of the ABI that it would expect a company to report on whether its remuneration policy related to ESG performance. Some companies do this as a matter of course – but these tend to be companies that are more attuned to CSR matters. This requirement was more broad ranging than CSR, and its emphasis on ESG risks meant that it was positioned in the role of what is right for a business rather than what is good for a business to do (as may be voiced by NGOs).

The second recommendation was verification of ESG statements in the annual report. The guidelines took matters further by suggesting that in terms of best practice, independent external verification of ESG disclosures would be regarded by shareholders as a significant advantage, but that credible other means of verification could be achieved by other means, including internal audit. Companies are expected to explain their reasons for the choice of method used.

The ABI recommendations are only guidelines, and as such are voluntary. Some company secretaries suggest that the importance of the ABI has changed compared with five or six years ago. Membership of the ABI represents only 25–30% of the UK market's capitalisation. The type of investor has changed, with smaller investment houses, smaller teams and highly research-led companies now in existence. There are many more US-style investors, including hedge funds that were not even dreamt of five years ago.

However, whilst there may be truth in comments about the changing style and nature of the investment market, the ABI's voice is still strong and regarded highly by UK directors. The likelihood is that the new guidelines, including the focus on ESG as part of the remuneration strategy and ESG statement verification, will come to be accepted as part of the normal procedures of corporate reporting over the next two to five years.

Development of ISAE3000

In 2002 the European Federation of Accountants produced a discussion paper, 'Providing Assurance on Sustainability Reports'. Whilst focused on CSR and sustainability reporting, and linked to Accountability's AA1000 Assurance Standard, the paper clearly has a role in the verification of Business Reviews where matters of ESG statements arise.

In June 2006, the European Federation of Accountants published a further discussion paper, 'Key Issues in Sustainability Assurance – An Overview',[8] which analysed Swedish, French, Dutch and German standards for assurance on sustainability reports. The analysis was structured by reference to the international framework and the generic standard for assurance issued by the International Federation of Accountants (IFAC). It also included reference to ISAE3000 – one of the engagement standards issued by IASB. This is a standard for assurance engagements by auditors relating to reviews or audits of information other than historical (and typically financial) information. The standard gives guidelines on how an assurance or verification engagement should be undertaken and how the assurance report should be written.

ISAE3000 should be considered in the context of two of the future developments covered earlier.

The first development is that of the Big Six Summit, whose second proposal featured the recommendation for the inclusion of non-financial information as part of the corporate reporting data set. Added to this was the message that investors would have to adjust to different levels of assurance than those to which they are currently accustomed.

The second development is the ABI's recommendation of independent verification of ESG statements included in annual reports.

The clear implication is that non-financial information is here to stay – on an international basis – and that investors will expect some form of assurance regarding reports that include ESG statements. Whether this type of verification and assurance will be undertaken by auditors as part of their normal audit is difficult to gauge, but the existence of ISAE3000 suggests that accounting firms are ready and willing to take up the commercial opportunities offered. The likelihood is that multinational companies will decide to utilise accounting firms for ESG verification and cause other smaller listed companies to follow their lead.

Report Leadership initiative

The Report Leadership initiative[9] was the output of a multi-stakeholder group that aimed to challenge the established thinking on corporate reporting. The stakeholders participating in the initiative are the Chartered Institute of Management Accountants (CIMA), PricewaterhouseCoopers, Radley Yeldar (the corporate communication design agency) and Tomkins plc. The initiative is intended to be ongoing and on which third parties can contribute via its website. Remarkably it was launched in November 2006, a few days after the Big Six Summit. However, there seemed to be little in the way of linking what was said at that summit (by PricewaterhouseCoopers amongst others) with this initiative.

The initiative took as its starting point the need to improve annual reports, on the basis that they should be more informative and accessible by providing information that investors want, without swamping them with unnecessary detail. Its objectives were to:

- help companies report in ways that are more relevant and informative to their primary audience;
- encourage investors to push for the information they want;
- prompt standards setters to consider how they might foster beneficial change.

The initiative recognised that companies spend significant time aggregating and recalculating internal data to produce regulatory information – a process described as wasteful and ineffective. Instead, a blueprint was developed for corporate reporting that aligns external reporting more closely with management reporting, acknowledges business complexities, is capable of being adapted to other media, and offers relevance and accessibility to investors.

The blueprint covers the following aspects of corporate reporting:

- effective communication:
  - structure;
  - messaging;
  - navigation.

- modelling the future:
  - value creation;
  - forward-looking orientation;
  - business environment;
  - strategy;
  - key performance indicators.

- Rethinking the financials:
  - revenue and costs;
  - segmental disclosure;
  - pensions;
  - analysis of net debt.

The underlying intention of the blueprint is to provide greater contextual information, based on research that current reporting approaches are considered too backward looking and too compliance driven. It starts from the perspective of making the annual report more relevant by ensuring that more of the content informs investors of what they want to know. It lines up with the outputs from another initiative – the Corporate Reporting Users Forum (CRUF) – which has produced guiding principles[10] on what analysts really want from accounts. This includes a cash flow statement that can be reconciled to the profit and loss statement, a profit and loss that differentiates between recurring and non-recurring activities, and a balance sheet that reflects the capital invested in the business, rather than its 'fair value'.

The strength of the Report Leadership initiative was not only that it attempted to prescribe a course of action, but that it produced a draft company report – for an imaginary company, Generico – so that the audience for whom the initiative was intended could touch and feel the concepts.

Initiatives like this – especially calling as it does for an avoidance of jargon ('don't spin and don't fudge the tricky bits' as one of the interviewees, featured later, described it) – will have an impact on corporate reporting.

However, it is unlikely that any one initiative will succeed on its own. The outcome will depend on how each initiative contributes to other ideas (such as that of CRUF). If successful, the effect will become like an unstoppable avalanche of new thought processes, considered positive by all parties and ready to be implemented.

Discussions about private equity firms' disclosure

The intrusion of private equity firms into the stock market has been one of the main phenomena of the early years of the twenty-first century. At the beginning of 2007 the largest ever deal was achieved with the buyout of TXU, the US utility, for nearly £23 billion by Texas Pacific, Kohlberg Kravis Roberts and Goldman Sachs. There was also a putative bid for J Sainsbury for £10 billion and, as this book was being written, Alliance Boots was under consideration of a private equity bid. Very few companies are able to consider themselves invincible from a private equity bid.

Apart from the fact that these deals are highly leveraged with debt capital (and hence may be more susceptible to failure over the long term), the real issue is the different standards of disclosure between private equity companies and listed companies. Both parties are large entities and as a result will have to produce Business Reviews, but the standards of disclosure within the Reviews are different, and listed companies' Reviews will be regulated more thoroughly by the FRRP than is likely to be the case for private equity. Added to this, the Combined Code does not apply to the private equity companies (although most would ensure that best practice applies).

Private equity firms argue that their level of disclosure to investors is much higher, and indeed more transparent than would be the case for almost any other part of the financial services industry, and that investors in hedge funds or pension plans are left in the dark by comparison. In addition, they claim that their business approach is more effective – often because when taken behind closed doors, they can drive change and growth more effectively than in the full blaze of publicity.

However, against this argument is the fact that public opinion distrusts and even abhors privacy. This is particularly the case when the company being bought out is in the public eye, as would be the case with Sainsbury or Boots, with issues relating to public health, food safety, environmental issues and openness about supply chains. These are issues on which a private equity owner would be unlikely to report and certainly would not be required to do so. Remarkably, Damon Buffini of Permira, regarded as being very reclusive from the public eye, went on television and radio in February 2007 to defend the role of private equity and even invited leaders of the GMB union (who have been critical of private equity destroying British jobs) to meet with him to discuss the issues.

For this reason, the private equity trade association, British Venture Capital Association (BVCA), has agreed to form a voluntary code to improve its disclosure.[11] Its concern is that if the industry is perceived as being too closed, government may decide to intervene with regulatory action.

Rod Selkirk, Chairman of BVCA, stated that:

> this initiative reflects the coming of age of the private equity industry as a mainstream asset class in the UK. We recognise that the industry's success has led to growing and legitimate interest in its activities. We plan to build on our existing high standards of transparency and openness to our investors by increasing the level of disclosure to a wider group of stakeholders.

Perhaps some of that government intervention is already on its way with the announcement that Ed Balls, the Economic Secretary of the UK Treasury, is to establish a review of the tax relief given on shareholder loans in highly leveraged deals.

The question, of course, is not whether there will be higher levels of disclosure, but how far it will go. This is likely to be resolved by political decision, rather than purely investment considerations. The final decision may not be in the hands of the UK Government, but determined within the EU, where Franco-German opposition to private equity is far stronger.

Conclusion

In this chapter, seven possible developments have been considered in terms of their impact on corporate reporting. Only time will tell how far each will develop – as well as whether other developments will have greater impact but which are as yet unforeseen.

What is clear is that the future of corporate reporting will be significantly different from the present and dramatically different from that in place at the turn of the millennium. To understand how these changes may develop, Chapters 12–14 feature the outcome of a series of interviews with 24 individuals who are at the forefront of corporate reporting today.

NOTES

1. Presentation made to the New York Economic Club, 20 November 2006.
2. Irwin Stelzer, *Sunday Times*, 11 February 2007.
3. Quoted in Irwin Stelzer's column, *Sunday Times*, Business News, 21 January 2007.
4. Lombard, *Financial Times*, 8 November 2006.

5   XBRL stands for Extensible Business Reporting Language – more details can found on its website at www.XBRL.org.

6   A copy of *Investing in Responsibility – Risk and Opportunities* (the original ABI report in which the first guidelines were promulgated) can be found on the ABI website at www.abi.org.uk.

7   The guidelines are available on the ABI's website at www.abi.org.uk/NewsReleases.

8   A copy of this paper can be found on the FEE website at www.fee.be.

9   More details about the initiative can be found on its website at www.reportleadership.com.

10 Details of CRUF's activities, including its guiding principles, can be found on its website at www.cruf.co.uk.

11 Details of BVCA's approach can be found on the BVCA website at www.bvca.co.uk.

CHAPTER **12**

Current state of corporate reporting – views from the users

KEY ISSUES

- Background
- Introduction to interviewees
  - Regulators
  - Company secretaries and in-house legal
  - Investors
  - Advisers
  - Communicators and commentators
- Current state of corporate reporting
  - Impact of abolition of OFR
  - Effect of IFRS
  - How good is corporate reporting?
  - Quality of the content
  - Which companies are better at reporting?
  - Progress over the past five to 10 years
- Value and purpose of annual reports
  - Who reads which document?
- Best practice in corporate reporting
  - Reporting style
  - Meeting investor needs
  - Corporate communications

Background

As the planning for this book progressed, it was clear that with so many different parties involved in the operation and implementation of corporate reporting, it was essential that the views of some of the experts and practitioners in the field should be canvassed. As a result, a range of in-depth interviews were undertaken.

The objective was to address three key areas:

1. the current state of corporate reporting, in terms of quality of reports and how it has moved over the past five to 10 years;
2. the challenges posed by the 2005 Business Review, together with the additional information required under the Companies Act 2006 version of the Business Review;

3. the future of corporate reporting over the next five to 10 years, together with the impact of electronic communications and the suggestions for real-time reporting, made by the head of the Big Six accountancy firms.

In addition, as a close to the interviews, a general discussion was undertaken about whether any other aspects of corporate reporting were relevant. In many respects, this closing discussion provoked a range of comments on burning issues, as well as continuing bugbears, which were extremely illuminating in terms of how the future would develop.

This chapter will cover the views of the interviewees in terms of the current state of reporting. The subsequent chapters will cover their perceptions of how the Business Review (both the 2005 and 2006 versions) is being handled, their thoughts on future reporting, and other aspects they had decided to raise. Chapter 15 will offer some concluding thoughts on the way forward.

Introduction to interviewees

Those interviewed were extremely generous with both their time and thoughts – but it is important at the outset to emphasise that comments attributed to them are based on their own personal views and should not be considered to be representative of the organisations for which they work or reflect any of the views of those organisations. In all, 22 interviews were conducted, involving a total of 24 interviewees. The numbers interviewed are not considered as being representative statistically, but the richness of the comments help to provide a deep insight into the views of the wide range of individuals involved in the development of corporate reporting.

The views of the regulators (two were interviewed) were regarded as important, as were the views of company practitioners – company secretaries and legal officers who are directly involved in corporate reporting. Interviewees ranged from individuals with experience of FTSE30, FTSE100 and FTSE250 companies, representing market capitalisation totalling around £100 billion;[1] and investors, to ensure a greater understanding of how they used annual reports, and how they felt that these compared with other forms of corporate reporting. In this respect, individuals from two of the largest pension funds (representing nearly £80 billion in funds) were included, as well as individuals advising fund managers and high net worth private investors. Professional advisers are of great importance to companies preparing their annual reports. Interviewees were from accounting practices (with experience of a wide range of companies from medium-sized unlisted to the very largest FTSE companies) and experts from the relevant professional institutes. In a similar light, the views of those who advise companies on corporate communications were important, particularly in terms of their experience in developing annual reports and their web counterparts. In addition commentators on corporate reporting and its future direction were included – either from an academic standpoint or as part of a commercial advisory service. The categories and names of all those who contributed are as follows:

Regulators

- **David Loweth**, Technical Director of the Accounting Standards Board.
- **Richard Thorpe**, Head of Accounting, Auditing Capital and Groups Policy, Financial Services Authority.

Company secretaries and in-house legal

- **Simon Bicknell**, Company Secretary, GlaxoSmithKline.
- **Simon Enoch**, Company Secretary, Kesa Electrical.
- **Helen Jones**, Director of Governance & Corporate Services, Kingfisher.
- **Robert Aitken**, Global Head of Legal and Compliance, Man Investments.
- **Richard Seaman**, Director of Compliance and Legal, Man Financial.
- **Paul Griffiths**, Company Secretary, Rentokil Initial.
- **Rosemary Martin**, Company Secretary and General Counsel, Reuters Group.

Investors

- **Peter Elwin**, Head of Accounting and Valuation Research, Cazenove Equities.
- **Paul Lee**, Director, Hermes Investment Management.
- **Ian Greenwood**, Manager, Governance & Engagement, Hermes Investment Management.
- **Nicholas Hodson**, Head of Investments, Lloyds TSB Private Bank.
- **Dr Daniel Summerfield**, Co-Head of Responsible Investment, Universities Superannuation Scheme.

Advisers

- **Paul Moxey**, Head of Corporate Governance and Risk Management, ACCA.
- **Giles Peel**, Director, Policy & Development, ICSA International.[2]
- **Tom Ward**, Partner, Moore Stephens.

- **David Chopping**, Partner, Moore Stephens.
- **David Phillips**, Senior Corporate Reporting Partner, PricewaterhouseCoopers LLP.

Communicators and commentators

- **Sallie Cooke Pilot**, Director of Corporate Reporting, Black Sun.
- **Nick Smith**, Senior Partner, The Smith Partnership.
- **Jonathan Hynes**, Senior Partner, The Smith Partnership.
- **Seamus Gillen**, Partner, h2glenfern and Course Director, ICSA training on Narrative Reporting in Practice.
- **Tim Ambler**, Fellow, London Business School.

On the four occasions where interviews were with two representatives from the same organisation, the views expressed in the subsequent chapters are attributed to only one of them – hence where Paul Lee is quoted, this refers to views expressed in the interview with Paul Lee and Ian Greenwood, and similarly for Jonathan Hynes (representing himself and Nick Smith), Tom Ward (representing himself and David Chopping) and Robert Aitken (representing himself and Richard Seaman). This has been done for ease of reading, and in no way reflects on the individuals not quoted.

Current state of corporate reporting

In this chapter, a variety of topics on corporate reporting are covered, with comments and quotes from each of the interviewees. These comments are included without trying to present a conclusion where there are contrasting statements, although some thoughts about the ways forward are offered in Chapter 15.

In starting with a view of the position of corporate reporting as it stands in 2006/2007, the purpose was to gauge interviewees' views before the impact of the full affect of the 31 December year-end Business Reviews had been felt. In particular, it was important to understand how the interviewees considered that reporting had developed over the past five to 10 years, as a means of establishing later how they believed corporate reporting would develop in the future.

Needless to say, views differed, often dependent upon the level of the individual's involvement in developing the annual reports. In this respect, the key differentiator was the extent to which the individuals had experienced developing corporate reporting at first hand.

Nevertheless, there were consistent views – including the many comments on the length of company reports. Often the length of the most recent HSBC report[3] (over 400 pages with no pictures) was given as an example to reinforce an overall comment that annual reports have become far too long. One comment was that often company reports were:

> pretty hard to wade through, let alone to find the profit numbers. Far too much data and probably not enough information . . .

Impact of abolition of OFR

The abolition of the OFR was much discussed, particularly issues relating to the confusion caused by the change to the statutory nature of the OFR following the Chancellor's intervention in November 2005. David Loweth commented that companies first asked what they were supposed to do and then took differing approaches. He suggested that some stopped, some took stock, and some just carried on with the OFR they had already planned. Rosemary Martin, reflecting the opinion of many interviewees, suggested that had the Review come in as scheduled, people would just have got on with it. People are now impatient about the long-drawn-out development of the Business Review.

Effect of IFRS

David Phillips believed that the effect of IFRS has had a big impact, suggesting that IFRS has been a bigger change than people realised. He considered it to have been a step change that caused people to question the direction in which financial reporting is going – and at the same time questions have been raised around convergence with the United States. Normally, he suggested, change occurs through drip, with which people become familiar over time. However, pension accounting and the IFRS are so significant that they have opened everyone's mind and forced people to be more considered about the challenges of reporting. Added to this was his view that there has been a growing consensus of stakeholder views coming together. He suggested that investors use the information in annual reports selectively and corporates do not use the information as the basis for running their businesses – even regulators have been voicing their concerns. Greater awareness of the issues and a realisation of the inefficiencies of reporting have evolved.

How good is corporate reporting?

The general view was that there have been some positive changes – although companies could do better overall. Tim Ambler suggested that things are getting progressively better, but not particularly quickly. However, within these overall comments, views were expressed that whilst the content of reports have improved there are still challenges. Helen Jones commented that it is difficult to see the wood for the trees. There is too much data, which means that the real information can get overlooked.

Simon Enoch commented that for the majority of readers, reports are very wordy, overly financial dependent, and only comprehensible to a very small minority. Jonathan Hynes commented that too often the final outcome of a report has been an impenetrable data dump. The challenge is to achieve the simple message:

> The problem is that often the decision-maker is not a communications person.

Quality of content

Quality of content was criticised by the investors. Daniel Summerfield criticised its lack of a joined-up approach, suggesting that whilst various aspects have improved, some companies are reporting in silos and sections are not necessarily integrated to offer a holistic overview of the companies' performance.

Paul Lee was particularly critical of some companies' reports that did not add value for the investor, suggesting that they were almost the same, year after year. For example, little detail was provided about how their strategy has evolved – just the numbers changed:

> They are "lazy" because they are not trying to add value. This is of limited use to the investors who review long-term issues to drive value.

Which companies are better at corporate reporting?

This subject was discussed with several of the interviewees, because it is important to understand whether particular categories of companies are better at corporate reporting than others. Most commented that some companies in the FTSE100 are not regarded favourably, but that some in the FTSE250 are seen as very credible.

Most seemed to share Paul Griffiths' view that FTSE30 and 100 companies probably need to do relatively little to improve their quality. Others, he suggested, including some FTSE100s and many below that, need to upgrade what they are doing, quite significantly in some cases.

However, some specific categories have already addressed the challenges of greater disclosure. There was recognition across the board that dual listed (UK and US) companies have already increased the levels of disclosures and as such have improved the quality of reporting. This is also the case with financial services companies, as was noted by Robert Aitken, who commented that these companies have higher accounting standards because of the capital requirement to which they needed to adhere, including standards to ensure greater transparency.

Progress over the past five to 10 years

One of the questions posed was how companies have developed in terms of corporate reporting over the past five to 10 years.

Sallie Cooke Pilot emphasised that, having formally tracked the quality of corporate reporting over the past four to five years, there has been steady progress and more effective communication, although this has not been helped by the confusion and uncertainty over OFR legislation and regulation. Over the past few years, she believed that best practices reporting standards will emerge for different sectors, and that there will probably be a period of stability.

However, David Phillips suggested that companies have made a big step in the last 12 months. This, he believed, is particularly helpful because financial reporting does not fulfil the needs of investors, and hence the changes the Business Review has made are much more relevant:

> The lack of a narrative context had undermined the whole reporting model for some time; a period of evolutionary change is now occurring.

Giles Peel regards corporate reporting as more sophisticated than five to 10 years ago because the audience has become more sophisticated – but it is also much easier to tick the boxes. A contrasting view came from Jonathan Hynes, who said that the compliance approach has made reporting less valuable since it is more negative than the regulators would have wanted to achieve, with more compliance and less communications. In the mid-1990s, he suggested, things were much more about telling the investors' story. He thought that it is odd that the regulators, in trying to achieve more, have also made some people more nervous of corporate reporting than they used to be.

Another criticism of the success of the regulators was that government has been prevailed upon to produce many unnecessary pieces of legislation, and company law should not be driven by concerns for social justice:

> Company law is about a set of principles that govern the relationships between the owners of capital and the people that manage that capital for them.

A concern voiced by many was the extent to which boards may be driven to focus on issues that are not really important in terms of the way they run their company. This was amplified by others, who addressed the related issue of the frequency of reporting.

Value and purpose of annual reports

Discussion subsequently focused on the value and purpose of annual reports. Common threads emerged from the various groups of interviewees about how helpful annual reports are, especially given the extensive amount of information content included within the preliminary announcements. A particularly strong comment was made by Nicholas Hodson, who stated that reports are more gloss and investor oriented:

> But I don't spend too much time reading the glossies because they are already out of date.

He went further when asked about the importance of the investor relations teams in contributing to investment analysts' accessibility to and understanding of a company's performance. When asked to compare an annual report with an investor relations team, in terms of what gave him the better value, his answer was 'an investor relations team, undoubtedly'.

Another investor, Daniel Summerfield, questioned the purpose of annual reports. Like Nicholas Hodson, he suggested that for most investors the report is out of date and served limited use in making investment decisions.

If these comments come from institutional investors, what did interviewees think about the value of the annual report to the retail investors? Simon Enoch commented that the wordier the document, the less inclined people are to read it:

> Most annual report and accounts get thrown in the bin without even being opened.

Who reads which document?

Simon Bicknell commented on his experience of shareholders where there had been an option to receive a summary report. He stated that less than 5%

requested the full report and, surprisingly, none of his US-based shareholders had requested the full report (although, of course, 20-F reports are available on line via EDGAR[4]).

This may be due to the dependence on the preliminary announcements by investors who are traders. Nicholas Hodson said that prelims are much better sources of information, even though the front page highlights the good and low-lights the bad.

However, it would be wrong to suggest that these views represent a complete investor perspective. Peter Elwin considered that the annual report should be seen as a broadcast medium covering a wide range of audiences. He suggested that the best approach is to let the reader sort out what they want. The retail investor may want 100 out of 300 pages, the institutional investor and sell-side analysts (both debt and equity) may want 295 out of the 300 pages, but not necessarily all on the same day. The market will dictate what gets read and when.

Paul Lee offered an alternative perspective when he said that the value of annual reports is very high, but that a lot of cynicism is aroused in people who consider them an irrelevance. He considered that for an investor who is not just a trader, the annual report is a crucial document. He believed that the report should be the first port of call as it can be a 'shop window' for investors – not just institutions but also retail investors:

> The information in the financials goes far beyond the results announcements. The notes to the accounts give huge amounts of information not available in the financial announcements.

This was reflected by Robert Aitken, who said that he uses the report with a whole range of outsiders – new regulators and people doing due diligence, e.g. banks and distributors. He suggested that for complex companies, the report and accounts are where all aspects of the company come together and that no other tool can be used as completely with third parties.

Best practice in corporate reporting

When asked about best practice in corporate reports, there was great consistency in replies, which focused on effective communications, with words and phrases used such as 'truthful', 'honest', 'well written', 'sticking to the main issues', 'succinct', 'freshly articulated information', 'more forward looking' and 'much franker discussion of risks and prospects'.

Overwhelmingly all interviewees referred to best practice as telling a story or painting a picture. Peter Elwin stated that his perception of best practice was covering performance and risk, and working out the strategy and its development. He considered that anything that supports this is worth having, and anything that detracts is not worth having. However, it must also be relevant, rather than repeating the previous year's format.

This was extended by Paul Lee who suggested that companies should not assume that everyone knows what the company does. In addition, he believed that the management style of the company can be reflected in the report:

> The way it is written is very important. You can tell from the report the quality of thinking and the process that has gone into it. That tells you a great deal about the quality of thought and processes which drive strategy and operational management in the company as a whole.

Reporting style

Reporting style was considered an important factor, and several company practitioners commented favourably on the Report Leadership initiative. In contrast, Simon Bicknell suggested that as every company is very different, their reports should reflect these differences, in terms of designs and emphasis, and that it is fundamentally important that boards decide what is appropriate for the companies they manage.

Some caveats were placed on the importance of honesty and fairness in best practice. Helen Jones commented that there is not a need to disclose everything, but that what is disclosed gives an honest picture. This was reinforced by Robert Aitken, who said that best practice is about being clear, fair and not misleading. Several of the company practitioners emphasised the need to edit the annual report to ensure that it is easy to understand and has a more human tone.

However, there was a recognition that some parts of the annual report are less valuable than others. In particular there was criticism of the statements of the chairman and chief executive at the front of the report:

> The Chairman's statement is fluff (with a little bit about board development). There is no point having the CEO and the FD sections alongside the Business Review.

Meeting investor needs

Giles Peel focused on the reality of the circumstances of active retail shareholders, stating that it is important to remember that most retail investors own more than one set of shares, making it burdensome for them to review lots of annual reports. He suggested that companies should consider investors' needs more, and that companies do not consider the multiple shareholders as much as they should. Best practice involves simplicity – by which he means the use of the English language:

> It is very easy to get into tortuous language in annual reports ... institutional investors do not view annual reports as "for them" but the language used by companies is aimed at them and therefore not really retail investor friendly.

David Phillips commented that as an accountant, he is concerned with the deficiencies of reporting. Unlike many of his colleagues, who thought that these deficiencies can be addressed through better measurement, he believed that the key is creating a better information set. He built on this theme with regard to meeting the investor needs, suggesting that what investors want is better information sets to populate their valuation models, without having to unbundle the accounts in order to get to key base information:

> They are frustrated over the formal reporting not giving them the information set they want.

His view of best practice reporting began with the recognition of the demand to comply with the regulatory model (Nicholas Hodson also emphasised that there should be strict adherence to IAS or GAAP standards), but then continued with the importance of presenting a joined-up picture of the company from strategy to performance bringing to life how the company is actually run. In terms of how good companies are at doing this, he suggested that there is significant room for improvement. Companies that can achieve this aim tend to be those that are well run and that can articulate their strategy clearly. In this respect, good quality external reporting is very closely related to what happens internally:

> The first question a board should ask is can they put this picture together internally – if they can't then they need to ask themselves some really serious questions. This is not about legislation – it's about how well companies are managed.

Paul Moxey related the annual report to corporate governance reporting and suggested that many producers of the governance statement in the annual report may have forgotten that the Combined Code states that the report should describe how the corporate governance principles are applied. He suggested that there is increasing interest from investors as to how the principles are applied.

Corporate communications

Sallie Cooke Pilot believed that the annual report is only a part of the corporate reporting communications exercise. She suggested that there is a need to look at best practice from a communications standard, which would consider the wider remit of messaging across all investor materials, including websites, presentations and other tools. Her experience was that the key strategic messages are often inconsistent and not featured in the annual report, and the task is to ask companies why they are not doing so.

Seamus Gillen added to this, emphasising the importance of continuous, and consistent, communications:

> There should not be a chink between different corporate communications – the annual report should only be the fixed time equivalent of real time investor relations communications.

Perhaps the lesson for best practice can be taken from Tim Ambler, who commented that the problem with lots of corporate reports is that they are fudged up by PR people – ending up with gloss instead of insight.

NOTES

1 As at week ending 24 February 2007.
2 Subsequent to this interview, Giles Peel took up the position of Managing Director of Capita's Company Secretarial Services division.
3 Robert Bruce, in the *Financial Times* Accountancy Column, 22 February 2007, stated that the Post Office had refused to deliver the HSBC annual report and accounts on health and safety grounds – it was deemed too heavy for staff to carry and deliver.
4 EDGAR stands for Electronic Data Gathering, Analysis and Retrieval System, and more information can be found at www.sec.gov/edgar.shtml.

CHAPTER 13

Challenges of the Business Review – views from the users

KEY ISSUES

- 2005 Business Review – process and experience
  - The process
  - Developing the Business Review
  - Experience of the first Business Review
- Forward-looking statements
  - A step into the unknown
  - Investor expectations
  - Views of advisers
- Reporting – KPIs and risks
  - KPIs
  - Risks
- Style of Business Review
- Impact of Companies Act 2006 on Business Review
  - New definition of directors' duties
  - New reporting requirements
  - Issue of safe harbour
- Best practice for Business Review reporting
  - Benefits of good quality Business Review reporting

Introduction

From the current state of corporate reporting, discussion with the interviewees moved on to their views on how companies are dealing with the Business Review – first under the 2005 Business Review Regulations, and, secondly, under the Companies Act 2006 Business Review. As before, comments are included without trying to present a conclusion where there are contrasting statements, to enable the reader to gain a flavour of the issues involved and some of the contrasting positions.

2005 Business Review – process and experience

The 2005 Business Review affects all sizes of companies and, in particular, causes the small and middle-sized listed companies to address issues that, previously, only their larger listed cousins may have had to consider in their reporting.

The process

Tom Ward is experienced in auditing both small and mid-cap companies, as well as a plethora of unlisted companies. His view on the challenges for listed companies was that the current situation has created very substantial problems for directors. His experience suggests that directors are concerned about how much they should be disclosing. In his view, there is a leaning towards copying what other people do, rather than being creative and divulging more about their own businesses.

He had not observed any great changes for unlisted companies as the result of the introduction of the Business Review:

> They do what the regulations tell them and no more. They do it because they have to do so.

However, interviewees thought that some unlisted companies may do more than is required, but that these are few and far between because of the nature of their shareholder base, for example companies with shareholders who are not on the board, or where companies have longer-term ambitions to be quoted. However, some unlisted companies may use the annual report as a tool for recruitment of senior managers and, as such, realise the importance of providing more information than just the financial accounts.

Developing the Business Review

One of the challenges acknowledged by most interviewees was the relative lack of guidance for companies in terms of how they should develop their Business Review. David Loweth explained the position of the ASB:

> We had some pressure to offer process guidance, but resisted it – on the basis we are not in the business of telling companies how to do reporting.

The extent to which companies are likely to feel challenged by the Business Review was seen to be dependent on their previous experience and background.

This experience included how familiar companies were with narrative reporting, and this related especially to companies that had completed OFRs in the past and to the nature of the business, including how widely their business activities were dispersed. It was felt that companies with many different business activities (including international operations) would be more likely to find the Business Review challenging than, for example, a UK-based property company, with a limited range of business activities.

Of the company practitioners interviewed, four were in the process of completing their Business Reviews for the first time, under 2005 Regulations. For some, previous preparations were holding them in good stead. Helen Jones commented that she had been through the process 18 months previously as last year's accounts had been prepared in anticipation of the OFR. As such, she did not foresee any significant changes in compiling the Business Review this year.

For others facing the task for the first time, it is having an almost cathartic effect. Paul Griffiths suggested that it has caused companies to consider how they are reporting to shareholders. In a similar vein, Rosemary Martin commented that on the whole it has been a positive move, and the biggest challenge has been how to structure the annual report.

Simon Bicknell considered that it has been more of a steady-as-you-go progress, commenting that his Business Review will be a summary of everything that has already been in the annual report in the past, with the addition of certain KPIs. He suggested that the general principle is that 'we know our shareholders best, and know how to communicate with them'.

This view was similar to that of Simon Enoch, who suggested that the challenge for company secretaries is to stop their boards thinking that they are providing more data than hitherto:

> If we look at what we give in the public domain – including analysts' presentations, etc., we already provide details that we can put in the annual report and comply with the regulation.

Experience of the first Business Review

Reviewing companies that had already produced their first Business Reviews did not lead all investors to be as confident as the company secretaries in terms of companies' abilities to produce them. Paul Lee suggested that whilst the approach at this stage is not to be openly critical, but to focus on examples of good practice, his experience of most Business Reviews indicates that companies have not found it easy to compile them:

> This may demonstrate something about the quality of strategic thinking at board level. Some cases suggest that the quality of thinking doesn't go on at board level, which is really quite concerning for an investor.

Both Peter Elwin and Nicholas Hodson were more favourably inclined towards the Business Reviews they had seen, but Daniel Summerfield and Peter Elwin commented on the problems of there being no firm guidance for companies. Daniel Summerfield suggested that the Business Review is so generalised that it will take some time for companies to understand how to populate and draft it.

Some of these views were shared by the advisers. David Phillips said that some companies have found the process harder than others. He considered that some companies have found the process difficult from a behavioural perspective, whilst others have seen it as an opportunity to describe more effectively what they are already doing. Others, he suggested, view it as more red tape, believing that no one reads an annual report, and so they are not concerned with its contents. He believed that the bigger companies are more in tune, but there are good examples across the board:

> I think the Business Review is more important and more valuable for the small caps and the mid caps to get it right – because it is almost like you're writing the brokers' reports for them.

Like Paul Lee, Paul Moxey discussed the extent to which boards have the information available and the potential risk of continuing a silo mentality in developing a Business Review. He considered that many boards probably do not have the inherent information themselves (especially non-executives). Yet he suggested that they would find the information very useful for themselves, for example providing clarity about strategy, how the organisation is going to achieve the strategy, and managing the risks. He was concerned that bringing all the information together does not happen at board level – and perhaps not at management board level either:

> They tend not to think strategically but focus on details and the solving of crises. They rarely have the luxury to sit back and look at it from the business perspective.

Giles Peel suggested that companies have coped very well with the Business Review, but he emphasised that the Review is intended to reflect the view of the board. He considered this aspect to have been one of the challenges, in so far as it is supposed to be the directors' own view. He suggested that previously, the culture was to get other people to write the report – hence the difficulty now. He believed that the OFR was a shock when it became statutory because it demonstrated a true line of accountability for the first time. He felt that the Business Review is less rigorous but still makes directors think more about running a business and how to report upon it. In his view corporate governance forces directors to conform and probably contrasts with the entrepreneurial spirit. Whilst he recognised that in practical terms it is easy to be repetitive, the real innovators have avoided repetition – and for the reader the report is easier to comprehend.

Amongst the communicators and commentators, Sallie Cooke Pilot and Seamus Gillen felt that companies are moving in the right direction with their first Business Reviews, although, like Daniel Summerfield, Seamus Gillen commented that it will take a year or two for companies to get to grips with what is required and how they can deliver it. He suggested that many companies do not necessarily want to be leading edge – for them, the first year is one of trial and error, and cautious positioning.

The challenges for smaller listed companies were touched upon by Jonathan Hynes. He gave as an example one chairman of a FTSE250 company who, whilst compiling the report, consequently had a lot of reading to do over Christmas to find out what was required. As a result, the chairman realised that writing the report will now take longer and needs to be more structured.

This example demonstrates clearly that the Business Review has been more problematic for those with fewer available resources than for larger companies.

Seen from the perspective of the communicators and commentators, there is evidence that the process of completing the Business Review is showing benefits. Sallie Cooke Pilot suggested that there is now more management of the process, engaging boards at an earlier stage. She considered that one of the benefits of the Business Review approach is the ability to align internal messages and the views of senior management on the key drivers of long-term value with the material for external communication. She believed that there has been a greater development between the two. She considered that the process of getting the information and communicating the information externally has improved, and as a result of increased transparency there has been a better alignment internally on the key elements of a company's strategy, such as KPIs and risk.

Forward-looking statements

The regulators[1] recognised that two of the areas that posed the most challenges to companies were the need to provide forward-looking statements and the need to provide KPIs. Clearly, there needs to be a better understanding of what is meant by a forward-looking statement. David Loweth suggested that in terms of forward-looking statements, investors were not looking for things such as profit forecasts, but that KPIs should be well stated and include targets so that the investors can see progress. He suggested that certainly more was needed in a forward-looking statement than was provided in one January 2006 annual report, in which the chairman's response to the section on 'Outlook for the Business' was the single word 'Good'.

A step into the unknown

Simon Enoch stated that there is a cautious approach towards forward-looking statements, with a reluctance to provide full disclosure on day one:

> Everyone feels that disclosure is rather like going into a shark's mouth – it's a one way process – there's no going back.

Helen Jones stated that the process has not been as difficult for her as it has for others. She commented that companies such as her own are regularly in the process of disclosing new openings in various parts of the world and are used to making this type of future announcement. However, she pointed out that there is nothing, even in the old OFR, that requires disclosure of dividend trends or future profits.

Paul Griffiths suggested that the process is more challenging when a company is in transition. He pointed out that for a company in transition, it has to be 'big picture stuff', because some of the planned actions may never happen – or at least not as contemplated. Consequently, he suggested that a 'broad stroke' approach is needed. However, Rosemary Martin acknowledged that one of the real difficulties arise because things change so quickly:

> The challenge is that even with forward-looking statements, almost as soon as you print the annual report it's out of date.

Investor expectations

The investors acknowledge that forward-looking statements are a potentially difficult area. Peter Elwin suggested that when talking to investors most companies are already giving forward-looking statements. He considered that the best approach may be to use the analysts' presentation as part of the Business Review.

Paul Lee suggested that his company had pushed very hard for resolution on liability because they are keen that directors should not be looking over their shoulders for lawyers and are making sensible judgments on what they can say. However, he would be concerned if, over a few years, there is no marked improvement in forward-looking statements:

> If this is the case, there may be some pressure from investors for a removal of the safe harbour provision . . . because it will not have done what it's there to do – encourage discussion about forward-looking prospects.

Daniel Summerfield went further, questioning whether companies are dealing with forward-looking statements comprehensively and effectively. He thought that what many investors are looking for is a projection of risks and opportunities and strategic direction. In his opinion, the best approach is to provide a holistic overview of these issues and how companies will deal with them going forward. But he recognised that some companies are concerned with issues that are perceived to be commercially sensitive.

Views of advisers

Amongst the professional advisers, David Phillips suggested that forward-looking statements are proving difficult because this area has been totally misunderstood:

> It's about building a picture of the future of the business, explaining its strategy, talking about lead indicators. There is a way to provide a medium-term view. It is not about making a forecast.

He believed that over time the Business Review will deliver real economic value to British industry and society by making transparent how companies are run and by providing information that will change behaviours and practices.

The communicators and commentators had observed companies' concerns about how to deal with forward-looking statements. Sallie Cooke Pilot described her own recommendation that companies deal with these statements by using external data to substantiate trends, possibly data from the public domain, as with BAA using external forecasts of passenger traffic over the next 10 years. In her view, investors are looking for more contextual information about the issues rather than detailed forecasts and future solutions. Her experience is that, even with the safe harbour provisions, companies are still concerned about putting themselves at a competitive disadvantage, but that, from what she has observed, when one company breaks ranks the others follow.

This need to take a rational approach towards forward-looking statements was amplified by Jonathan Hynes, who suggested that no one is willing stand up and say, for example, 'in five years we will be there'. For him, the timescale is the key, and more important is a statement of intent for the next 12 months, together with 'what is our strategy and how will it pan out', but he does not anticipate forward-looking statements requiring numbers.

Reporting – KPIs and risks

KPIs

KPIs were one of the biggest issues for company practitioners. Depending on the nature of the company, however, compiling information on KPIs was not regarded as challenging. Some companies, especially holding companies, are used to providing such information and its context.

Simon Bicknell confirmed that data are not the problem. He described the process that GSK had pursued in the development of its Business Review, which resulted in the disclosure of KPIs that had been used for some time by the board – turnover, earnings per share and total shareholder return. He stated that the Business Review contains a double page that shows the links between the three KPIs and the strategy strands, and the deliverables for each strategy, which demonstrate the company's achievements throughout the year.

He also indicated that some companies disclose KPIs because they feel they have to have them, but which are not used by the board in the management of the business. He considered that KPIs should be a genuine management tool and not simply a disclosure or PR exercise:

> There are lots of PIs – the focus should be on disclosing those that are Key.

Some concerns were voiced over the challenges of developing non-financial KPIs that are meaningful to both investors and the executive management, particularly if the issues looked at by investors are strategy related, and the issues faced by companies are operational.

For Rosemary Martin and others, the challenges of measurement have been considerable. Helen Jones' approach has encompassed more KPIs, but the challenge is reducing the list to meaningful KPIs that businesses can start reporting. She stated that each company measures CO_2 in different ways, which requires a co-ordinated approach. Yet, she suggested that this is not sympathetic to the way her business operates, which is that each company has its own consumer markets and knows what is best in those markets – not those individuals at the centre in group headquarters.

Similarly the legal nature of using non-financial KPIs poses some problems, as described by Paul Griffiths, who considered that the challenge is for companies to ensure that, when they move from using KPIs internally and include them in a legal document, there is an underlying quality platform.

KPIs can be an important tool for investors. Daniel Summerfield commented on the importance of non-financial KPIs, describing them as absolutely key for providing investment guidance, although companies are not used to reporting on them. One difficulty may be the interpretation of 'non-financial'. He used the term 'extra financial' instead of non-financial because individuals may consider that non-financial means 'not financial' (and hence not relevant), and 'extra financials' include intangibles. However, the disadvantage of using this term is that individuals discount intangible assets as these cannot be measured.

The choice of KPIs must be based on business criticality. In this respect Peter Elwin commented that there are risks for investors regarding KPIs. He was concerned that the temptation for a company is to go back to boiler plate, which is not particularly informative. He recognised that the challenge is striking a balance between what investors want to know and what the company is prepared to divulge, suggesting that investors want clarity and a continuity of consistent and relevant information:

> Investors will refer to KPIs if they feel the companies believe in them . . . I hope businesses use the KPIs that they tend to use in analysts' presentations – but if the KPIs are used only for the Business Review, and not for managing the business, then analysts will ignore them.

Professional advisers recognised that KPIs were new to some companies. Tom Ward cited one listed client who is taking advice on non-financial KPIs because standard KPIs are not those used to manage his business. Tom Ward suggested that the legislation is very vague and that the approach of unlisted companies will be to refer to the minimum KPIs possible.

In contrast, Giles Peel stated that he would be surprised if determining KPIs was difficult because KPIs are part of the way the business is managed. However, he considered that finding the right level would be challenging for companies.

David Phillips concluded that all companies have struggled with the concept of KPIs. He did not consider that an income statement was a KPI.

Risks

One of the bigger challenges for companies that are dual listed in the United Kingdom and United States relates to risks because such companies must produce a 20F report to meet US requirements.

Rosemary Martin stated that unlike the UK regulations, the US regulations require that the list of risks should not include a description of the mitigation of those risks. She suggested that this could result in the absurd position of describing risks with mitigations in the front of the document, with the US risk review being formally disclosed at the back.

However, Robert Aitken considered that currently existing legal requirements for the financial services industry were of benefit when it came to reporting on risk indicators as a result of the introduction of the Capital Requirements Directive 2003. He indicated that he always examines KPIs and how they can be improved. His company has a one-and-a-half-year track record, which has been an iterative process, paring down risks to those that are meaningful.

For companies dealing with KPIs for the first time, however, the process has been a learning curve, as was described by Paul Griffiths, who said that articulating risk factors is something that has not been done thoroughly in the past.

Amongst the investors, Paul Lee suggested that the area of risks is probably one of the weakest areas of reporting. He expected to see only the principal risks (not 'everything bar the kitchen sink') and a short statement about their mitigation:

> More than 5–6 and this indicates the Board may not be managing or in control.

This was reflected in comments by Daniel Summerfield who suggested that some companies are reporting on risks in a way not necessarily designed to enable investors to utilise them easily in their decision-making.

The professional advisers recognised that companies were having difficulty describing business risks. David Phillips suggested that risks are badly reported, ranging from nothing to the US 'kitchen sink' approach.

Tom Ward suggested that smaller listed companies may not report risks very effectively, often because of a lack of resources.

Style of Business Review

David Loweth commented on the importance of the correct balance in reporting. Good and bad news should be included, as relevant, and a description of the resources of the business – especially given that over 70% of the value of FTSE100 is represented by intangibles.

The company practitioners considered that style was important. Their boards had been used to the more familiar annual report format, and some practitioners considered that a significant challenge lay in familiarising boards with the new requirements and ensuring that they were comfortable with the process.

Helen Jones referred to the need to help executives to get used to style changes. She indicated that the challenge has been to get directors to think carefully about the structured way in which the Business Review requires information to be presented.

Rosemary Martin talked about developing the style of the report in a way consistent with the factual (not 'fluffy') business approach of her company's business. Her intention is that the Business Review represents the views of the board (written by people, as humans). She believes that this makes the Review more personal, in contrast to the way in which the company reported previously.

Simon Enoch considered that the best approach was for company secretaries to stress to their boards that all the data had been previously available in the public domain, but was now being collated in the annual report.

The challenges included how to handle the statements of the chairman and chief executive.

Helen Jones suggested that the chairman's letter should be retained because of its PR qualities, highlighting aspects of the year's results and thanking people. She expects that the CEO's review will introduce the Business Review.

Several practitioners had considered using the independent audit approach. Paul Griffiths been able to construct a Business Review using this approach, which incorporated the conventional chairman/CEO letter.

Nicholas Hodson commented that from the point of view of style, a glossy annual report was 'sometimes good and sometimes bad'. He suggested that the contents are pulled out of the analysts' presentation, so there is not very much over and above the preliminary results.

Impact of Companies Act 2006 on Business Review

New definition of directors' duties

The first question was to consider how the new definition of director's duties in the Companies Act 2006 would impact, including in relation to reporting responsibilities.

Richard Thorpe commented that anecdotally he had heard that audit committees are taking the new responsibilities very seriously, and that they have given rise to more serious debates between auditors and audit committees.

Many company practitioners felt that this was more of a codification of existing case law rather than 'new' legislation, with many suggesting that it would make little difference in their companies, and possibly not even in the bigger world. However, some considered that it would take time before the true impact could be identified. Some suggested further that new processes will be put in place, including changing minutes to formally record when 'account had been taken of all the areas and on balance [it was] found it to be in the best interests of the shareholders'.

This more cautious approach may reflect concerns that, whilst the strict legal approach may indicate no change, the biggest concern of all businesses is their reputation. Simon Enoch suggested that these duties may give statutory help to NGOs and other splinter groups, even if this is not legally a sustainable action.

Robert Aitken related directors' duties to the need to ensure the integrity of non-executive directors. The desire and willingness of people to be non-executives may change accordingly.

All the investors believed that the new duties will have relatively little impact, although Peter Elwin suggested that they will subtly alter behaviour, albeit not in terms of corporate behaviour.

An interesting perspective, perhaps more from the position of smaller listed and unlisted companies, was given by Tom Ward. He suggested that directors may not have realised the impact of case law on directors' duties. He gave as an example the responsibility for employees which has existed for many years, but will be brought more into focus under the new duties. He considered that directors' behaviour will change through a new awareness of their responsibilities under the Act.

Giles Peel suggested that directors have been very dependent on advisers but that different legal views are held even within the same profession. As a result some companies are very relaxed, whilst others are concerned that board minutes are written in particular ways.

David Phillips suggested that there would continue to be a high degree of polarity. He expected that boards will fall into two camps – those that are confident in their own judgment and those that will be challenged by the legislation. However, he is optimistic that companies are run today with a clear view of their stakeholders, and with the interests of customers, staff, suppliers, etc. clearly in mind:

> But I do worry about the risk of increased litigation and it is something everyone from Government down must be wary of.

New reporting requirements

In addition to the new definition of directors' duties, the Act requires a more rigorous set of requirements for listed companies in relation to the Business Review. Overall, the attitude of the company practitioners was that the new requirements will not pose any additional strains, although the issue of forward-looking statements is clearly not fully resolved by the advent of the safe harbour provision. For the professional advisers, Giles Peel suggested that the new regime will roll forward reasonably well, but that there is constant pressure to dumb down because advisers are risk averse.

David Phillips and Seamus Gillen compared the OFR with the 2006 Business Review. David Phillips suggested that the Business Review is essentially the OFR, absent the requirement to report on strategy. However, he said that, as the ASB has pointed out, most companies are reporting on strategy since this is the critical foundation on which all reporting is built. Seamus Gillen considered that this will not cause turbulence. David Phillips considered that the main challenge of the Business Review will be in helping people understand the requirements of the legislation. He suggested that it was easier to comply with the old OFR because of RS1, which put some flesh on the bones of primary legislation. This direct link no longer exists under the Business Review, but his advice to companies is to continue to use RS1 as key guidance.

Sallie Cooke Pilot suggested that companies are currently bringing forward 2006 requirements into their current Business Reviews. She believes that this will focus companies' sights on complying with an external standard, with the annual report providing an opportunity for companies to demonstrate how directors are fulfilling their duties.

Issue of safe harbour

The issue of safe harbour is causing some difficulties. The regulators' view was that the safe harbour provision should help companies with forward-looking statements. However, David Loweth suggested that the danger is that a boiler plate approach may be taken, which provides very little information.

Similarly, regulators stated the need for companies to comment on policies and their effectiveness, and the expectation is that companies will tread cautiously. However, some companies may see the value in having to make the s. 404 Sarbanes Oxley attestation that controls are in place and are effective.

The company practitioners were concerned about the links between derivative actions and statutory liability regime. Helen Jones suggested that this may have knock-on effects to D&O insurance policies and that single issue NGOs may take derivative actions.

In relation to what was described as the Rumsfeld test – whereby all directors are required to certify to the auditors that they have been provided with all the information they need to know about the company – concern was voiced about the ability of the board to sign off this certification, which may require an elaborate process to be put in place so that management can certify to the board that it has provided all the necessary information. However, as was acknowledged, all non-executives must rely on that statement, trusting management and the internal controls in place.

Amongst the professional advisers, Tom Ward suggested that directors are more concerned about statements doing harm to their companies' reputation rather than the potential of being sued. In this respect, he regarded the safe harbour provisions as the most extreme route.

Best practice for Business Review reporting

When asked about views on best practice in company reporting, a common theme was the use of the OFR's Reporting Statement as the basis for best practice reporting. In particular its consistency of approach was considered to be important. It was even suggested that buy-side analysts had looked at the predictions made in the previous year's OFR, evaluated how well they had been achieved, and used the degree of success as a basis for evaluating the current year's OFR predictions.

Sallie Cooke Pilot put the use of the Reporting Statement in a context that enabled all sizes of companies to apply it to their own Business Review. She recommended the OFR Reporting Statement as best practice:

> But not in a prescriptive manner . . . OFR or BR, it doesn't matter what it's called; what matters is the content – and using the guidelines helps.

Perhaps as a means of making the Reporting Statement more applicable to all sizes of listed companies, David Loweth suggested that the ASB may consider whether it can be more closely aligned with the 2006 Business Review by means of updates.

The more important issue was the content and style of the Business Review. Helen Jones commented that best practice had more to do with structure of the way the Business Review is written. Similarly, Rosemary Martin said that the Review should represent a readable document that people can use, clearly articulating the business, the direction in which it is going, and the risks associated with it, to the best of the company's ability.

Paul Griffiths emphasised that studious following of best practice may not be the route forward, and that what is right for one company may not be right for another. He considered that the Review should be more about the business – not generic or boiler plate – because it represents a company's communications to its shareholders. Simon Bicknell was concerned about overuse of the term 'best practice' because in reality it is subjective, and practitioners differ in their views and approaches.

Paul Griffiths commented on Business Review reporting from the point of view of subsidiaries. He considered that what a group has reported for external purposes may not be as relevant for subsidiaries, which will use either generic (PwC-based) or business-specific models. From his perspective, subsidiaries should get advice and guidance from the parent.

Tom Ward considered that in relation to poor and best practice, it is easier to say what amounts to poor practice, which in his opinion overemphasises the historical perspective of information. Too many companies ignore the fact that investors invest in other companies – and that they can manage risk through their portfolios.

David Loweth suggested that, to an extent, the development of Business Reviews will be investor led. This would require more consultation with investors through bodies such as the Corporate Reporting Users Forum:

> Investors recognise they haven't got their act together in the past and acknowledge they haven't really engaged.

Paul Lee suggested that guidance was needed as to what investors can do to help companies make their reporting more relevant:

> We are doing what we can to get investor-led guidance for companies out in the market-place – guidance on the right approach, not a prescribed format or list of contents. We and our peers need to find the mechanism to get our messages across as to what we are expecting, and celebrate good practice when we find it.

Daniel Summerfield suggested that investors will take a view on reporting in June or July based on the 31 March year-end reports, at which time they will make a decision of the extent to which companies have risen to the challenge. As a consequence, investors will need to provide feedback to companies and consider whether it is necessary to develop guidelines.

Benefits of good quality Business Review reporting

Paul Lee suggested that the good quality of Business Review reporting will be very beneficial:

> It should drive better strategic thinking because the process drives the board to talk about the issues, have them formally on board agendas and so ensure that all directors are more fully engaged in the process.

Sallie Cooke Pilot said that she has always been a huge advocate of reports as a tool to communicate the investment proposition – how much value has been created, how that value was generated and why the company is well placed to continue to create value. She believed that companies are now beginning to see the benefit of better reporting. She considered that businesses will gain with significant internal benefits, as a result of better decision-making and more joined-up thinking between internal and external messaging.

Seamus Gillen added that the more emotional empathy that goes into the report, the more the company will communicate its value proposition. He suggested that this acts as a proxy for the focus and commitment of the management team, and the strength of the company culture. He believed that this approach will encourage a deeper strategic perspective about managing business-critical issues, and that there is a deepening realisation that the company may not have been playing all its cards to its advantage.

David Phillips emphasised that the Business Review gives financial reporting a context, and that, for example, whilst it is helpful to know that a company is growing 10% year on year, more helpful is to know that the market has grown by 20% or that the company's growth has arisen through price increases and not volume.

Seamus Gillen commented about companies not taking full credit for their actions:

> There has been too much that is silent information.

However, he also considered that with this information set, the annual report has greater value and relevance. He commented that research with investors shows that some investors rely only on the prelims of the report, but that more considered and analytical investors utilise the annual report extensively.

Richard Thorpe made reference to the importance of narrative reporting in helping to understand 'fair value'. Being particularly involved with the financial services sector, he considered it important that readers of reports are informed about the underlying assumptions behind values derived from financial models – such as future interest rates, inflation and rates of growth. These, combined with the management perception of the level of risk in their business and the risk in the economy, help inform readers of the strength of the company's performance in the future.

Paul Moxey commented on the importance of understanding how well the company is governed, together with risk reporting and the company's strategy. He referred to the first principle of the Combined Code, which includes matters such as setting and monitoring the achievement of objectives, the setting of company values and how embedded these are. He believed that companies should be reporting on these matters.

He considered that best practice requires companies to report on the whole picture. From the investors' view, the Business Review has the potential of describing everything in a balanced and articulate manner, with a full overview of the organisation and its prospects:

> A story of results, prospects, where it wants to go and how well it has done, information on risks, and on its business environment.

NOTE

1 It should be noted that the FSA has no formal view or interest on corporate reporting – its obligation is to ensure that the information shareholders need is made available to the market.

CHAPTER **14**

Future of corporate reporting – views from the users

KEY ISSUES

- What is the future for corporate reporting
  - Expectations
  - What they thought would happen
  - Value of company report and accounts
- Opportunities offered by electronic communications
  - Default to electronic communications
  - Web used as part of corporate reporting format
- Real time reporting and other new forms of reporting
  - Possible introduction of real time reporting
  - Quarterly management statements
  - Management commentary
- Other issues
  - Role and practice of auditors
  - Nature of regulation
  - Verification
  - Private equity

Introduction

A key area of interest of the interviewees (see Chapters 12–14) was how they expected corporate reporting to develop. Companies will become familiar with the Business Review over the next few years and how they can use it to their advantage. For this purpose, the interviewees were asked their views on likely developments over the next five to 10 years (both in terms of what they hoped will arise and what they think is most likely to occur), their thoughts on how electronic communications may affect corporate reporting, and their views on the likelihood of the Big Six's prediction that real time reporting will come to fruition. They were also asked whether there were any other issues that they believed merited discussion.

What is the future for corporate reporting?

Expectations

David Loweth suggested that in terms of corporate reporting companies will highlight key issues, have a more innovative approach towards using the web, and produce shorter reviews. He suggested that the summary report could include the Business Review, with a series of supplements on the web providing fuller detail, and the full set of the annual report and accounts consequently becoming more of a filing requirement.

Some of the company practitioners hoped for a calming down after a raft of new legislation. Paul Griffiths expected a settling down of the new regime. This was similar to Simon Enoch's hope that no new requirements are introduced, but perhaps less aspirational than Simon Bicknell's hope that companies will be left alone to get on with doing what they are good at.

Amongst the professional advisers, Giles Peel extended the view of shorter and web-based communication into a hope for greater interactivity. He suggested that the entire shift has to be a mirror image of what is happening on the internet. He hoped that corporate reporting will be forced down the route of producing more informal and more frequent information. Further, he suggested that the biggest revolution may be more two-way communication between companies and the people to whom they report.

Amongst the communicators and commentators, many of whom echoed the hope for brevity and succinctness, Sallie Cooke Pilot suggested reordering information in the report to reduce repetition, and that information be included more selectively. Most importantly she emphasised that information should focus on the material issues affecting a business:

> If you started from scratch, it would be fundamentally different – I think you'd have a very different style of report with a more common sense approach to setting the framework for the company story.

What they thought would happen

In discussing the reality of what would happen to reporting over the next five to 10 years, a more sanguine approach emerged. David Loweth suggested that the reality will be evolutionary rather than revolutionary – and it will take longer than 10 years because companies are fundamentally cautious.

There was a relative consistency of views between the company practitioners. One suggestion was that with the fullness of time, when activists realise that the changes have not achieved what they expected, the Government will be under lobbying pressure to do more.

Helen Jones was concerned with the possible development of a nanny state approach to amending the legislation should the strategy fail.

This was echoed by Simon Enoch who said that politicians and professional bodies are pushing for more disclosure, and may only be satisfied once they have realised the SEC's desire for real time reporting.

This was reflected to some extent by Robert Aitken who, although he could not envisage the level of reporting reaching US levels, considered that UK and European requirements are increasing as business is becoming more complex. He suggested that the complexity of modern business drives the need for greater regulation.

Amongst the investors Nicholas Hodson believed that regulation will continue at the present trend. He suggested that the idea of 'letting the market decide' is still a possibility but that regulators are pressing for more information more frequently.

However, Peter Elwin suggested that the annual report will remain a central document – probably electronically with hyperlinks. In this respect, he expected companies to be forced to use XBRL[1] because the US SEC wants this, although he was sceptical about the technology.

Daniel Summerfield believed that an integration of silos is necessary, and that remuneration reporting is often written out of context with the company's strategic reporting. He gave as an example one company's remuneration report that stated that targets were being achieved easily, contrasting with the statements in the chairman's report.

Paul Lee's concern echoed that of the company practitioners when he said that regulators would get too involved, making it a difficult compliance-driven process, rather than allowing the board to write the story as it sees it.

Amongst the professional advisers, Tom Ward suggested that listed and unlisted companies will take different approaches. He believed that unlisted companies' reports will be reduced and simplified, but that listed companies will continue with the same levels of disclosure because analysts read the report. He emphasised that reports are not intended for shareholders. Instead, he suggested that shareholders will move more to summary versions, and that in a few years' time only analysts will receive full reports.

Paul Moxey considered that companies will only go part of the way towards providing better governance reporting. Giles Peel considered that because companies are always 'looking over their shoulder' in relation to corporate reporting, the likelihood is that they will tend, over time, to go for the least-information approach on the basis that this is what they can get away with – a lowest common denominator philosophy.

However, David Phillips believed that there will be a big step change in terms of internal thinking because of the development of competitive pressures within industry, the introduction of external mechanisms such as benchmarking of companies' performance, and regulation from the FRRP. The latter, he believed, has teeth, although he hoped that the FRRP will let practices evolve. At the same time he recognised that there will be issues around consistency of measures, for example retail indicator of sales per square foot, which can be interpreted differently by different companies.

Like many of the company practitioners, the concern of Jonathan Hynes in relation to communicators and commentators was that there would be an even thicker wedge of compliance regulations. He suggested that reports will become more rather than less opaque and that there will be an increase in the sheer volume of detail:

> The approach will be a Lego Brick approach to corporate reporting – make up your own investment story out of the following component parts.

Tim Ambler commented on the long-term trend towards increasing transparency – beginning with the 1906 Act, which provided legislation on balance sheet reporting. He believed that business accepts that this is a long-term trend and that more transparency is a good thing. At the same time, however, he considered that the excessive size of reports, together with the boiler plating manner in which they are compiled, does not help the purpose of annual reports, which is to provide a clear description of the company as seen by the directors.

Value of company report and accounts

Richard Thorpe recognised that the report provides the ability to predict future cash flows, and that if investors are going to evaluate the residual stewardship responsibility of directors, a set of annual accounts is needed.

He went on to say that the introduction of fair value in accounting practice changes the value of annual accounts, because they are likely to be no longer relevant two days after their preparation. However, he believed that there is a benefit in having an annual statement from the directors to shareholders stating that:

> this is what we have done with [your] money and this is what we believe we should be able to do going forward.

David Loweth suggested that instead of looking at just the issue of narrative reporting there was a need to step back and consider the total reporting picture, questioning what is required from corporate governance reporting. He commented that annual reporting has become confusing:

> There has been an Elastoplast approach of incremental additions to annual reports that came with each new regulation.

Many company practitioners questioned the value of greater disclosure. Helen Jones suggested that the reality is that the more disclosure, the less people see: 'they don't even read the summary accounts'. She believed that shareholders read details on only the profit, dividends and directors' remuneration, and provided the first two are going up and the third is going down, they are content. Shareholders will be happy to see directors' remuneration rise only if it does so at a rate commensurate with profit and dividends.

Rosemary Martin commented upon legal issues, stating that there is a big question over directors' liability, with two matters moving in opposite directions. She suggested that, on the one hand, markets are requiring more information, available electronically and related to investors' interests, whilst, on the other hand, directors have more awareness of the need to provide more accurate and verifiable information provided in a formal business document. She is uncertain how these two trends will play out.

In addition, she also questioned the purpose of the annual report. However, in her view investors do not get all the information they need from the annual report, instead acquiring this from sources such as analysts' presentations and information on blogs. She commented that some investors are looking for 'accurate enough', very up-to-date information, rather than 100% accurate but old information. As a result, she believed that the annual report is becoming less meaningful, and that there is more reliance on informal reporting. Overall, she felt that corporate reporting may become less important since a company's formal documents will be only one thread in a rich tapestry of information available to investors:

> A lot of information will not be on our websites – but on those of other people, including blogs.

Robert Aitken made a similar point when he stated that financial reports are difficult to follow, and that analysts, investors and the credit analysts are looking for different types of information in the reports. However, he questioned the purpose served by annual reports, and at what audience they are aimed. He considered that there is opportunity to acquire more information from other forms of financial reporting, such as the financial media, rather than from a set of historic information. Simon Bicknell thought that investors should express their opinions more directly about what they want from annual reports:

> There should be a framework relationship between the owners and the managers of their capital.

Sallie Cooke Pilot suggested that the challenge for companies is to develop reporting to improve stakeholder relationships and increase business benefits. She believed that the best reporting focuses more on trends and how the company is positioning the business to capitalise on these trends, rather than the results themselves.

Seamus Gillen suggested that one of the benefits of the narrative report is the way in which the process used to construct it can help companies unearth the value locked in their business, which is a precondition for leveraging further value. He saw the opportunity for far better communication of the value proposition to people who matter most – the investors.

Opportunities offered by electronic communications

The issue of electronic communications touches upon two areas. First, the Companies Act 2006 enables companies to move to a default position, whereby they advise shareholders that they will communicate company reports electronically, and make them available for access via electronic means. The second relates to the consequence of such a move, and whether, if the annual report is available only via the web (unless specifically requested by shareholders in a hard copy format), companies can maximise its effectiveness.

Default to electronic communications

For the corporate practitioners, Paul Griffiths commented that by defaulting to electronic communications, the requirement to produce a hard copy report could be as low as 5–10% of the register. He suspected that for small print runs (less than 5,000), the marginal cost of copies would be disproportionately large. Instead he suggested that the approach may be to develop a desk-top published solution, provided this was produced professionally.

In contrast, Helen Jones commented that even with previous attempts to incentivise shareholders to move to a summary report, only about 15% responded positively. She suggested that moving to a default electronic communication could represent a potentially high reputation risk amongst retail shareholders. She was not convinced that shareholders will read over 60 pages on screen – and that they will not be prepared to use their own facilities to print it out.

Simon Bicknell did not share this view, commenting that there was unlikely to be a strong response from shareholders, given the extent of their lack of interest in the annual report.

This view was shared by Simon Enoch, who commented that the potential print production savings would be negligible because of high set-up costs, but pointed out that with postage costs at £5 or more per report, this is the area where cost savings could be made.

Tim Ambler thought that those shareholders who opt not to receive the full report and accounts – but go instead to the summary version – will not receive the Business Review or the OFR. He believed that the summary version should have the Business Review (or OFR) included.

However, Sallie Cooke Pilot said that it will be impossible to reduce print entirely, and suggested that there is a need for a more integrated approach to reporting. In her opinion the challenge will be to have a more joined-up communications effort and integrate electronic communications as appropriate. Communicating key messages for many companies will still be pertinent, especially if the company's shareholders are also customers, for example in the utilities sector.

This view was backed up by Jonathan Hynes, who thought that the printed annual report will remain. He suggested that the death of the printed report is greatly exaggerated because it serves an entirely different need, with a chairman presenting to an investment committee, etc. His view was that the printed version used in conjunction with a fit-for-purpose, rewritten, re-edited electronic version would provide extra avenues in which to communicate to audiences.

Seamus Gillen considered that using electronic communications to drive value was a benefit, although he did not think that the hard copy would disappear. He suggested that e-communications would increasingly allow people to ask for and, eventually, view the content how and when they required it:

❝ Narrative is about content and content drives value. ❞

Web used as part of corporate reporting format

Using the web as part of the corporate reporting format provoked the most discussion amongst the interviewees. Most company practitioners suggested that there would be few changes because everything is already on screen, i.e. the annual report, analysts' presentations, and video and web casts.

Robert Aitken suggested that flexible use of the website will offer more interactivity, not as a chat room but as making available more segmented information. However, he expressed concern that information is only as good as the people producing it, and with it comes the need for a process of validation.

Simon Bicknell highlighted the potential problems for extending web-based information for dual listed companies. He suggested the production of an annual report that has links to other parts of the website, for example to more detailed environmental information. He indicated that, essentially, everything on the web should be brought within the confines of the reporting document. His concern was that the whole website could become a reporting document in US terms, whereby a reference to another part of the web incorporates that information into the annual report. As a result, a US shareholder may be entitled to rely on the veracity of the information at any given time, based on a process of due diligence and verification. However, he also considered that the information on the web can become out of date very quickly.

Rosemary Martin thought that the approach to web communications should be cautious, avoiding anything that would give rise to legal issues. More corporate responsibility KPIs could be put on the website. In this respect, she suggested that the report could link to other documents. The website version of the report will therefore be more interesting than the printed version, perhaps with links to comments that do not form part of the formal report.

In the opinion of the investors, it was clear that the web was not necessarily the answer to their needs. Nicholas Hodson pointed out that some very good fund managers do not use electronic communications, such as Bloomberg, Reuters or the internet, but instead use the *Financial Times* and the annual report.

Peter Elwin emphasised the importance of understanding the management's views – at first hand. He considered that the market wants to assess the management's credibility face to face in order to evaluate their ability to deal with Rumsfeld's unknown unknowns.[2] Directors should explain their position with a few very focused messages, which they do effectively on a face-to-face basis but not so well in the annual report. At the same time, he accepted that it would be more sensible for the compliance document to be available on the web, with relevant pictures. However, he stated that the annual report is not dead, suggesting that investors want companies to describe themselves in the round. He believed that shareholders want to be able to view one document that gives details of the company's performance, risks and strategy, avoiding boiler plate and advertising puff.

Daniel Summerfield was more supportive of electronic communications, to provide investors with real time comprehensive information about companies. He considered that XBRL has a role to play and that companies need to provide a wider range of information. David Phillips was also an advocate of XBRL. He saw its potential in terms of avoiding audited accounts being disaggregated by intermediaries, which can distort and corrupt information. However, he saw the value of information being tagged by XBRL because it can be passed directly from the company to the spreadsheet of any analyst interested in that company's stock.

Paul Lee suggested that more information will be available on the web and there will be much less reliance on printed annual reports:

> It may be the end of the printed report as we know it – but not the annual report and accounts as such, which will always prove to be necessary.

For the professional advisers, Paul Moxey emphasised that, in theory, anything price sensitive must be released immediately, but that there should be better two-way communications between company and shareholders. Companies are happy to talk to institutional investors on a confidential basis, but do not want other retail investors asking questions. Whilst institutional investors are more aware of their fiduciary duties towards the people who actually fund them, he believed that there is a long way to go from awareness to actual accountability to the people who are the real investors.

Perhaps unsurprisingly, the communicators and commentators saw real potential in greater use of electronic communications. Sallie Cooke Pilot said that there is an opportunity for more targeting, viewing stakeholders as part of a company's marketing approach and using database management. She emphasised the importance of assessing the success of the communications programme for the annual report:

> Imagine if a Marketing Director walked into a room and was asked how the annual report went down and said "Oh well, no news is good news" – it would be unacceptable – no results, no impact, no nothing – that's ridiculous.

The need for improved quality of communications on the web was considered by Jonathan Hynes, who related it to the SEC's suggestion that electronic voting should be available to companies and shareholders, and commented that in order to have better, more enfranchised voting, shareholders need to be better informed. He considered that the logical conclusion of more enfranchisement is the need for better reporting, because the existing annual report format is not good enough for that purpose:

> The book is linear – the web isn't! Offer shareholders the opportunities to follow the information they are interested in – it will be self-driven discovery.

Real time reporting and other new forms of reporting

Possible introduction of real time reporting

The possibility of introducing real time reporting was discussed by the heads of the Big Six accounting practices, and provoked an almost resounding view amongst the interviewees of its impracticality. The company practitioners commented on the issues around technology and of managing accounting adjustments on a more frequent basis.

Interestingly, the investors were very much against the introduction of real time reporting. Nicholas Hodson commented that he would prefer to have an event he can trade around, and questioned why anyone would suggest that real time reporting is a good thing.

Several questioned the level of detail required by investors. Peter Elwin suggested that investors want the management view, including that on risks and rewards:

> They are paying the managers to run the business – they don't want the general ledger.

In addition Paul Lee commented that the potential danger of real time reporting is that it will focus companies on short-term behaviour in the investment markets. This issue was also mentioned by David Phillips, who expressed his concern about its likely resulting volatility, although he pointed out that companies are required by the listing rules to report any new material information that arises.

There was a strong sense amongst the communicators and commentators of the challenges regarding the number of times companies are already reporting. For smaller companies, with investor relations departments of two or less, even compiling the annual report is a challenge. More frequent reporting would be overburdensome.

Simon Enoch pointed out that he is already in direct communication with the market in one form or another every eight weeks or so with pre-close statements, prelims, full booklets, and quarter 1 and 3 results and half year. He believed that the market is kept fully informed of his sales trends all the way through the year. He added that the quality of real time information is questionable and that he could see no real benefit for investors or companies.

Quarterly management statements

Quarterly management statements are formally required under the Companies Act 2006, resulting in companies reporting more frequently than at present. For the company practitioners, Helen Jones spoke positively about the experience of producing these statements 'because ours are voluntary'. She stated that once people start producing the quarterly statement under the Transparency Directive, they can also include quarterly sales and profit. She pointed out that her company does not report on net operating, post-tax or post-central expenses, but only to the level of retail profit (because, in her view, this is what analysts understand), and offers guidance on changes in trends, for example if the interest charge is likely to be more than expected.

Simon Bicknell also commented favourably, based on his experience that his quarterly reports are driven by UK requirements rather than anything else. He believed that quarterly reporting gives a more transparent view of how the business is run and, whilst some people say that it gives a focus only on the short term, he does not consider this to be the case.

Robert Aitken emphasised the risk of data being taken out of context, suggesting that the key issue is how reliable the data are. For example, the annual bonus cycle can change the year-end figures significantly, and monthly profit and loss would only be an estimate.

Amongst the investors, Nicholas Hodson suggested that companies already report a lot of detail. He believed that increased reporting may cause increased volatility, as well as being an unwanted diversion for management:

> I would prefer management run the business rather than spend excessive time reporting on it.

Helen Jones questioned whether companies will continue to produce preliminary announcements, but concluded that such practice should be maintained as a means of getting information into the public domain that can be discussed in the analysts' presentations.

Management commentary

Regulators were supportive of the possible introduction of a management commentary. However, David Loweth noted that it would be some time before a final document saw the light of day. Whilst this would provide a framework for use globally, he believed that the key issue is whether it becomes a mandatory requirement or only part of practice guidelines. He suggested that the commentary is essentially the same as the OFR and the Reporting Statement, and that its key benefit would be common ground across the world. However, amongst the investors, Paul Lee was unhappy about its possible introduction. He stated that the IASB should not proceed with it because it is not an accounting standard as such, and that the IASB should concentrate instead on getting the existing accounting standards up to scratch.

Other issues

The interviewees were given the opportunity to raise any other issues they felt were important regarding corporate reporting.

David Loweth raised the issue of the inclusion of the Business Review as part of the directors' report, stating that the EAMD merely requires a Business Review to be included as part of the annual accounts as a whole and does not focus on the directors' report. If this were changed, it could allow more flexibility for companies to produce more constructive reports.

This focus on making the report more constructive was echoed by Paul Griffiths, who commented that key is making certain that the report is clear and not subject to boiler plating, with excessive use of model practices. It would also mean avoiding the US practice of 'looking over one's shoulder' for fear of litigation. It would also allow people to understand the nature of the company, what is important for the board and how the board runs the business.

David Phillips took a broader view of the role of report, looking beyond the annual report to understanding the data set. He considered that every form of communications should be built off this data set. In this respect he focused on what he regarded as the important question: who are we trying to serve? He suggested that the annual report is compiled for one reason and one reason only – to put information into the market:

> The questions we should be asking are whether this is the right information set, and are we delivering it with the frequency required? We have to fight this space and avoid moving ahead for regulatory purposes.

Robert Aitken commented on the fact that annual reports are serving a multiple audience, a role for which they were never designed – hence the scale issue. He considered that if investor surveys are conducted, the aim should be to see who is actually using the annual report and whether they are using all of it:

> If you can't comfortably answer that this is what the shareholder wants, then you should ask the question whether it is serving the right purpose.

Role and practice of auditors

In relation to the role and practice of auditors, Richard Thorpe touched upon the question of audit reports. He suggested that the pendulum swings backwards and forwards between the role of the auditor in reviewing everything in the accounts and then giving a clean opinion and the role of the auditor in commenting on what is in the accounts and then giving no opinion at all. He considered that the pendulum is swinging back towards some level of commentary. Paul Lee discussed the nature of audit reporting, saying that if this could be improved this would consequently improve the quality of the annual report. He referred to the Audit Quality Forum recommendations that suggest a more active than passive report, so that investors can see that they are getting more value out of the process:

> Currently audit reports don't say anything of value – at the moment we don't read them because there's no point.

Nature of regulation

Rosemary Martin commented that in her opinion the burning issue regarding regulation is the Elastoplast approach. She suggested that the remuneration report may change over the next five years because the United States has more stringent regulations. This means that remuneration reporting may be considered again by the regulators, taking into account such things as exit provisions, etc. Robert Aitken also referred to the Elastoplast situation in relation to the size of rule books:

> Regulatory rule books have grown with each regulation – there is a need to stand back and review it overall.

Verification

On the suggested verification of environmental, social and governance (ESG) statements within a company's annual report, based on the comments of the ABI, Tom Ward considered the practicalities of auditing ESG statements, stating that some areas are difficult to audit, for example disclosure of risk management. However, he suggested that if an ESG statement is put in the context of audited reports, it must be audited. He considered that accounting standards have moved away from the reading of accounts, and away from objectivity, which may lead to the potential for manipulation.

He suggested that very few people currently do any further form of verification of the annual report. One of those who does, Helen Jones, commented that she had organised verification to prospectus standards for the past 10 years, although she doubted whether more than 10% of companies do verify. ESG verification to that standard will, however, prove more of a challenge, but she and her team are working on this.

David Phillips took the view that if investors and bodies such as the ABI want this information verified, the profession should take up the challenge. While this may not be easy, he believed that it would provide an environment in which the profession can reinforce its value to the market and provide insights as to how it can address the expectation gap that still exists around financial reporting.

The key issues, as he pointed out, are to explain and validate the information that the company uses internally, to verify that all material aspects of it have been reported externally and, possibly, to comment on how this performance compares with best practice. He suggested, perhaps not surprisingly, that verification is key to the future of auditing:

> This model requires professionals to exercise judgment which I believe is critical to the long term future of the audit profession.

Peter Elwin stated that there has been considerable effort applied to get companies to give CSR information, but very little effort to link this to hard core financials, for example staff turnover and productivity, and sales revenue or profitability. In this respect, he considered that if the information starts out as being irrelevant to the company's strategy or its financials, there is little use in verifying it. Having said that, he believed that if the information is of significance, it should be independently verified.

David Phillips also described the reporting challenges as some of big issues that are only now beginning to impact the corporate agenda.

This was reinforced by Seamus Gillen who commented on the apparent unwillingness of investors to factor ESG issues into their models. He considered that the primary responsibility for resolving this impasse lies with companies who are best placed to deepen the rigour of the materiality analysis, to ensure reporting of business-critical ESG issues only. In return, he believed that analysts and investors need to signal their willingness to acknowledge companies' efforts. The outcome will be higher-quality engagement between investors and companies, based on greater levels of confidence, on both sides, that reporting is centred around issues of strategic relevance. Value lies in both directions, and investors who price in relevant ESG issues more accurately may place themselves at a competitive advantage. In this respect, he regarded the recent ABI guidance as important in focusing on the core issues that matter to investors:

> If what goes into the Business Review does not appear credible, investors will ignore it. Investors are looking for evidence of high-quality disclosures as a pre-requisite for well-informed investment decisions.

Paul Moxey discussed the importance of ethics as part of the internal control framework, saying that nobody appeared to be doing this in any comprehensive manner – even though the Reporting Statement and the Combined Code require it. He expected that this will become more important in the future – and referred to the first principle of the Combined Code, which requires information about how values are embedded. He considered that this matter was about compliance versus performance, with compliance being the US approach. One can comply with the rule rather than the performance. He commented that the authors of CoSo (Committee of Sponsoring Organisations of the Treadway Commission) identified that the foundation of internal control is the control environment. This includes team work, motivation and culture (including ethics). Policies will be set, but whether they will be implemented effectively depends on the culture.

Private equity

Discussion was raised about the nature of corporate reporting relating to private equity in the UK market, given its increased activity. Tim Ambler commented on the imbalance in reporting between listed companies and private companies. He suggested that it is very unfair for British disclosure requirements to force listed companies to disclose material that private companies or foreign competitors do not have to provide:

> Even with private equity (which is able to communicate directly to their shareholders) there should be a level playing field.

Seamus Gillen also commented upon the increasing trend and importance of private equity interests acquiring public companies. One of the key features of the phenomenon, he suggested, is agency dysfunction between owners and managers, and the resulting inefficiency and lack of alignment in interests. He suggested that high-standard disclosure narrows this gap by generating increased transparency, visibility of operations and accountability, and, as a result, potentially reduces some of the inefficiencies on which private equity take-outs thrive.

Simon Enoch referred to the issues of private equity and commented that capital markets are only one form of financing a business. He considered that no business in the United Kingdom is immune from private equity. However, he came back to the question of regulation, suggesting that too many different bodies are concerned with corporate reporting:

> Everyone feels they are quite entitled to lay the rules down and we are in danger of rearranging the corporate reporting deckchairs on the Titanic.

NOTES

1. XBRL stands for Extensible Business Reporting Language – more details can found on its website at www.XBRL.org.
2. Donald Rumsfeld, US Secretary of Defense, attempted to clarify a point in a US Department of Defense news briefing on Iraq by stating that 'there are known knowns; there are things we know we know. We also know there are known unknowns; that is to say we know there are some things we do not know. But there are also unknown unknowns – the ones we don't know we don't know' (2 February 2002).

CHAPTER **15**

Some thoughts on the way forward

KEY ISSUES

- Compliance or a tool for investors?
- Effective communications?
- Future for the annual report
- Does this all matter?

Introduction

Chapters 12–14 provided a rich seam of thinking about how the corporate reporting scene has developed over the past decade and where it might go over the next decade. In gathering the thoughts of those who were interviewed, it was important not to give one individual's views greater dominance or value over others. What was important was to see the contrasts between their views and, as a result, to understand how these contrasts may be resolved over time.

However, now is the opportunity to make some judgments on what has been discussed and to provide some thoughts on the possible ways forward over the next decade, particularly in trying to balance the views of investors and company practitioners.

Compliance or a tool for investors?

The Business Review should be seen first in its position as a compliance document. If the board of a company seeks to give a limited view of its risks and information regarding its involvement with aspects such as the environment or its employees, then it is within its right to do so.

However, the clear message from the regulators and the investors (including the ABI) is that more is expected of companies than a mere compliance approach. The key issue appears to be the extent to which forward-looking statements will represent a quality comment on behalf of the board, and the extent to which they will be of value to investors as part of their investment decision-making.

Clearly, there seems to have been misunderstanding, as well as misgivings, amongst companies about what is expected from forward-looking statements, and the views expressed in Chapters 12–14 of regulators and investors should go some way (together with the safe harbour provision) to helping company practitioners determine how they should proceed with the statements. Whilst not expected to give detailed sets of figures, practitioners are expected to provide a contextual framework around which shareholders and potential investors can build their own valuation perspectives.

In this respect the description of risks (and the company's mitigations to help manage them) assists investors to determine how likely it is that the views included in the forward-looking statements will materialise. This forces companies to think in a joined-up manner. It also highlights the danger of chairmen deliberating on forward-looking statements in a vacuum apart from the risks inherent in the business. There should be a clear alignment between the forward-looking statement and the risks. In this respect, the comment of David Phillips that it is not about legislation but about 'how well companies are managed' comes into sharp focus.

Similarly, the inclusion of KPIs is critical in terms of investors being able to follow the forward thinking of the board. Companies that include KPIs that are not relevant to the way the business is managed will be seen by analysts as creating smoke screens. Analysts will use KPIs as trend indicators to evaluate the extent to which the company's ability to deliberate on future trends and developments is based on good or poor quality management skills, and value the company accordingly.

Undoubtedly, it will be helpful for companies to have more detailed guidance from the investment fraternity on the nature of the content expected to be included in Business Reviews. But ultimately how the board manages the business and demonstrates the strength of its internal management approach in its external reporting to its shareholders will be important. As David Phillips said:

> The UK has the best regulatory governance and reporting model in the world with the Combined Code and the Business Review – it is principles-based, allows companies to explain how they are run and provides the flexibility in reporting needed to get the right information set into the market.

Over the next five years the quality of Business Review reporting will improve in better meeting the needs of the shareholders and investors, but there may be some difficulties for boards along the way.

Effective communications?

Business Reviews will help improve the quality of information provision. However, what is particularly relevant from the comments in the previous chapters is the style of the production of the annual report itself. The guidance provided by the Report Leadership initiative, as well as, to a lesser extent, the approach of the Independent Audit, is of great value to companies.

Looking behind these guides, what comes across is not that annual reports should be glossy affairs. Instead, the emphasis is on making them readable and relevant to the reader. It seems that annual reports are rarely seen as part of a communication process. Instead, it appears that they are perceived as a compliance document, and, as such, not truly worthy of a communications evaluation.

Sallie Cooke Pilot's question about the extent to which annual reports are evaluated as part of a marketing campaign is a valid one. The fact that company practitioners regard their retail shareholders as not paying much attention to annual reports is not down to shareholder disinterest, but because shareholders do not see the content of the reports as relevant or useful to themselves.

The Report Leadership initiative uses strong management action words in each of its section headings, and the first of these is 'effective communications'. If nothing else comes out of the deliberations over new style reporting such as the OFR and the Business Review, the one change that it is reasonably confident to predict will arise in the next decade is that annual reports will improve in their quality of communication. Greater use of styles of reporting will make them more understandable, more readable and more relevant to their primary audience, the shareholders.

Future for the annual report

What was very striking about the comments of the interviewees in Chapters 12–14 was the apparent lack of value attached to the annual report. Institutional investors seemed to have mixed feelings about its value. Even amongst those who did consider annual reports to be important, such as Paul Lee, the focus was on certain elements (such as the notes to the accounts) being of particular value, with the remainder being of little use. Amongst the company practitioners, a common view seemed to be that retail investors saw little or no value in the annual report.

The importance of the annual report was emphasised in relation to the use of technology to link parts of the annual report on the web to other elements of particularly relevant interest to shareholders (or, even more importantly, of interest to other stakeholders). Discussion about the opportunities offered by XBRL to investors to tag specific parts of the report's data set, and download them onto their own spreadsheets, meant that the value of the annual report as a complete document became even more relevant.

With the likelihood of companies moving to electronic communications of results and reports as a default, the question that arises is what form of report is likely to be of greater use to a retail shareholder. It seems unlikely that shareholders will want to go to the time and expense of printing off a full version of the annual report. Instead, they are likely to favour the summary report.

On that basis, the nature of the annual report must be called into question. Why are companies still spending large amounts of money on glossy hard copy reports when they appear to be credited with such little value by either retail or institutional investors? The answer is probably that the hard copy report has become a traditional form of corporate communications, and, as such, not questioned.

How can companies best meet the needs of investors and shareholders? The following is one way in which corporate reporting and annual reports will move over time:

- **Full annual report** – the compliance and filing document – will be produced in Word format (without any pictures, but including graphs and charts) and will be posted only on the website. This format should allow reporting timescales to be reduced.
- **Summary report** (including a summary of the Business Review, and relevant pictures, graphs and charts) will be the default for shareholders and will be the document to which they are directed on the website.
- **Summary report** on the web will include links to other, more data-rich, areas of benefit if the user wishes to explore aspects in more detail. These will include thought pieces (perhaps from external observers) that will help elaborate on some of the discussion referred to in forward-looking statements. In addition, the CSR report will be held on the website, but only its business-critical performance indicators will be referred to within the annual or summary reports. There will be links available from the annual report to the CSR report for those who require greater detail.
- **Annual reports** will include XBRL links to enable investment analysts to create valuation models across companies based on the investment attributes they think are most relevant for them.

The above scenario will probably happen when a company (probably one of the larger companies) decides that it needs to take a more considered view of its corporate reporting communications. As part of this process, it will leave the path it has followed for the past 20 years, during which time technology has long since left it standing still. From that point on, other enlightened companies will break the established format of annual reports.

Does this all matter?

Some commentators will consider the outcomes of developments in corporate reporting to be irrelevant, since nothing will have changed in terms of the behaviour of the individuals or corporate bodies concerned. But there is evidence that attitudes in the corporate and the investment world are changing. One example is the acceptance of companies of the relevance of their own corporate social responsibility position as a potential factor in determining (or undermining) their own reputation, which subsequently impacts on their shareholder value.

At the same time, many commentators are addressing the issues of corporate governance and investor responsibility. One example is *The New Capitalists – How citizen investors are reshaping the corporate agenda*.[1] Written by individuals with great experience of the investment and corporate governance world, this suggests that the world's corporations are owned by the many, rather than the few, and that these owners are individuals whose assets are held in pension funds and the like.

The authors suggest that there is a new capitalist circle of accountability, involving corporations, institutional investors and boards of directors. They consider that corporations are facing pressure to transform themselves into institutions that are accountable to their citizen owners, and that investors are beginning to act as responsible proprietors.

They suggest that there are six key players who will act out the drama of the civil economy:

- company boards and managers, which need to be accountable;
- investment funds, which need to be responsible;
- monitors, who need to be independent;
- standards and measures, which need to be relevant;
- civil society groups, which need to be open to earn market access;
- lawmakers and regulators, who need to empower new capitalists.

The reader may argue about the extent to which the world of the new capitalist will come about. However, for business to be successful in any economy requires trust and credibility. The underlying message of some commentators is that trust and credibility can only be attained through ensuring effective corporate governance and relevant, transparent and accessible corporate reporting. These are the driving forces for both economic growth and a healthy respect between business and the other constituents of our society. The changes and developments in place now will deliver this growth and respect.

NOTE

1   Davis, Lukomnik and Pitt-Watson (Harvard Business Press, 2006).

Appendix 1
Form and content of company accounts as established under Companies Act 1985

The following is the format for balance sheets and profit and loss accounts under the Companies Act 1985, although an item need not be listed in this format if, for the year in question, there is no amount to be shown.

BALANCE SHEET

Two formats were permitted for this purpose. The first is shown below. The second is the more traditional 'assets and liabilities' format. To save excessive repetition, only the main headings are shown under format 2.

Format 1
A. Called up share capital not paid (1)
B. Fixed assets
   I. Intangible assets
      1. Development costs
      2. Concessions, patents, licences, trade marks and similar rights and assets
      3. Goodwill
      4. Payments on account
   II. Tangible assets
      1. Land and buildings
      2. Plant and machinery
      3. Fixtures, fittings, tools and equipment
      4. Payments on account and assets in the course of construction
   III. Investments
      1. Shares in group companies
      2. Loans to group companies
      3. Shares in related companies
      4. Loans to related companies
      5. Other investment other than loans
      6. Other loans
      7. Own shares

C. Current assets
  I. Stocks
    1. Raw materials and consumables
    2. Work in progress
    3. Finished goods and goods for resale
    4. Payments on account
  II. Debtors
    1. Trade debtors
    2. Amounts owed by group companies
    3. Amounts owed by related companies
    4. Other debtors
    5. Called up share capital not paid
    6. Prepayments and accrued income
  III. Investments
    1. Shares in group companies
    2. Own shares
    3. Other investments
  IV. Cash at bank and in hand
D. Prepayment and accrued income
E. Creditors
    1. Debenture loans
    2. Bank loans and overdrafts
    3. Payments received on account
    4. Trade creditors
    5. Bills of exchange payable
    6. Amounts owed to group companies
    7. Amounts owed to related companies
    8. Other credits including taxation and social security
    9. Accruals and deferred income
F. Net current assets (liabilities)
G. Total assets less current liabilities
H. Creditors: amounts falling due after more than one year
    1. Debenture loans
    2. Bank loans and overdrafts
    3. Payments received on account

    4. Trade creditors
    5. Bills of exchange payable
    6. Amounts owed to group companies
    7. Amounts owed to related companies
    8. Other credits including taxation and social security
    9. Accruals and deferred income
I. Provisions for liabilities and charges
    1. Pensions and similar obligations
    2. Taxation including deferred taxation
    3. Other provisions
J. Accruals and deferred income
K. Capital and reserves
    I. Called up share capital
    II. Share premium account
    III. Revaluation reserve
    IV. Other reserves
        1. Capital redemption reserve
        2. Reserve for own shares
        3. Reserves provided for by the articles of association
        4. Other reserves
    V. Profit and loss account

Format 2 (main headings only)
ASSETS
A. Called-up share capital not paid
B. Fixed assets
    I. Intangible assets
    II. Tangible assets
    III. Investments
C. Current assets
    I. Stocks
    II. Debtors (included prepayment and accrued income)
    III. Investments
    IV. Cash at bank and in hand

LIABILITIES
A. Capital and reserves

    I. Called up share capital
    II. Share premium account
    III. Revaluation reserve
    IV. Other reserves
    V. Profit and loss account
B. Provisions for liabilities and charges
C. Creditors
D. Accrual and deferred income

PROFIT AND LOSS ACCOUNT

Four formats were permitted for this purpose. The first is shown below, and is familiar as a summary version of the profit and loss account. The second is the more detailed format. Within this detail are included breakdowns of changes in stocks, staff costs depreciation and write-offs. The third and fourth are based on the concepts of charges and income. To save excessive repetition, only the first format is shown.

Format 1

1. **Turnover**
2. Cost of sales
3. **Gross profit or loss**
4. Distribution costs
5. Administrative expenses
6. Other operating income
7. Income from shares in group companies
8. Income from shares in related companies
9. Income from other fixed asset investments
10. Other interest receivable and similar income
11. Amounts written off investments
12. Interest payable and similar charges
13. Tax on profit or loss on ordinary activities
14. **Profit or loss on ordinary activities after taxation**
15. Extraordinary income
16. Extraordinary charges
17. Extraordinary profit or loss
18. Other taxes not shown under the above items
19. **Profit or loss for the financial year**

Appendix 2

Comparing the requirements of the OFR and Business Review (Companies Act 1985 and Companies Act 2006)[1]

	OFR	2005 Business Review – SI 2005 3442	2006 Companies Act Business Review
Status	Now voluntary (except for certain public sector bodies)	Statutory – effective for all financial years starting on or after 1 April 2005	Statutory – effective on 1 October 2007
Companies affected	UK listed – plus any other organisations that purport to prepare an OFR	All large and medium UK registered companies (listed and unlisted) plus EU and EEA registered companies (under EAMD)	Additional requirements for UK listed
Reporting basis	ASB's Reporting Statement – as guidelines	No basis except for that declared in the SI	No basis except for that declared in the Companies Act
Principles	<ul><li>Directors' view</li><li>Matters material to members</li><li>Forward looking</li><li>Complement financial statements</li><li>Comprehensive and understandable</li><li>Balanced and neutral</li><li>Comparable over time</li></ul>	<ul><li>Balanced and comprehensive</li><li>Consistent with size and complexity of the business</li></ul>	<ul><li>*Statutory purpose of the BR – to help members assess how directors have performed their duty to promote the success of the company for the benefits of the members as a whole but having regard to long-term consequences, employees' interests, business relations with supplies and customers, impacts on community and environment, reputation for high standards of*</li></ul>

	OFR	2005 Business Review – SI 2005 3442	2006 Companies Act Business Review
	■ No disclosures required if these are seriously prejudicial		*business conduct, and acting fairly between shareholders* ■ No disclosures required if these are seriously prejudicial
Content – with KPIs for financial and non-financial matters – to the extent necessary (TTEN)	Description – nature of business, including objectives/strategies	A fair review of the business	
	Development and performance of the business – current year and future – based on business segments – no safe harbour (except in directors' report)	Development and performance of the business – current year and position at year end	Development and performance of the business – current year and future – *forward-looking statements* – *with safe harbour within the directors' report*
	Resources available, principal risks/ uncertainties affecting long-term value	Description of principal risks and uncertainties	
	Capital structure, treasury policies, cash flows and liquidity	Include where appropriate references to, and additional explanations of, amounts included in the annual accounts	
	TTEN – information about environmental matters	**TTEN –** information about environmental matters, plus KPIs	**TTEN –** information about environmental matters, plus KPIs – *if not, explain what is not contained*

	OFR	2005 Business Review – SI 2005 3442	2006 Companies Act Business Review
Content – with KPI's for financial and non-financial matters – to the extent necessary (TTEN)	**TTEN** – information about employees	**TTEN** – information about employees plus KPIs	**TTEN** – information about employees, plus KPIs – *if not, explain what is not contained*
	TTEN – information about social/community matters		**TTEN** – *information about social and community matters – if not, explain what is not contained*
	TTEN – information about persons with whom there are contractual or other arrangements		**TTEN** – *information about persons with whom there are contractual or other arrangements – suppliers, major customers, joint ventures – if not, explain what is not contained*
	TTEN – information about receipts from and returns to members in respect of their shares		
	Related to TTEN, describe related policies and extent to which successfully implemented		**Related to TTEN,** *describe related policies and their effectiveness*
Audit requirements	None – but the ASB recommends companies to state if the OFR has been completed in accordance with the Reporting Statement	Consistency between information in directors' report and information in annual accounts	

	OFR	2005 Business Review – SI 2005 3442	2006 Companies Act Business Review
Penalties for non-compliance	None	\multicolumn{2}{c}{**Criminal** – for all reports for financial years commencing on or after 1 April 2005 **Civil** – for all reports for financial years commencing on 1 April 2006 and beyond}
Enforcement	None	\multicolumn{2}{c}{Financial Reporting Review Panel from 1 April 2006}

NOTE

1 Reproduced with the agreement of The Virtuous Circle 2007©

Appendix 3
Financial Reporting Council Combined Code on Corporate Governance[1]

CODES OF BEST PRACTICE

SECTION 1 COMPANY
A. DIRECTORS
A.1 The Board

Main Principle

Every company should be headed by an effective board, which is collectively responsible for the success of the company.

Supporting Principles

The board's role is to provide entrepreneurial leadership of the company within a framework of prudent and effective controls which enables risk to be assessed and managed. The board should set the company's strategic aims, ensure that the necessary financial and human resources are in place for the company to meet its objectives and review management performance. The board should set the company's values and standards and ensure that its obligations to its shareholders and others are understood and met.

All directors must take decisions objectively in the interests of the company. As part of their role as members of a unitary board, non-executive directors should constructively challenge and help develop proposals on strategy. Non-executive directors should scrutinise the performance of management in meeting agreed goals and objectives and monitor the reporting of performance. They should satisfy themselves on the integrity of financial information and that financial controls and systems of risk management are robust and defensible. They are responsible for determining appropriate levels of remuneration of executive directors and have a prime role in appointing, and where necessary removing, executive directors, and in succession planning.

Code Provisions

A.1.1 The board should meet sufficiently regularly to discharge its duties effectively. There should be a formal schedule of matters specifically reserved for its decision. The annual report should include a statement of how the board operates, including a high level statement of which types of decisions are to be taken by the board and which are to be delegated to management.

A.1.2 The annual report should identify the chairman, the deputy chairman (where there is one), the chief executive, the senior independent director and the chairmen and members of the nomination, audit and remuneration committees. It should also set out the number of meetings of the board and those committees and individual attendance by directors.

A.1.3 The chairman should hold meetings with the non-executive directors without the executives present. Led by the senior independent director, the non-executive directors should meet without the chairman present at least annually to appraise the chairman's performance (as described in A.6.1) and on such other occasions as are deemed appropriate.

A.1.4 Where directors have concerns which cannot be resolved about the running of the company or a proposed action, they should ensure that their concerns are recorded in the board minutes. On resignation, a non-executive director should provide a written statement to the chairman, for circulation to the board, if they have any such concerns.

A.1.5 The company should arrange appropriate insurance cover in respect of legal action against its directors.

A.2 Chairman and Chief Executive

Main Principle

There should be a clear division of responsibilities at the head of the company between the running of the board and the executive responsibility for the running of the company's business. No one individual should have unfettered powers of decision.

Supporting Principle

The chairman is responsible for leadership of the board, ensuring its effectiveness on all aspects of its role and setting its agenda. The chairman is also responsible for ensuring that the directors receive accurate, timely and clear information. The chairman should ensure effective communication with shareholders. The chairman should also facilitate the effective contribution of non-executive directors in particular and ensure constructive relations between executive and non-executive directors.

Code Provisions

A.2.1 The roles of chairman and chief executive should not be exercised by the same individual. The division of responsibilities between the chairman and chief executive should be clearly established, set out in writing and agreed by the board.

A.2.2[2] The chairman should on appointment meet the independence criteria set out in A.3.1 below. A chief executive should not go on to be chairman of the same company. If exceptionally a board decides that a chief executive should become chairman, the board should consult major shareholders in advance and should set out its reasons to shareholders at the time of the appointment and in the next annual report.

A.3 Board Balance and Independence

Main Principle

The board should include a balance of executive and non-executive directors (and in particular independent non-executive directors) such that no individual or small group of individuals can dominate the board's decision taking.

Supporting Principles

The board should not be so large as to be unwieldy. The board should be of sufficient size that the balance of skills and experience is appropriate for the requirements of the business and that changes to the board's composition can be managed without undue disruption. To ensure that power and information are not concentrated in one or two individuals, there should be a strong presence on the board of both executive and non-executive directors.

The value of ensuring that committee membership is refreshed and that undue reliance is not placed on particular individuals should be taken into account in deciding chairmanship and membership of committees. No one other than the committee chairman and members is entitled to be present at a meeting of the nomination, audit or remuneration committee, but others may attend at the invitation of the committee.

Code provisions

A.3.1 The board should identify in the annual report each non-executive director it considers to be independent.[3] The board should determine whether the director is independent in character and judgement and whether there are relationships or circumstances which are likely to affect, or could appear to affect, the director's judgement. The board should state its reasons if it determines that a director is independent notwithstanding the existence of relationships or circumstances which may appear relevant to its determination, including if the director:

- has been an employee of the company or group within the last five years;
- has, or has had within the last three years, a material business relationship with the company either directly, or as a partner, shareholder, director or senior employee of a body that has such a relationship with the company;
- has received or receives additional remuneration from the company apart from a director's fee, participates in the company's share option or a performance-related pay scheme, or is a member of the company's pension scheme;
- has close family ties with any of the company's advisers, directors or senior employees;
- holds cross-directorships or has significant links with other directors through involvement in other companies or bodies;
- represents a significant shareholder; or
- has served on the board for more than nine years from the date of their first election.

A.3.2 Except for smaller companies,[4] at least half the board, excluding the chairman, should comprise non-executive directors determined by the board to be independent. A smaller company should have at least two independent non-executive directors.

A.3.3 The board should appoint one of the independent non-executive directors to be the senior independent director. The senior independent director should be available to shareholders if they have concerns which contact through the normal channels of chairman, chief executive or finance director has failed to resolve or for which such contact is inappropriate.

A.4 Appointments to the Board

Main Principle

There should be a formal, rigorous and transparent procedure for the appointment of new directors to the board.

Supporting Principles

Appointments to the board should be made on merit and against objective criteria. Care should be taken to ensure that appointees have enough time available to devote to the job. This is particularly important in the case of chairmanships. The board should satisfy itself that plans are in place for orderly succession for appointments to the board and to senior management, so as to maintain an appropriate balance of skills and experience within the company and on the board.

Code Provisions

A.4.1 There should be a nomination committee which should lead the process for board appointments and make recommendations to the board. A majority of members of the nomination committee should be independent non-executive directors. The chairman or an independent non-executive director should chair the committee, but the chairman should not chair the nomination committee when it is dealing with the appointment of a successor to the chairmanship. The nomination committee should make available[5] its terms of reference, explaining its role and the authority delegated to it by the board.

A.4.2 The nomination committee should evaluate the balance of skills, knowledge and experience on the board and, in the light of this evaluation, prepare a description of the role and capabilities required for a particular appointment.

A.4.3 For the appointment of a chairman, the nomination committee should prepare a job specification, including an assessment of the time commitment expected, recognising the need for availability in the event of crises. A chairman's other significant commitments should be disclosed to the board before appointment and included in the annual report. Changes to such commitments should be reported to the board as they arise, and included in the next annual report. No individual should be appointed to a second chairmanship of a FTSE 100 company.[5]

A.4.4 The terms and conditions of appointment of non-executive directors should be made available for inspection. The letter of appointment should set out the expected time commitment. Non-executive directors should undertake that they will have sufficient time to meet what is expected of them. Their other significant commitments should be disclosed to the board before appointment, with a broad indication of the time involved and the board should be informed of subsequent changes.

A.4.5 The board should not agree to a full-time executive director taking on more than one non-executive directorship in a FTSE 100 company nor the chairmanship of such a company.

A.4.6 A separate section of the annual report should describe the work of the nomination committee, including the process it has used in relation to board appointments. An explanation should be given if neither an external search consultancy nor open advertising has been used in the appointment of a chairman or a non-executive director.

A.5 Information and Professional Development

Main Principle

The board should be supplied in a timely manner with information in a form and of a quality appropriate to enable it to discharge its duties. All directors should receive induction on joining the board and should regularly update and refresh their skills and knowledge.

Supporting Principles

The chairman is responsible for ensuring that the directors receive accurate, timely and clear information. Management has an obligation to provide such information but directors should seek clarification or amplification where necessary. The chairman should ensure that the directors continually update their skills and the knowledge and familiarity with the company required to fulfil their role both on the board and on board committees. The company should provide the necessary resources for developing and updating its directors' knowledge and capabilities. Under the direction of the chairman, the company secretary's responsibilities include ensuring good information flows within the board and its committees and between senior management and non-executive directors, as well as facilitating induction and assisting with professional development as required. The company secretary should be responsible for advising the board through the chairman on all governance matters.

Code Provisions

A.5.1 The chairman should ensure that new directors receive a full, formal and tailored induction on joining the board. As part of this, the company should offer to major shareholders the opportunity to meet a new non-executive director.

A.5.2 The board should ensure that directors, especially non-executive directors, have access to independent professional advice at the company's expense where they judge it necessary to discharge their responsibilities as directors. Committees should be provided with sufficient resources to undertake their duties.

A.5.3 All directors should have access to the advice and services of the company secretary, who is responsible to the board for ensuring that board procedures are complied with. Both the appointment and removal of the company secretary should be a matter for the board as a whole.

A.6 Performance Evaluation

Main Principle

The board should undertake a formal and rigorous annual evaluation of its own performance and that of its committees and individual directors.

Supporting Principle

Individual evaluation should aim to show whether each director continues to contribute effectively and to demonstrate commitment to the role (including commitment of time for board and committee meetings and any other duties). The chairman should act on the results of the performance evaluation by recognising the strengths and addressing the weaknesses of the board and, where appropriate, proposing new members be appointed to the board or seeking the resignation of directors.

Code Provision

A.6.1 The board should state in the annual report how performance evaluation of the board, its committees and its individual directors has been conducted. The non-executive directors, led by the senior independent director, should be responsible for performance evaluation of the chairman, taking into account the views of executive directors.

A.7 Re-election

Main Principle

All directors should be submitted for re-election at regular intervals, subject to continued satisfactory performance. The board should ensure planned and progressive refreshing of the board.

Code Provisions

A.7.1 All directors should be subject to election by shareholders at the first annual general meeting after their appointment, and to re-election thereafter at intervals of no more than three years. The names of directors submitted for election or re-election should be accompanied by sufficient biographical details and any other relevant information to enable shareholders to take an informed decision on their election.

A.7.2 Non-executive directors should be appointed for specified terms subject to re-election and to Companies Acts provisions relating to the removal of a director. The board should set out to shareholders in the papers accompanying a resolution to elect a non-executive director why they believe an individual should be elected. The chairman should confirm to shareholders when proposing re-election that, following formal performance evaluation, the individual's performance continues to be effective and to demonstrate commitment to the role. Any term beyond six years (e.g. two three-year terms) for a non-executive director should be subject to particularly rigorous review, and should take into account the need for progressive refreshing of the board. Non-executive directors may serve longer than nine years (e.g. three three-year terms), subject to annual re-election. Serving more than nine years could be relevant to the determination of a non-executive director's independence (as set out in provision A.3.1).

B. REMUNERATION

B.1 The Level and Make-up of Remuneration

Main Principle

Levels of remuneration should be sufficient to attract, retain and motivate directors of the quality required to run the company successfully, but a company should avoid paying more than is necessary for this purpose. A significant proportion of executive directors' remuneration should be structured so as to link rewards to corporate and individual performance.

Supporting Principle

The remuneration committee should judge where to position their company relative to other companies. But they should use such comparisons with caution, in view of the risk of an upward ratchet of remuneration levels with no corresponding improvement in performance. They should also be sensitive to pay and employment conditions elsewhere in the group, especially when determining annual salary increases.

Code Provisions

Remuneration policy

B.1.1 The performance-related elements of remuneration should form a significant proportion of the total remuneration package of executive directors and should be designed to align their interests with those of shareholders and to give these directors keen incentives to perform at the highest levels. In designing schemes of performance-related remuneration, the remuneration committee should follow the provisions in Schedule A to this Code.

B.1.2 Executive share options should not be offered at a discount save as permitted by the relevant provisions of the Listing Rules.

B.1.3 Levels of remuneration for non-executive directors should reflect the time commitment and responsibilities of the role. Remuneration for non-executive directors should not include share options. If, exceptionally, options are granted, shareholder approval should be sought in advance and any shares acquired by exercise of the options should be held until at least one year after the non-executive director leaves the board. Holding of share options could be relevant to the determination of a non-executive director's independence (as set out in provision A.3.1).

B.1.4 Where a company releases an executive director to serve as a non-executive director elsewhere, the remuneration report[7] should include a statement as to whether or not the director will retain such earnings and, if so, what the remuneration is.

Service Contracts and Compensation

B.1.5 The remuneration committee should carefully consider what compensation commitments (including pension contributions and all other elements) their directors' terms of appointment would entail in the event of early termination. The aim should be to avoid rewarding poor performance. They should take a robust line on reducing compensation to reflect departing directors' obligations to mitigate loss.

B.1.6 Notice or contract periods should be set at one year or less. If it is necessary to offer longer notice or contract periods to new directors recruited from outside, such periods should reduce to one year or less after the initial period.

B.2 Procedure

Main Principle

There should be a formal and transparent procedure for developing policy on executive remuneration and for fixing the remuneration packages of individual directors. No director should be involved in deciding his or her own remuneration.

Supporting Principles

The remuneration committee should consult the chairman and/or chief executive about their proposals relating to the remuneration of other executive directors. The remuneration committee should also be responsible for appointing any consultants in respect of executive director remuneration. Where executive directors or senior management are involved in advising or supporting the remuneration committee, care should be taken to recognise and avoid conflicts of interest. The chairman of the board should ensure that the company maintains contact as required with its principal shareholders about remuneration in the same way as for other matters.

Code Provisions

B.2.1 The board should establish a remuneration committee of at least three, or in the case of smaller companies, two members, who should all be independent non-executive directors. The remuneration committee should make available its terms of reference, explaining its role and the authority delegated to it by the board. Where remuneration consultants are appointed, a statement should be made available of whether they have any other connection with the company.

B.2.2 The remuneration committee should have delegated responsibility for setting remuneration for all executive directors and the chairman, including pension rights and any compensation payments. The committee should also recommend and monitor the level and structure of remuneration for senior management. The definition of 'senior management' for this purpose should be determined by the board but should normally include the first layer of management below board level.

B.2.3 The board itself or, where required by the Articles of Association, the shareholders should determine the remuneration of the non-executive directors within the limits set in the Articles of Association. Where permitted by the Articles, the board may however delegate this responsibility to a committee, which might include the chief executive.

B.2.4 Shareholders should be invited specifically to approve all new long-term incentive schemes (as defined in the Listing Rules) and significant changes to existing schemes, save in the circumstances permitted by the Listing Rules.

C. ACCOUNTABILITY AND AUDIT

C.1 Financial Reporting

Main Principle

The board should present a balanced and understandable assessment of the company's position and prospects.

Supporting Principle

The board's responsibility to present a balanced and understandable assessment extends to interim and other price-sensitive public reports and reports to regulators as well as to information required to be presented by statutory requirements.

Code Provisions

C.1.1 The directors should explain in the annual report their responsibility for preparing the accounts and there should be a statement by the auditors about their reporting responsibilities.

C.1.2 The directors should report that the business is a going concern, with supporting assumptions or qualifications as necessary.

C.2 Internal Control

Main Principle

The board should maintain a sound system of internal control to safeguard shareholders' investment and the company's assets.

Code Provision

C.2.1 The board should, at least annually, conduct a review of the effectiveness of the group's system of internal controls and should report to shareholders that they have done so. The review should cover all material controls, including financial, operational and compliance controls and risk management systems.

C.3 Audit Committee and Auditors

Main Principle

The board should establish formal and transparent arrangements for considering how they should apply the financial reporting and internal control principles and for maintaining an appropriate relationship with the company's auditors.

Code provisions

C.3.1 The board should establish an audit committee of at least three, or in the case of smaller companies, two, members, who should all be independent non-executive directors. The board should satisfy itself that at least one member of the audit committee has recent and relevant financial experience.

C.3.2 The main role and responsibilities of the audit committee should be set out in written terms of reference and should include:

- to monitor the integrity of the financial statements of the company, and any formal announcements relating to the company's financial performance, reviewing significant financial reporting judgements contained in them;
- to review the company's internal financial controls and, unless expressly addressed by a separate board risk committee composed of independent directors, or by the board itself, to review the company's internal control and risk management systems;
- to monitor and review the effectiveness of the company's internal audit function;
- to make recommendations to the board, for it to put to the shareholders for their approval in general meeting, in relation to the appointment, re-appointment and removal of the external auditor and to approve the remuneration and terms of engagement of the external auditor;
- to review and monitor the external auditor's independence and objectivity and the effectiveness of the audit process, taking into consideration relevant UK professional and regulatory requirements; to develop and implement policy on the engagement of the external auditor to supply non-audit services, taking into account relevant ethical guidance regarding the provision of non-audit services by the external audit firm; and to report to the board, identifying any matters in respect of which it considers that action or improvement is needed and making recommendations as to the steps to be taken.

C.3.3 The terms of reference of the audit committee, including its role and the authority delegated to it by the board, should be made available. A separate section of the annual report should describe the work of the committee in discharging those responsibilities.

C.3.4 The audit committee should review arrangements by which staff of the company may, in confidence, raise concerns about possible improprieties in matters of financial reporting or other matters. The audit committee's objective should be to ensure that arrangements are in place for the proportionate and independent investigation of such matters and for appropriate follow-up action.

C.3.5 The audit committee should monitor and review the effectiveness of the internal audit activities. Where there is no internal audit function, the audit committee should consider annually whether there is a need for an internal audit function and make a recommendation to the board, and the reasons for the absence of such a function should be explained in the relevant section of the annual report.

C.3.6 The audit committee should have primary responsibility for making a recommendation on the appointment, reappointment and removal of the external auditors. If the board does not accept the audit committee's recommendation, it should include in the annual report, and in any papers recommending appointment or re-appointment, a statement from the audit committee explaining the recommendation and should set out reasons why the board has taken a different position.

C.3.7 The annual report should explain to shareholders how, if the auditor provides non-audit services, auditor objectivity and independence is safeguarded.

D. RELATIONS WITH SHAREHOLDERS

D.1 Dialogue with Institutional Shareholders

Main Principle

There should be a dialogue with shareholders based on the mutual understanding of objectives. The board as a whole has responsibility for ensuring that a satisfactory dialogue with shareholders takes place.

Supporting Principles

Whilst recognising that most shareholder contact is with the chief executive and finance director, the chairman (and the senior independent director and other directors as appropriate) should maintain sufficient contact with major shareholders to understand their issues and concerns. The board should keep in touch with shareholder opinion in whatever ways are most practical and efficient.

Code Provisions

D.1.1 The chairman should ensure that the views of shareholders are communicated to the board as a whole. The chairman should discuss governance and strategy with major shareholders. Non-executive directors should be offered the opportunity to attend meetings with major shareholders and should expect to attend them if requested by major shareholders. The senior independent director should attend sufficient meetings with a range of major shareholders to listen to their views in order to help develop a balanced understanding of the issues and concerns of major shareholders.

D.1.2 The board should state in the annual report the steps they have taken to ensure that the members of the board, and in particular the non-executive directors, develop an understanding of the views of major shareholders about their company, for example through direct face-to-face contact, analysts' or brokers' briefings and surveys of shareholder opinion.

D.2 Constructive Use of the AGM

Main Principle

The board should use the AGM to communicate with investors and to encourage their participation.

Code Provisions

D.2.1 The company should count all proxy votes and, except where a poll is called, should indicate the level of proxies lodged on each resolution, and the balance for and against the resolution and the number of abstentions, after it has been dealt with on a show of hands. The company should ensure that votes cast are properly received and recorded.

D.2.2 The company should propose a separate resolution at the AGM on each substantially separate issue and should in particular propose a resolution at the AGM relating to the report and accounts.

D.2.3 The chairman should arrange for the chairmen of the audit, remuneration and nomination committees to be available to answer questions at the AGM and for all directors to attend.

D.2.4 The company should arrange for the Notice of the AGM and related papers to be sent to shareholders at least 20 working days before the meeting.

SECTION 2 INSTITUTIONAL SHAREHOLDERS

E. INSTITUTIONAL SHAREHOLDERS[8]

E.1 Dialogue with Companies

Main Principle

Institutional shareholders should enter into a dialogue with companies based on the mutual understanding of objectives.

Supporting Principles

Institutional shareholders should apply the principles set out in the Institutional Shareholders' Committee's 'The Responsibilities of Institutional Shareholders and Agents – Statement of Principles'[9] which should be reflected in fund manager contracts.

E.2 Evaluation of Governance Disclosures

Main Principle

When evaluating companies' governance arrangements, particularly those relating to board structure and composition, institutional shareholders should give due weight to all relevant factors drawn to their attention.

Supporting Principle

Institutional shareholders should consider carefully explanations given for departure from this Code and make reasoned judgements in each case. They should give an explanation to the company, in writing where appropriate, and be prepared to enter a dialogue if they do not accept the company's position. They should avoid a box-ticking approach to assessing a company's corporate governance. They should bear in mind in particular the size and complexity of the company and the nature of the risks and challenges it faces.

E.3 Shareholder Voting

Main Principle

Institutional shareholders have a responsibility to make considered use of their votes.

Supporting Principles

Institutional shareholders should take steps to ensure their voting intentions are being translated into practice. Institutional shareholders should, on request, make available to their clients information on the proportion of resolutions on which votes were cast and non-discretionary proxies lodged. Major shareholders should attend AGMs where appropriate and practicable. Companies and registrars should facilitate this.

© Financial Reporting Council. Reproduced with permission.

NOTES

1 It should be noted that this appendix covers only Sections 1 and 2 of the Code – the subsequent schedules are not included.
2 (Combined Code footnote 5): Compliance or otherwise with this provision need only be reported for the year in which the appointment is made.
3 (Combined Code footnote 6): A.2.2 states that the chairman should, on appointment, meet the independence criteria set out in this provision, but thereafter the test of independence is not appropriate in relation to the chairman.
4 (Combined Code footnote 7): A smaller company is one that is below the FTSE350 throughout the year immediately prior to the reporting year.
5 (Combined Code footnote 8): The requirement to make the information available would be met by making it available on request and by including the information on the company's website.
6 (Combined Code footnote 9): Compliance or otherwise with this provision need only be reported for the year in which the appointment is made.
7 (Combined Code footnote 12): As required under the Directors' Remuneration Report Regulations.
8 (Combined Code footnote 21): Agents such as investment managers, or voting services, are frequently appointed by institutional shareholders to act on their behalf and these principles should accordingly be read as applying where appropriate to the agents of institutional shareholders.
9 (Combined Code footnote 22): Available at www.investmentuk.org.uk.

Appendix 4
Company Secretary Checklist – annual report and accounts

The following is a summary extract of a checklist that has been compiled by Addleshaw Goddard LLP, Solicitors, for company secretaries of listed companies. It should be noted that this summary is based on the December 2006 version of the checklist that Addleshaw Goddard updates and publishes each December. The checklist is in two parts – the first, covering certain legal and non-accounting aspects of the annual report and accounts, is reprinted here; the second covers details of the procedures for notice of the annual general meeting, and this is not included within this appendix. The full document can be viewed by going to www.addleshawgoddard.com/view.asp?content_id=946&parent_id=911.

THE BASICS

- Is the company's name in the same form as the certificate of incorporation (or current certificate of incorporation on change of name)?
- Are the accounts made up to the correct date?
- Have the accounts been approved by the board and signed on behalf of the board by a director?
- Has the preliminary statement of annual results been published as soon as possible after board approval and in any event within 120 days of the year end?
- Does the preliminary statement of annual results comply with the requirements of the Listing Rules?
- Does the balance sheet state the name of the director who signed it on behalf of the board?
- Is the balance sheet dated with the date of approval by the board?
- Are the accounts being published as soon as possible following approval and in any event within six months of the year end?
- Have two copies of the accounts and notice of AGM been forwarded to the FSA at the time of issue?
- Are copies of the accounts, directors' report, DRR and auditors' report being sent to every member, every debenture-holder and every person entitled to receive notice of general meetings, including the auditors and directors?
- Has a copy of the accounts, on plain white matt paper, without pictures or shading, with a balance sheet signed by a director on behalf of the board, been filed with the Registrar of Companies, together with a copy of the directors' report and the DRR, each signed by a director or the secretary on behalf of the board, and the auditors' report, stating the name of the auditors and signed by them, within seven months of the financial year end?

- Has the annual information update (AIU) been prepared and filed with the FSA (by notification to a Regulatory Information Service) within 20 working days of the date on which the annual report and accounts were filed with the FSA?

DIRECTORS' REPORT

- Has the directors' report been approved by the board?
- Does it state the name of the director or secretary who signed it?
- Does it present a balanced and understandable assessment of the company's position and prospects?
- Does it state the names of the persons who were directors of the company at any time during the year?
- Does it state the principal activities of the group in the course of the year?
- Does it state the amount (if any) that the directors recommend should be paid by way of dividend?
- Does it contain a fair review of the group's business and a description of the principal risks and uncertainties it faces?
- Does it contain a statement to the effect that, so far as the directors who are in office at the time when the directors' report is approved are aware, there is no relevant audit information of which the auditors are unaware and that each such director has taken all reasonable steps to make himself aware of any relevant audit information and to establish that the auditors are aware of that information?
- Does it state whether any qualifying third party indemnity provision is in force at the time when the directors' report is approved or was in force during the year?
- Does it provide an explanation of the difference, where there is a difference of 10% or more between the actual figures in the accounts and any previously published, unaudited financial information, profit forecast or profit estimate (which must be reproduced in the accounts)?
- Does it incorporate details of important group events since the financial year end, likely future developments in the business of the group, the group's R&D activities and the group's overseas branches?
- Does it contain a statement of any significant difference between the market value of any interests in land of the group and the amount at which those interests are included in the balance sheet?
- Does it contain details of any arrangements whereby a shareholder has waived or has agreed to waive any dividends, future dividends and/or dividends for the period under review?
- Does it contain a statement of the beneficial and non-beneficial interests of the directors in shares in or debentures of the company or its subsidiaries as at the beginning and end of the year?

- Does it contain a statement of any options in respect of shares in or debentures of the company or its subsidiaries granted to or exercised by a director or his immediate family during the year?
- Does it contain a statement about changes in directors' beneficial and non-beneficial interests in shares and debentures between the end of the financial year and a date not more than one month prior to the date of the AGM notice, or an appropriate negative statement?
- Does it contain a statement about other disclosable share interests notified to the company as at a date not more than one month prior to the date of the AGM notice, or an appropriate negative statement?
- Does it contain particulars of any political or charitable donations?
- Does it contain an indication, in relation to the use by the group of financial instruments, of the group's financial risk management objectives and policies, and of its exposure to price, credit, liquidity and cash-flow risk, unless such information is not material in assessing the group's assets, liabilities, financial position and profit or loss?
- Does it contain the required particulars of any purchases or proposed purchases by the company of its own shares during the year or since the year end or sales or proposed sales of treasury shares during the year and of any shareholders' authority existing at the year end for the purchase by the company of its own shares (including treasury shares)?
- Does it provide a statement on the policy and practice regarding payment of the company's creditors, including the number of 'creditor days'?
- If the average number of employees of the company exceeded 250 in each week during the financial year, is there a statement:
    - On the company's policy on equal opportunities for disabled employees?
    - On employee involvement?
- Does it contain detailed information, by reference to the financial year end, on:
    - The structure of the company's capital, including the rights and obligations attaching to each class of shares and, where applicable, the percentage of the total share capital represented by each class?
    - Any restrictions on the transfer of securities in the company, including limitations on the holding of securities and requirements to obtain approval for a transfer of securities?
    - For each person with a significant direct or indirect holding of securities, such details as are known to the company of the identity of the person and the size and nature of the holding?
    - For each person who holds securities carrying special rights with regard to control of the company, the identity of the person and the nature of the rights?
    - Where the company has an employees' share scheme in relation to which their shares are with rights with regard to control of the company which are not exercisable by the employees, how those rights are exercisable?

- Any restrictions on voting rights, including limitations on voting rights of holders of a given percentage or number of votes; deadlines for exercising voting rights; and arrangements by which, with the company's co-operation, financial rights carried by securities are held by a person other than the holder of the securities?
- Any agreements between holders of securities known to the company which may result in restrictions on the transfer of securities or on voting rights?
- Any rules that the company has about appointment and replacement of directors and amendment of the articles of association?
- The powers of the directors, including in relation to issuing or buying back shares?
- Any significant agreements to which the company is a party that take effect after or terminate upon a change of control following a takeover bid, and the effects of any such agreements?
- Any agreements between the company and its directors or employees providing for compensation for loss of office or employment (whether through resignation, purported redundancy or otherwise) that occurs because of a takeover bid?
- Does the directors' report contain any necessary explanatory material with regard to information required to be included in the report by CA schedule 7 part 7?

DIRECTORS' REMUNERATION

In respect of directors' remuneration:

- Has a report been prepared on behalf of the board?
- Has the report been approved by the board and signed by a director or the secretary and is their name stated in the report?
- Does the report cover the details of the remuneration of all those who served as director during the financial year?
- Has a resolution approving the report been drafted to be put to shareholders at the AGM?

In relation to the remuneration committee required under the Combined Code, does the report:

- Name those who served on the committee during the financial year?
- Name those who provided advice or services to the committee and state (except in the case of directors) whether they were appointed by the committee?
- State the nature of any other services provided to the company by those persons (other than directors)?
- Contain a statement of the company's policy on directors' remuneration for the following and subsequent financial years?
- Does the policy statement give details of any performance conditions to which each director's entitlement to share options or under long-term incentive plans (LTIPs) is subject?

- Does the policy statement cover the company's policy on the granting of options or awards under its employees' share schemes and other long-term incentive schemes, explaining and justifying any departure from that policy in the period under review and any change in the policy from the preceding year?
- Does the policy statement explain the relative importance of performance-related and non-performance-related elements of remuneration for each director?
- Are the policies on duration of contracts, notice periods and termination payments summarised and explained?
- Does the report explain and justify if pensionable earnings include elements of remuneration other than basic salary?

Are the following details of any performance conditions given:

- An explanation of why they were chosen?
- A summary of the methods to be used to assess whether they have been met and why those methods were chosen?
- Details of any external factors (e.g. other companies or stock market indices) used for comparison?
- A description of, and an explanation for, any significant amendment proposed to be made to the terms and conditions of entitlement of a director to share options or under LTIPs?
- If no performance conditions apply, the reason why not?

PERFORMANCE GRAPH

- Is there a performance (line) graph, showing the total shareholder return of the company against a suitable, named index, for each financial year in the relevant period (usually the last five financial years)?
- Are reasons given for the choice of index?

SERVICE CONTRACTS

- Are details provided for each director of the date of any service contract (or contract for services), any unexpired term and any notice period?
- Are details provided of any rights to receive compensation on early termination, in sufficient detail to enable members to estimate any liability in the event of early termination?
- Are details provided of any service contract which provides for, or implies, a notice period in excess of one year or pre-determined compensation on termination exceeding one year's salary and benefits in kind and the reasons for such notice period?
- Is there a statement of the unexpired term of the service contract of any director proposed for election or re-election at the AGM or, where applicable, a statement that any such director has no service contract?

INDIVIDUAL REMUNERATION

Does the report give details, in tabular form, with explanatory notes as necessary, of each element in the remuneration package, for each director by name, showing:

- Salary and fees?
- Annual bonuses?
- Deferred bonuses?
- Sums paid by way of expense?
- Compensation for loss of office and payments for breach of contract or other?
- Termination payments?
- Estimated money value of benefits in kind?
- Total individual remuneration (i.e. the sum of the above) for the financial year and the previous financial year?
- The nature of any element of remuneration which is not in cash?

SHARE OPTIONS

Does the report give details, in tabular form, differentiating between share options with different terms and conditions, with explanatory notes as necessary, for each director, containing:

- The number of shares under option at the beginning of the year (or the date of appointment, if later)?
- The number of shares under option at the end of the year (or the date of cessation of appointment, if earlier)?
- Information identifying options awarded, exercised, lapsed unexercised or the terms of which have been changed during the year?
- For each unexpired option:
  - The price paid, if any, for its award?
  - The exercise price?
  - The date from which the option may be exercised?
  - The expiry date?
- A description of any change made during the year to the terms to which any option is subject?
- A summary of any performance criteria upon which the grant or exercise of any option is conditional and any changes to those criteria during the year?
- For any options exercised during the year, the market price of the shares at the time of exercise?
- For options unexpired at the end of the year, the market price of the shares at the end of the year, together with the range of market prices during the year?

LTIPS

- Does the report give details, in tabular form, for each director by name, of LTIPs (other than share options disclosed above), including interests at the start and end of the period under review (or date, or cessation, of appointment, as appropriate, if either occurred during the year), entitlements and awards granted during the year (including number of shares, market price of the shares at the date of grant and applicable performance conditions), details of performance conditions and the period over which such conditions have to be met and changes in the terms and conditions made during the year?
- In respect of awards vesting during the financial year, are details given of any shares, cash or other benefits receivable, together with, in the case of awards of shares, the number of shares, the dates of awards, market value at the time of the award and at the time of vesting and details of applicable performance conditions?
- Are details provided of any single director LTIPs?

RETIREMENT BENEFITS

Does the report contain details, for each director, of pension entitlements earned during the year, for **'defined benefit' (final salary) schemes**, as follows:

- Any change in accrued benefits during the year?
- The amount of accrued benefits at the end of the year?
- The transfer value, calculated in a manner consistent with applicable actuarial professional guidelines, of accrued benefits, at the end of the year?
- The transfer value so calculated contained in the previous year's remuneration report or, if there was no such report or the report did not contain any such value, the transfer value so calculated of accrued benefits at the beginning of the year?
- The increase in the transfer value over the year less any contributions made by the director?

For **'defined contribution' (money purchase) schemes**, does the report contain details, for each director, of pension entitlements earned during the year, as follows:

- Details of the company's contributions paid or payable for or during the year?

EXCESS RETIREMENT BENEFITS

In respect of 'excess retirement benefits', does the report show:

- The total amount of any increase in the pension paid to or receivable by any director or former director (awarded after the later of the date on which the pension first became payable and 31 March 1997) which is not covered by the scheme's normal contribution

recommendations and which would not have been awarded on the same basis to all members of the scheme?
- The nature of any non-cash retirement benefit improved in this way and the estimated money value of the improvement?

COMPENSATION FOR PAST DIRECTORS

- Are details provided of any significant payments or awards to former directors during the year?

SUMS PAID TO THIRD PARTIES FOR A DIRECTOR'S SERVICES

- Are details provided of payments made, including the estimated monetary value of any non-cash benefit given, to any third party in respect of a director's services as a director of the company or any subsidiary?

CORPORATE GOVERNANCE

- Is there a statement of how the company has applied the principles set out in section 1 of the Combined Code?
- Is there a statement of compliance with the provisions set out in section 1 of the Combined Code?
- Has any non-compliance been disclosed and explained?
- Have the auditors reviewed the company's statement of compliance with the Combined Code to the extent required?
- Is there a statement by the directors that the business is a going concern, giving any necessary supporting assumptions or qualifications, and has this statement been reviewed by the auditors?
- Is there a statement of how the board operates, including a high-level statement of which types of decisions are to be taken by the board and which are to be delegated to management?
- Are the chairman, deputy chairman (where applicable), chief executive, senior independent director and the chairmen and members of the nomination, audit and remuneration committees identified?
- Does the statement record the number of meetings of the board and of those committees and individual attendance by directors?
- If, exceptionally, a board has decided that a chief executive should become chairman (contrary to the principle of paragraph A.2.2 of the Combined Code), is the board's reasoning (which should have been set out to shareholders at the time of the appointment) set out?

- Are the other significant commitments of the chairman, and any changes to them during the year, identified?
- Are the non-executive directors considered by the board to be independent identified as such and are reasons provided as to why the board has determined directors to be independent notwithstanding the existence of relationships or circumstances which may appear relevant to its determination?
- Are sufficient biographical details (and any other relevant information) given in respect of directors submitted for election or re-election?
- Is there an explanation by the directors of their responsibility for preparing the accounts and a statement by the auditors about their reporting responsibilities?
- Is there an explanation as to how performance evaluation of the board, its committees and its individual directors has been conducted?
- Is there a statement of the steps the board has taken to ensure that members of the board, and in particular the non-executive directors, develop an understanding of the views of major shareholders about their company?
- Is there a separate section describing the work of the audit committee in discharging its responsibilities?
- Where there is no internal audit function, are the reasons for the absence of such a function given?
- Where the board has not accepted the audit committee's recommendation on the appointment, reappointment or removal of the external auditors, is there a statement from the audit committee explaining the recommendation and has the board set out the reasons why it has taken a different position?
- Is there an explanation of how, if the auditor provides non-audit services, auditor objectivity and independence is safeguarded?
- Is there a statement by the directors as to how the board has maintained a sound system of internal control to safeguard shareholders' investment and the company's assets?
- Do the directors report that they have reviewed the effectiveness of the group's system of internal controls, including financial, operational and compliance controls and risk management systems?
- Does the board's statement on internal control include such meaningful, high-level information as the board considers necessary to assist shareholders' understanding of the main features of the company's risk management processes and system of internal control and avoid giving a misleading impression?

Does the report include:

- A section describing the work of the nomination committee, including the selection process it has used in relation to board appointments and an explanation if neither an external search consultancy nor open advertising has been used in the appointment of a chairman or a non-executive director?
- A description of the work of the remuneration committee as required under the DRR

Regulations, including, where an executive director serves as a non-executive director elsewhere, whether or not the director will retain such earnings and, if so, what the remuneration is?

Do the disclosures on internal controls cover the following:

- Confirmation that there is an ongoing process for identifying, evaluating and managing the significant risks faced by the company, that it has been in place for the year under review and up to the date of approval of the annual report and accounts, that it is regularly reviewed by the board and that it accords with Turnbull?
- An acknowledgement by the directors of their responsibility for the company's system of internal control and for reviewing its effectiveness?
- An explanation that the system of internal control is designed to manage rather than eliminate the risk of failure to achieve business objectives and can only provide reasonable and not absolute assurance against material misstatement or loss?
- A summary of the process applied in reviewing the effectiveness of the system of internal control?
- Confirmation that necessary actions have been or are being taken to remedy any significant failings or weaknesses identified from the review?
- The process applied in dealing with material internal control aspects of any significant problems disclosed in the annual report and accounts?
- Where relevant, an explanation as to why it has not been possible for the board to make one or more of the disclosures required by Turnbull paras 34 and 36?
- Details of any material joint ventures and associates which have not been dealt with as part of the group for the purposes of applying Turnbull?

NOTES TO THE ACCOUNTS AND OTHER LISTING RULES REQUIREMENTS

- Is there an explicit and unreserved statement that the financial statements comply with IFRS or, if there has been a departure from the requirements of IFRS, has the necessary disclosure been made?
- Are the required details of each class of share capital disclosed, either on the face of the balance sheet or in the notes?
- Is the required information given about the basis of preparation of the financial statements and the specific accounting policies used?
- Are the required details of dividends disclosed?
- Are the additional details in relation to the company's domicile, legal form, country of incorporation, registered office address, operations and principal activities and parent and ultimate parent disclosed (to the extent that any such information is not disclosed elsewhere in the report and accounts)?

- Has adequate disclosure been made, where appropriate, of any subsidiaries, joint venture companies or associated undertakings?
- Has adequate disclosure been made of any significant holding of the parent company in an undertaking which is not a subsidiary undertaking, a joint venture or an associated undertaking?
- Is there a statement of any interest capitalised, including an indication of the amount and treatment of related tax relief?
- Are details given of any arrangement under which a director has waived emoluments or future emoluments from a group company?
- For shares allotted for cash during the year to non-shareholders or on a non-pre-emptive basis and where any such allotment has not been specifically authorised by the shareholders, have details been given of the classes of shares allotted, for each class the number allotted, their aggregate nominal value and the consideration received by the company for their allotment, the names of the allottee (or, if more than six in number, a generic description of each new class of equity holder) and the market price of the shares on the date on which the terms of issue were fixed (which date must be stated)?
- Has the same information been given for any unlisted major subsidiary undertaking of the company?
- Are details given of the participation of the company's parent undertaking (if any) in any placing of the company's shares?

Are details given of any contract of significance subsisting during the period under review:

- To which any group company is a party and in which a director of the company is or was materially interested and between any group company and a controlling shareholder?
- Are details given (subject to the specified exceptions) of any contract for the provision of services to a group company by a controlling shareholder?
- Are details given of small related party transactions?
- Has the necessary disclosure been made of the nature of any services provided by the auditors, whether in their capacity as auditors or otherwise, or by their associates and of the amount of any remuneration received or receivable by the auditors or their associates in respect of any such services?

CORPORATE SOCIAL RESPONSIBILITY

Does the annual report contain a statement confirming whether the board takes into account the ABI Guidelines and:

- Takes regular account of the significance of social, environmental and ethical (SEE) matters to the business of the company?
- Has identified and assessed any significant risks to the company's short and long-

term value arising from SEE matters and considered any potential to enhance value by responding to SEE issues appropriately?
- Has received adequate information to assess SEE issues and to ensure that SEE issues are covered in the training of directors? and
- Has ensured that the company has effective systems for managing significant SEE risks, including, where relevant, performance management systems and remuneration incentives?

In addition, does the annual report follow the ABI Guidelines and:

- Include information on SEE-related risks and opportunities that may significantly affect the company's value and how these risks may impact on the business; describe the company's policies and procedures for managing risks to value arising from SEE issues and, if there are no such policies and procedures, provide reasons for their absence?
- Include information about the extent of compliance by the company with those policies and procedures?
- Describe the procedures followed for verifying SEE disclosures which should afford a reasonable level of credibility to those disclosures?

© Addleshaw Goddard.

About The Virtuous Circle

A specialist management consultancy, The Virtuous Circle (TVC) works with national and international businesses in three areas:

- enhancing shareholder value through effective corporate reporting;
- building the reputation of businesses through developing and implementing their CSR strategies;
- building an understanding of non-financial risks and their management.

Recent projects completed by the TVC team (based throughout the United Kingdom and in Brussels) include:

- developing non-financial reporting strategies for clients, including identifying business critical KPIs;
- writing, implementing and communicating codes of ethics;
- undertaking CSR audits and developing CSR strategic positioning;
- developing and writing CSR reports;
- assisting client submissions for surveys, including carbon Disclosure Project, DJSI, BitC and EIRIS;
- developing risk management systems for non-financial activities.

Complementing its corporate work, TVC also works with major UK institutions on research studies.

It has published research reports in association with The Work Foundation and the Royal Society of Arts (RSA), the Chartered Institute of Personnel and Development (CIPD), and supported the Accounting Standards Board (ASB) with its narrative reporting studies.

Further information on The Virtuous Circle can be obtained on its website at www.thevirtuouscircle.co.uk or by e-mail to its Chief Executive, Tony Hoskins at thoskins@thevirtuouscircle.co.uk.

May 2007

Index

Abbreviated accounts 26, 38–9, 51, 56
Accountability 67, 238, 256–8
Accountability's AA1000 Assurance Standard 183
Accounting Standards Board (ASB) 6, 7, 10, 16–17, 28, 121–4, 155
   see also Operating and Financial Review (OFR)
   Business Review 157, 167–73, 202
   Reporting Statement 7, 18–24, 28, 120, 122, 124, 157, 167, 213, 214
Accounts see annual accounts
Action Fund Management 177
Activists 62, 126–7
Addleshaw Goddard 110
Admission documents 98, 101
Aitken, Robert 191, 195, 197, 198, 210, 212, 220, 222–3, 225, 228, 230
Alternative Investment Market (AIM) 9, 37, 46, 85, 96–102, 136, 137
Ambler, Tim 192, 193–4, 221, 224, 232
Annual accounts 1, 3, 4, 35–7
   see also audit
   abbreviated 26, 38–9, 51, 56
   approval 41, 44, 50
   Business Review 124, 159, 160–1, 170–1
   checklist 261–72
   circulation 42
   Companies Act 1985 240–3
   company duties 39–43
   CRUF guidance 185
   discussion 221–3
   enforcement 51–2
   filing 43
   revision 43
   time schedule 110–13
   types 37–9
Annual reports 1, 3, 15
   AIM 97
   checklist 261–72
   Combined Code 69–70
   design 115–18
   development 109–18, 119–42
   discussion 229–30, 236–8

downloading 179
ESG 182
Listing Rules 85–8
Transparency Directive 102–3
value and purpose 196–7
Apple 177
Asset-rich companies 160, 161, 264–5
Association of British Insurers (ABI) 79, 181–3
Audit 246
   Combined Code 67, 256–8
   exemptions 55–7
   financial statements 103
   path 132
   requirements 54–64
   standards convergence 179
Audit committee 68, 70–5, 111–13, 256–8
Auditors 3
   appointment 57–8
   assessment 111–12
   Combined Code 68
   directors' duties 34
   duties 59–62
   eligibility 61
   liability 61
   rights 62–3
   role 230
   statement 38
Auditors' report 47, 58–9
   accounts 37
   signing 61, 62
   small companies 44
   special 56, 60–1
Audit Quality Forum 230
Authorisation orders 52

Balanced and comprehensive analysis 159, 162, 168–9, 172
Balance sheet 14, 15, 37, 40, 240–3
   abbreviated 38
   auditors 58
   small companies 44
   total, company size 35, 36
Balls, Ed 187

Banking companies 36
BDO 178
Best practice 197–200, 214–17, 284–60
Bicknell, Simon 191, 196–7, 198, 203, 208, 215, 219, 223–5, 228
Big Six summit 177–9, 183, 184, 190, 227
Board
  see also directors
  Combined Code 69–70
  nomination committee 80–2
  performance evaluation 81
Board of Trade 5
BP 177–8
British Venture Capital Association (BVCA) 186–7
Browne, Lord 177–8
Brown, Gordon 18, 120
Buffini, Damon 186
Business impact areas 128
Business Link website 39
Business Review 16, 17–18, 20, 24–8, 31, 41–2, 110, 119–42, 179, 189
  directors' duties 34
  discussion 193, 201–17, 229, 234–6
  key steps 140–1
  private equity firms 186
  quoted companies 46
  reporting requirements 154–74
  route map 127
  small companies 44
  statutory purpose 127
Business Review Regulations 2, 24, 25, 27, 28, 157–9

Cadbury Report 66
Capital Requirements Directive 210
Capital structure, Business Review 171
Cash flow, Business Review 171
CBI 18
Chairman's statement 138–9
Charities 2
Chartered Institute of Management Accountants (CIMA) 184
Chief executive's statement 138–9
Chopping, David 192
Circulars 92–6
Civil penalties 51–2
Climate change 123
Codes of Governance 65–82
Coloplast 150–2

Combined Code 3, 65–82, 115, 186, 248–60
  annual reports 85
  discussion 200, 232
Committee of European Securities Regulators (CESR) 179–80
Committee of Sponsoring Organisations of the Treadway Commission (CoSO) 232
Companies Act 1985 5, 6, 13–29, 120, 240–3, 244–7
Companies Act 1989 5, 14, 15
Companies Act 2006 1, 2, 6, 13–14, 120, 189, 244–7
  audit requirements 54–64
  Business Review 125–7
  forward-looking statements 20
  impact 30–53
  non-compliance penalties 47–51
Companies House 2, 5, 26
Company Law Reform Steering Group 146, 147
Company Secretaries Checklist 110, 261–72
Comply or explain requirement 15, 66
Comprehensive income 8
Constitution, amendment 105
Contractual arrangements 126–7, 157–8, 171
Control review 112, 113, 114
Cooke Pilot, Sallie 192, 195, 200, 205, 207, 213, 214, 216, 219, 223, 224, 226, 236
Co-operative bodies 2
Copy writers 117
Corporate governance 3, 238, 268–70
Corporate Reporting User Forum (CRUF) 185, 215
Corporate social responsibility (CSR) 155, 182, 183–4, 231, 271–2
Court orders 51–2
Cox, Chris 176, 180

Debenture holders 43, 47, 49
Deloitte 8–9, 135, 178
Department for the Environment and Rural Affairs (DEFRA) 19
Department of Trade and Industry (DTI) 9, 17, 18
Directors
  auditor appointment 57–8
  benefits 41, 49
  Business Review 158
  Combined Code 248–55
  duties 33–4, 211–12
  remuneration 40–1, 264–5, 266
  retirement benefits 267–8

Rumsfeld test 214
shareholder value 32
Directors' remuneration report 46–7, 78–80, 264–5
 auditors 59, 60
 non-compliance penalties 49, 50–1
 Regulations 2002 78
Directors' report 15–16, 25, 26, 41–2, 110, 262–4
 abbreviated accounts 38
 approval 51
 Business Review 119–21, 124, 159, 168
 enhanced *see* Business Review
 FRRP review 27–8
 groups 26–7
 non-compliance penalties 48, 50–1
 small companies 44
Disclosure
 Checklist 135
 Combined Code 69–70
 discussion 195
Dividends
 preliminary statement 86
 small companies 44
Dormant companies 56, 57

Electronic communications 33, 116, 223–7
Elwin, Peter 191, 197, 198, 204, 206, 209, 212, 220, 225, 227, 231
E-money issuers 36
Employees 35, 36, 44
 annual report 109
 Business Review 123, 126, 157, 171
 information, accounts 40
Enoch, Simon 191, 194, 203, 206, 211, 212, 219, 220, 224, 227–8, 233
Environment
 Business Review 123, 126, 157, 170, 171
 OFR 19
 reporting 146
Environmental, social and governance reporting (ESG) 181–4, 231–2
Equity changes 8
Equity share capital 45–6
Ernst and Young 178
European Accounts Modernisation Directive (EAMD) 6, 14, 17–18, 24–5, 120, 136, 157, 229
European Economic Area (EEA) states 36, 46, 91
European Federation of Accountants 183–4

European Union
 Business Review 24–5, 26
 Directive on Audits 5
 harmonisation 5, 6, 14
 IFRS 9, 180–1
 Lisbon Summit 24
 Management Commentary 180
 Prospectus Directive 80
 regulations 14
 Seventh Company Law Directive 5, 14
 Takeovers Directive 31
 Transparency Directive 31, 86, 87–8, 102–5, 228
Euros 26, 43

Fair review 14, 25, 121–2, 159, 162, 168
Fair value measurement 9
Financial Accounting Standards Board (FASB) 179, 180
Financial Reporting Council (FRC) 6–7, 52, 110–11, 167, 248–60
Financial Reporting Review Panel (FRRP) 7, 27–8, 34, 155, 186, 221
Financial Services Act 1986 5
Financial Services Authority (FSA) 66, 83–5, 88, 89, 176
 circulars 92
 Handbook 83–4
 prospectuses 90–1
 responsibility statement 103
 Transparency Directive 104–5
Financial Services and Markets Act 2000 26, 36, 46, 84–5, 120
Financial statements
 audit committee 73
 Business Review 27
 production 112
 remuneration committee 114
 summary 27, 38, 47, 49
 Transparency Directive 103
Forward-looking information 170, 173
Forward-looking statements 20–1, 205–8, 234–5
Frank, Barney 177
Free Enterprise Action Fund 177
FTSE 17, 157, 194

General Electric 177
Generally accepted accounting principles (GAAP) 7–10, 59, 179
Gillen, Seamus 192, 200, 205, 213, 216, 223, 224, 231–2, 233

Glietzmann, Miles 148
Governance 3, 238, 268–70
  codes 65–82
  ESG 181–4, 231–2
Government
  bodies 2
  review 3
Grant Thornton 178
Green approach 177
Greenbury Report 66
Greenwood, Ian 191, 192
Griffiths, Paul 191, 194, 203, 206, 209, 210, 211, 215, 219, 223, 229
Groups
  see also subsidiaries
  Business Review 120
  directors' report 26–7

Half-yearly reports 87–8, 103–4
Hampel Committee 66
Higgs Report 66, 75, 80
Hodson, Nicholas 191, 196, 197, 199, 204, 211, 220, 225, 227, 228
Hynes, Jonathan 192, 194, 205, 208, 221, 224, 226–7

ICSA 76, 77, 115
Independent Audit Ltd 134, 138, 236
Indirect investors 33
Insolvency Acts 5
Institute of Chartered Accountants in England and Wales (ICAEW) 10
Institute of Practitioners in Advertising (IPA) 138
Institutional ownership 148
Insurance companies 26, 36
Insurance market activity 120
Intangibles, Value Reporting 149–50
Interim management statements (IMS) 104
Interim statements 1
International Accounting Standards (IAS) 14, 36, 37, 59, 86
International Accounting Standards Board (IASB) 7–8, 10, 158, 179, 180, 183–4, 229
International Federation of Accountant (IFAC) 183
International Financial Reporting Standards (IFRS) 7, 8, 9–10, 14, 36, 46, 104, 177–8, 179, 180–1, 193
International Governance Network 178

Internet 179, 237
  see also websites
  electronic communications 33, 116, 223–7
  real time reporting 178, 190, 220, 227–9
  web-based reporting 219, 220
  XBRL 179, 226, 237
Investor valuation 150
ISAE2000 183–4
ISD investment firms 36

Jenkins Committee 5
Jobs, Steve 177
Joint Stock Companies Act 4–5
Jones, Helen 191, 194, 198, 203, 206, 208, 211, 214–15, 220, 222, 223–4, 228, 231

Kanjorski, Paul 177
Key performance indicators (KPIs) 22–4, 25, 26, 122–3, 126, 129–33, 137
  Business Review 159, 163–5, 167, 169–70, 171, 172, 206
  discussion 208–10, 235
KPMG International 178

Lee, Paul 191, 192, 194, 197, 198, 203, 204, 206–7, 210, 215, 216, 220, 226, 227, 229, 230, 236
Limited Liability Act 5
Limited liability partnerships (LLP) 2, 38
Liquidity, Business Review 171
Listing prospectus 1
Listing Rules 14, 65, 66, 83–96
Long-term incentive plans (LTIPS) 267
Loweth, David 191, 193, 202, 206, 210–11, 213, 214, 215, 219, 222, 229

Management Commentary 180, 229
Management report 103
Management statements, quarterly 228
Martin, Rosemary 191, 193, 203, 206, 208, 210, 211, 215, 222, 225, 230
Material KPIs 129–30
Mineral companies 89
Minority interests 8
Montagnon, Peter 181
Moxey, Paul 191, 200, 204, 217, 220, 226, 232

National Association of Pension Funds (NAPF) 79

National Association of Securities Dealers Automated Quotations (NASDAQ) 2, 36, 46
National Grid 20–1
Nominated advisers (Nomads) 96, 101–2
Nomination committee 80–2, 115
Nominee holdings 33
Non-executive directors 34, 81
Non-profit-making companies 56
Non-quoted companies 65
Non-statutory accounts 37, 43, 56–7

Offences
  fraud 3
  non-compliance penalties 47–51, 247
  statement to auditors 63
Operating and Financial Review (OFR) 7, 16–24, 27, 120, 121, 122–3, 126, 132, 136, 138 146–7, 177, 179
  Business Review 157–9, 165–6, 173, 244–7
  Disclosure Checklist 135
  discussion 193, 214
  storyboard approach 134, 135
Opportunities, Business Review 128–9, 131–2

Paulson, Hank 175–6
Peel, Giles 191, 195, 199, 204–5, 209, 212, 213, 219, 220–1
Pension Investment Research Consultants (PIRC) 79–80
People-rich companies 160, 161, 164–5
Performance graph 265
Performance indicators, key *see* key performance indicators (KPIs)
Periodic reporting 102
Phillips, David 192, 193, 195, 199, 204, 207, 209, 210, 212–13, 216, 221, 226, 227, 229, 231, 235
Photography 117
Policies
  Business Review 133
  review 112, 114
Pre-announcement documents 97
Preliminary statement 86, 197
Price sensitive information, AIM 99
PricewaterhouseCooper (PwC) 135, 136–7, 145, 149–52, 178, 184
Private companies 44–5, 57
Private equity firms 186–7, 232–3
Profit and loss account 14, 15, 37, 243
  abbreviated 38

auditors 58
small companies 44
Proofreading 118
Prospectus Directive 90
Prospectuses 88–91, 97–8
Prospectus Rules 91

Qualified reports 59
Quality, reporting 145–53, 194–5, 216–17
Quoted Companies Alliance (QCA) 134, 137

Radley Yeldar 184
Rake, Mike 178
Real time reporting 178, 190, 220, 227–9
Records
  accounts 39
  non-compliance penalties 48
Registered office, EEA states 36
Registrar of Companies 5, 37, 43, 44, 45
Regulatory impact assessment (RIA) 136
Regulatory information service (RIS) 86, 88, 91, 93
Related party circulars 94–5
Related party transactions 99–100
Related undertakings 40, 49
Remuneration
  Combined Code 254–6
  directors 40–1, 264–5, 266
  directors' remuneration report 46–7, 49, 50–1, 59, 60, 78–80, 264–5
Remuneration committee 75–80, 113–15, 182
Report Leadership initiative 184–7, 198, 236
Resources, Business Review 170–1, 172–3
Responsibility statement 103
Retirement benefits 267–8
Reverse takeovers, AIM 99
Risks
  audit committee 72, 74–5, 111, 112
  Business Review 122, 128–9, 131–2, 159, 162–3, 169, 171, 172
  discussion 210
  KPI 23–4
Robust KPIs 129–30
Rumsfeld test 214

Safe harbour provision 20, 213–14
Sarbanes Oxley Act 2002 (SOX) 175–6, 213
Scientific research-based companies 89
Seaman, Richard 191
Secretary of State 52, 62

Securities and Exchange Commission (SEC)
    8, 84, 176, 177, 179–80, 226
Segment information reporting 8
Selkirk, Rod 187
Service contracts 265
Shareholders
    annual report 109
    Business Review 27
    communication 3, 109
    communications 91, 105
    electronic communications 116
    engagement 32–3
    enlightened value 32, 33–4, 146–7
    institutional 259–60
    OFR 19
    relations 258–9
    US rights 177
Shares
    acquiring own 95
    options 266
    rights 105
Size of company 2
    abbreviated accounts 38
    accounts 35–6, 44
    Business Review 26, 120, 121–2
Small companies 45, 57
    abbreviated accounts 38
    accounts 44
    audit 55–6, 60–1
    Business Review 26, 120
    group size 35–6
Smith Guidance 70, 71, 72, 73, 74–5, 113
Smith, Nick 192
Smith Report 66
Social issues 126, 146, 157, 171, 181–2, 231–2
Sole traders 2
South Sea Company 4
Stakeholders
    information 3
    OFR 19
Statutory accounts 37, 43
Statutory instruments (SI) 31
Stelzer, Irwin 176
Stock Exchange rules 83–106
Storyboard approach 133–5
Strategic goals/objectives 128

Strategic impacts 131–2
Subsidiaries 15, 20, 25, 27, 34, 136
Summary financial statements 27, 38, 47, 49
Summary reports 223–4, 237
Summerfield, Daniel 191, 194, 196, 204, 205, 207, 209, 210, 215, 220, 225–6
Suppliers, Business Review 126–7
Sustainability reporting 183

Takeovers Directive 31
Tate & Lyle 20–1
Tax charges 3
Templates 134, 135
'Think Small First' 35, 136
Thorpe, Richard 191, 212, 216–17, 221, 230
Tomkins plc 184
Total shareholder return (TSR)
    benchmarking 77–8
Transparency 148, 150–2, 221
Transparency Directive 31, 86, 87–8, 102–5, 228
Turnover, company size 26, 35, 36

Undertaking for collective investment in transferable securities (UCITS) 36
United States
    developments 175–7
    GAAP 8–9, 179
    regulations 210
Unlisted equity instruments 8–9
Unqualified reports 59
Unquoted companies 38, 43, 45–7

The Virtuous Circle 133, 155–67, 172–3
Vodafone 20–1

Ward, Tom 192, 202, 209, 210, 212, 214, 215, 220, 231
Websites 1
    see also Internet
    accounts publication 42, 47, 50
    annual report 116
    discussion 224–7
    summary reports 237
Worshipful Company of Marketers 138

XBRL 179, 226, 237